SEÑORITAS IN BLUE

Sussex Studies in Spanish History

General Editor: Nigel Townson, Universidad Complutense, Madrid

Consultant Editor: José Alvarez-Junco, Universidad Complutense, Madrid

Advisory Editors: Pamela Radcliff, University of California, San Diego
Tim Rees, University of Exeter

Published

José Alvarez-Junco, *The Emergence of Mass Politics in Spain: Populist Demagoguery and Republican Culture, 1890–1910*

Tom Buchanan, *The Impact on the Spanish Civil War on Britain: War, Loss and Memory*

David Messenger, *L'Espagne Républicaine: French Policy and Spanish Republicanism in Liberated France*

Inbal Ofer, *Señoritas in Blue: The Making of a Female Political Elite in Franco's Spain*

Elizabeth Roberts, *"Freedom, Faction, Fame and Blood": British Soldiers of Conscience in Greece, Spain and Finland*

Nigel Townson, *The Crisis of Democracy in Spain: Centrist Politics under the Second Republic, 1931–1936*

Forthcoming

Hugo Garcia, *The Truth about Spain!: Mobilizing British Public Opinion, 1936–1939*

Raanan Rein, *Repercussions of the Spanish Civil War in Palestine: History and Memory*

SEÑORITAS IN BLUE

THE MAKING OF A FEMALE
POLITICAL ELITE IN FRANCO'S SPAIN

INBAL OFER

sussex
ACADEMIC
PRESS

BRIGHTON • PORTLAND

Copyright © Inbal Ofer, 2009

The right of Inbal Ofer to be identified as Author of this work has been asserted in accordance with the Copyright, Designs and Patents Act 1988.

2 4 6 8 10 9 7 5 3 1

First published 2009 in Great Britain by
SUSSEX ACADEMIC PRESS
PO Box 139
Eastbourne BN24 9BP

and in the United States of America by
SUSSEX ACADEMIC PRESS
920 NE 58th Ave   Suite 300
Portland, Oregon 97213-3786

British Library Cataloguing in Publication Data
A CIP catalogue record for this book is available from the British Library.

Library of Congress Cataloging-in-Publication Data
Ofer, Inbal.
Señoritas in blue : the making of a female political elite in Franco's Spain : the national leadership of the Sección Femenina de la Falange (1936–1977) / Inbal Ofer.
p. cm.
Includes bibliographical references and index.
ISBN 978-1-84519-314-0 (h/c : alk. paper)
1. Women in politics—Spain—History—20th century. 2. Women fascists—Spain—History—20th century. 3. Falange Española Tradicionalista y de las Juntas Ofensivas Nacional-Sindicalistas. Sección Femenina—History. 4. Elite (Social sciences)—Spain—History—20th century. 5. Spain—Politics and government—20th century. I. Title.
HQ1236.5.S7O36 2009
306.2082'0946—dc22

2008036891

Typeset & Designed by SAP, Brighton & Eastbourne.
Printed by TJ International, Padstow, Cornwall.
This book is printed on acid-free paper.

CONTENTS

Series Editor's Preface	vi
Acknowledgements	ix
Cover Illustrations in Formal Setting	xi
Introduction	1
Prologue – The Birth of a Female Political Elite	15
1 Nurses and Students: Education, Professional Training and the Civil War Experience in the Shaping of Two Generations of Leadership	21
2 *The National Syndicalist Woman*: The Genealogy of a Gender Identity	55
3 Bridging the Gap between Elitist and Mass Politics: Gender Legislation of the Sección Femenina de la FET	79
4 Am I that Body? Sección Femenina de la FET and the Struggle for the Institution of Physical Education and Competitive Sports for Women	104
Conclusions	128
Notes	135
Bibliography	151
Index	159

SERIES EDITOR'S PREFACE

Our knowledge and understanding of the Franco dictatorship of 1939–1975 have been enormously enhanced over the last two decades as more and more research on this crucial period in modern Spanish history has appeared. Still, much of this work has focused on the economy or high politics, especially during the regime's first decade, the 1940s. A great deal remains to be done. Thus the social and cultural history of the dictatorship has yet to be written, while its last thirty years have been subjected to little research in comparison with the first ten. In *Señoritas in Blue*, Inbal Ofer tackles both of these principal areas of neglect in her study of one of the most under-researched and least understood themes of all: the dictatorship's organization for women, the *Sección Femenina* or Women's Section. Not only does she reconstruct the political history of the SF, but she also recovers the organization's cultural and social dimensions. Moreover, she tells this story from the very outset of the regime in 1939 up to, and beyond, its demise in 1975. Consequently *Señoritas in Blue* tackles a major shortcoming in the historiography on the Franco dictatorship while contributing to the wider debate on the role of women within fascist or right-wing authoritarian regimes.

Prior to the 1990s, the Sección Feminina received scant attention from scholars. Within the overall context of studies on women in twentieth-century Spain, there was a certain amount on left-wing politicians such as Dolores Ibarruri, *La Pasionaria*, and progressive artists and intellectuals such as María Zambrano, but there was scarcely anything on conservative women, whether Catholic, monarchist or Basque and Catalan nationalists. Neither was there much on the lives and experiences of ordinary women. Those scholars who worked on the Sección Femenina tended to regard it as apolitical, thereby replicating the dictatorship's own dismissive discourse in which the political domain was strictly divorced from the social. The SF's alleged preoccupation with supposedly marginal matters, such as the Social Service for Women or classes in home economics, merely reinforced the impression that, within the grand scheme of the dictatorship, the SF was a purely peripheral entity.

In reassessing the SF, Inbal Ofer has drawn upon the new approaches to gender studies to have emerged over the last decade. Influenced not only by the debates within feminism but also by the research on women in the Mediterranean region and central Europe, she has moved beyond the so-called Anglo-Saxon paradigm, with its stress on the acquisition of the female suffrage and formal rights, in order to explore other channels for the empowerment of women. She contends that the SF did not blindly follow the dictates of a regime based on the exclusion of women from the public sphere, but eventually developed and defended its own, autonomous social and political agenda, though always within the framework of the regime.

In doing so, the SF managed to realize a number of reforms during the late Franco period that, in Ofer's words, "greatly improved" the lives of women. Thus the SF not only facilitated the entry of women into the labour market and higher education, but also encouraged them to fight for political representation and to lead economically independent lives. Certainly these reforms furthered the legal, professional and political rights of women throughout Spain. From this perspective, the SF pursued a gender policy that benefited millions of women and which was achieved despite the redoubtable restraints of the dictatorship. On the other hand, the SF was more concerned with the advancement of middle class, as opposed to working class, women. Indeed, this class bias was to be a salient characteristic of the organization. Even more importantly, the SF never acted against, or even outside, the Francoist system. Paradoxically, it was precisely because the SF was *not* perceived as a threat to the dictatorial order that it was able to achieve as much as it did.

Still, the SF was not simply a women's organization *per se*. On the contrary, the national leadership of the SF regarded itself as simply one more political actor within the Franco dictatorship. Accordingly, the SF competed with other groups within the regime, above all the Catholic church, with a view to advancing its own ideological agenda.

Señoritas in Blue therefore marks a radical rupture with the dominant narrative on the Franco dictatorship. What Edward Malefakis has dubbed the 'essentialist' vision of the regime maintains that Franco controlled all aspects of civil, economic and political life and that all of the regime groups were prepared to renounce their ideological and religious goals in exchange for the exercise of administrative power. By contrast, Ofer argues that each group possessed considerable autonomy and defended its own ideological and collective interests in the negotiations that characterized all policy-making under the dictatorship. Only in this way was the SF able to increase substantially the number of women in the labour market and to better their working conditions. Ofer also breaks with the dominant narrative by underlining the degree to which the regime, and with it the SF, actually evolved over time, as shown by the changing image of the "National Syndicalist Woman".

Señoritas in Blue, which draws on extensive primary research (including numerous personal interviews), enriches our vision of the Franco dictatorship in a number of ways. Not only does Inbal Ofer's pioneering work present a fundamental reappraisal of the SF under the dictatorship, but it also offers a more nuanced understanding of the regime itself. Finally, *Señoritas in Blue* is to be welcomed for broadening and deepening our understanding of the experiences and agency of women under fascist or right-wing authoritarian regimes.

Nigel Townson
Madrid

ACKNOWLEDGEMENTS

This book has been a long time in the making. My research on the Sección Femenina de la FET would not have been possible without the financial assistance of several institutions and foundations. I would like to thank the School of History, Tel Aviv University and the Rottenstreich Foundation for their generous support. I am also grateful to the "Yad Hanadiv" Foundation (Israel) for making the editing and publication of this book possible.

Of all the people who assisted me through eight years of research and writing I am especially indebted to Professor Raanan Rein. His great patience and vast knowledge were a constant inspiration. I would like to thank all those who never tired of reading, re-reading, commenting and clarifying: Professor Jeffery Lesser of Emory University, who read the entire manuscript and offered much advice. Dr. Gerardo Leibner, Atalia Shragai, Uri Rosenhack and Lior Ben David of the Sverdlin Institute for Latin American History and Culture, Tel Aviv University and to all members of the Institute's research seminar.

A special mention is in order of all the friends and colleagues who made Spain into my second home: To Dr. Nigel Townson for his friendship and time. For reading large parts of this manuscript and greatly encouraging me to publish it. To Julio, of the Real Academia de Historia, who made sure I would always find what I was looking for. To Tomas and Pilar, who for many years were my family away from my own family, and to Tamar Groves and Cristina Martinez for their friendship and many insights.

I would like to thank collectively all the people who were so generous with their time, sharing with me their thoughts and private memories: Victoria Eiroa, Teresa Loring, María Nieves Sunyer, Adelida del Pozo, Consuelo Salvo Guntín, María Sierra, Jaime Suarez and Consuelo Valcarcel. I am especially indebted to Andresa López, who assisted me in getting and staying in touch with all those people throughout the years. I am deeply sorry she did not live to see the publication of this book.

And finally I would like to thank my husband Ilan, who never tired of reading chapters, papers and presentations – the one person who truly knows everything there is to know about the Sección Femenina de la

Acknowledgements

Falange. I would not have been able to travel this long road without his love and support and that of my two children Adam and Arielle.

INBAL OFER
Yehud (Israel), 2008

General Francisco Franco and Pilar Primo de Rivera in Castillo de la Mota, Medina del Campo, 1939.

Physical education classes for women, Ciudad Universitaria, Madrid, 1960.

Physical education classes, Summer camp for girls "Marina Española", Playa de Sada, La Coruña, 1963.

INTRODUCTION

To those familiar with the history of Spain under the reign of General Francisco Franco, the title of this book – *The Making of a Female Political Elite in Franco's Spain* – might seem an exaggeration. To others the putting together of the phrases "Francoist Spain" and a "Female Political Elite" might seem to be an utter contradiction in terms. How can we talk of the existence of a female political elite within a regime that saw the exclusion of women from the public sphere as one of the preconditions for its existence? And even if one could conceive of a situation in which a female political elite might attempt to force its way into the heart of Francoist power, how can we claim this role for an organization that originated as the women's wing of Spain's fascist party – the Spanish Falange? Yet this is precisely the claim of the current study.

While acknowledging the deep organizational and financial ties, as well as the great ideological affinity, between the Sección Femenina de la FET (henceforth the SF) and the Franco regime, I shall demonstrate how its national leadership used its formal position in order to promote an autonomous social and political agenda. Despite the need to constantly maneuver between the cultural and legal dictates of the regime to which it adhered, the unique activities and personal experiences of SF members at the heart of Spain's political power became a model for an array of policies and reforms that greatly improved the lives of Francoist women.

The Spanish Falange, of which the SF was part, was founded in Madrid in October 1933 by José Antonio Primo de Rivera, son of the former dictator Miguel Primo de Rivera. The movement was formed in an attempt to provide solutions for some of the political and social problems faced by Spanish society during the years of the Second Republic. First and foremost amongst these problems was the ineffectiveness of the Spanish Traditional Right in facing what was perceived as a growing threat to Spain's territorial and religious unity. The SF, founded in June 1934, existed for 43 years, attaining in its heyday (at the end of the Spanish Civil War in 1939) over half a million members. During the four decades of its existence, the organization managed to seize authority over most of the sectors and associations in Francoist Spain in which women operated. It gained control of the Syndicate of Female University Students, the nurses' and teachers' syndicates, the Social Service for Women (Servicio Social de la Mujer) and others.

Yet despite the SF's size and importance, it received little attention from historians prior to the 1990s. This situation has changed in the last decade with the publication of new works dealing with the organization's activities in the different Spanish territories and its influence on the different female populations that came into contact with it.[1] But an examination of way in which the SF's policies were formulated and implemented at the macro level is still lacking. Following the rhetoric of the regime, many historians tended to see the SF as an apolitical organization. As such, its members were perceived as being occupied with a variety of marginal activities, such as providing home economics classes or administrating the obligatory Social Service for Women.[2] By highlighting the SF's supposedly apolitical nature, Spanish historiography has in effect reproduced Francoist discourse, which reinforced the distinction between the political and the social, and between the private and the public. This discourse, which in the past contributed to the exclusion of women from many centers of political and public power, now often serves to obscure and invalidate those efforts they did make to conquer the "public sphere."[3]

Women were not of course totally absent from the long and impressive list of works concerned with 20th century Spain. The "female angle" was deemed by many a worthy point of departure for research, but only in certain cases. High-ranking left-wing political activists, women intellectuals and artists and women prisoners or political exiles are only some cases in point. However, the everyday culture and experiences of ordinary women under the Franco regime have received less attention. And those women who were known to be public activists affiliated with the Catholic Church, with the movements of the Conservative Right or with those of Catalan or Basque Nationalism, are still largely absent from the existing literature.[4]

In view of these tendencies, the awakened interest in the SF in the mid-1990s must be placed in the wider context of new developments in the research on women and gender history. Such an interest has no doubt been influenced by the debates taking place within the feminist movement itself concerning the nature of feminism as a social and political phenomenon and by works that have examined different women's movements in central Europe and around the Mediterranean. Once the universality of the Anglo-Saxon feminist model – with its emphasis on formal equality and the central role of women's suffrage – started to be questioned, the way was opened to explore the significance of a wider variety of projects for the promotion of women. Historian Mary Nash, for example, claimed that Spanish feminism itself was made up of a variety of associations that fought for differentiated social and civil rights that would be accorded to all Spanish women in light of their status as potential mothers.[5] By fighting for improved education and working conditions for women, Spanish feminists contributed to the acknowledgment of women's basic rights. According to Nash, this discourse, which emphasized the complementary nature of women's role and rights, helped to make the demands of Spanish feminists heard within the political circles in which they moved.

In Spain and elsewhere, however, the attempt to include new collective experiments under the heading of feminist research raised a series of important questions: What is feminism? Who is a feminist? How do we understand feminism across national boundaries, cultures and centuries? And more to the point as far as the current book is concerned, what is the relationship between the promotion of women as a collective and feminism? Can every person or group that is engaged in promoting women's rights within specific social and political contexts be considered feminist?

Members of the SF rejected out of hand the label of *feministas* affixed to them by those within Nationalist Spain who viewed the promotion of women's professional, legal and political rights as undermining the stability of the Franco regime. While one cannot ignore such a rejection, it is important to situate it within the right political and cultural context. We must ask ourselves why women who championed their own and others' right to gainful employment, higher education, economic independence and political representation, and who were critically engaged with writings such as those of Simon de Beauvoir or Betty Friedman, recoiled so violently from being called feminists.

The answer, I believe, lies partially in the meaning assigned to the term at that time and the negative connotations attached to it within nationalist and Catholic circles. Members of the SF publicly defended a gender-based but egalitarian vision of social organization, which emphasized women's rights as defined primarily by their childbearing and/or nurturing capacities. Feminism, as they understood it defended more abstract concepts of human rights, celebrating the quest for personal independence in all aspects of life, while playing down or dismissing as insignificant all sex-linked qualities or contributions, including childbearing and its attendant responsibilities. Within the boundaries of such a definition, the hyper-nationalist SF, with its commitment to the promotion of the Spanish family and largely Catholic membership, was understandably ill at ease.

While it would be anachronistic to speculate how recent developments in feminist scholarship might have influenced the self-perceptions of SF members, there is no doubt they have made the actual role of these women within the Francoist system more "apparent" and their presence more "visible." The ability to discern the autonomous formulation and implementation of gender policies, which I view as a central attribute in the making of a female political elite, was much aided by the subtle working definitions of historian Karen Offen. Offen, in her now classical article

"Defining Feminism: a Comparative Historical Approach", pointed to two central modes of argumentation taken by the proponents of women's emancipation from male control – the "relational" and the "individualist":

> The term 'relational' seems advantageous (as compared say with 'familial' or 'maternalist') because it encompasses all relationship, implying at least the possibility of extension to other classes of people besides husbands, children and other immediate relatives. . . . Viewed historically, arguments in the relational feminist tradition proposed a gender based but egalitarian vision of social organization. They featured the primacy of a companionate, non-hierarchical, male-female couple as the basic unite of society, whereas individualist arguments posited the individual, irrespective of sex or gender, as the basic unite. Relational feminism emphasized women's rights as *women* (defined primarily by their childbearing and/or nurturing capacities) in relation to men. It insisted on women's distinctive contribution in these roles to the broader society and made claims on the common wealth on the basis of these contributions. By contrast the individualist feminist line of argumentation emphasized more abstract concepts of human rights and celebrated the quest for personal independence (or autonomy) in all aspects of life, while downplaying, deprecating or dismissing as insignificant all socially defined roles and minimizing discussion of sex-linked qualities or contributions, including child-bearing and its attendant responsibilities.[6]

As Offen pointed out in the French case, the key arguments of relational feminism culminated in the seemingly paradoxical doctrine of "equality in difference" or equity as distinct from equality. The fundamental tenets included the notion that there were both physiological and cultural distinctions between the sexes, a concept of a womanly or manly nature and a sharply defined gender division of labor, or roles, in the family. This definition, which emphasizes the differences and centrality of interpersonal relations in general, is of special relevance to any discussion concerning an organization such as the SF. Its greatest merit lies in the way it allows us to consider both the promotion of women as a collective and their commitment to a larger nationalist project within a single conceptual framework. In doing so it makes explicit the tensions which commitment to these two projects generated, while at the same time acknowledges the centrality of both to the lives and personal histories of SF members.

I would like to note, too, the importance of situating the current book within the vast field of studies examining lives and agency of women under fascist regimes. While I would not qualify the Franco regime as a fascist regime, one can not disregard the international context within which it came into life. The rebelling Nationalist forces in Spain would have been hard pressed to survive if not for the initial military support of Fascist Italy, and especially of Nazi Germany. Less than six months after the conclusion of the Spanish Civil War (Madrid, the last Republican stronghold, surrendered before the Nationalist army on March 28, 1939) the Second World War erupted. And while Spain hastened to declared its neutrality in this overpowering conflict the sympathies and support of the Franco regime clearly lay with the Axis powers. Furthermore, the SF itself originated within a self-denominated fascist movement. And while Falangism in its "purest" form never matured into a mass movement one can not ignore its ideological roots.

The first historians to turn their attention to the story of those women who actively supported and collaborated with the fascist regimes of Europe saw them as misguided, assigned to the status of an "out-group", and sexually marginalized by Fascism's heightened chauvinism.[7] In the past three decades, however, a more complex and nuanced picture has emerged, which takes into account the array of life experiences of women who were actively affiliated with different fascist movements.[8] Taken in conjunction these studies emphasis the central role played by women (both in qualitative and quantitative terms) in fascist organizations. Through combined structural and discursive analysis all studies point to a surprisingly (yet common) high level of female mobilization sustained over time. Despite the highly nationalistic and chauvinistic rhetoric of fascist movements such works also point to high levels of involvement of women in the formulation and implementation of national policies.

An analysis of the SF's activities on a national level reinforces many of these conclusions. It also offers a unique perspective on the interactions between issues of class, gender, religion and nationality far beyond the interwar years. By concentrating on the pervasiveness and evolution of gender concerns in the Spanish case, I hope to draw attention to their constitutive, yet changing influence on the evolution of the Franco regime. By examining the role class and nationality played in the consolidation of the SF's political position I wish to stress the way in which female agency worked to create its own "out-groups", reformulating the balance of power even within the most gender biased regimes.

The SF's symbiotic, and at the same time highly conflictive, relationship with the Franco regime raises questions concerning the latter's nature and functioning. Social scientist Juan Linz, in a 1964 article entitled "An Authoritarian Regime: Spain", initiated a debate that still rages today concerning the character of the Franco regime.[9] Linz coined the expression "authoritarianism" in order to describe regimes whose members exhibited a limited degree of ideological heterogeneity. According to Linz such regimes did not present a specific, coherent ideology, but their different sectors were characterized nonetheless by a shared mentality (in the Spanish case that of National Catholicism). Linz claimed that totalitarian regimes strove to maintain high levels of mobilization and attempted to penetrate and control all aspects of their subjects' everyday lives. Authoritarian regimes, on the other hand, presented low mobilization levels, except in times of major crisis. Furthermore, according to Linz, authoritarian leaders were often quite content to leave at least some aspects of everyday civic life under the control of different social groups, as long as these were perceived as having a vested interest in the regime's survival.

Since the 1980s, this view of the Franco regime has been repeatedly challenged by historians such as Paul Preston, who contends that the political entity that rose out of the Spanish Civil War attempted to involve itself in and control every single aspect relating to civil, political and economic life in post-1939 Spain. Historian Tzvi Medin, for example, claimed that the dictator was the final and supreme arbitrator and what seemed like ideological heterogeneity was no more than limited freedom of action accorded to state bureaucrats.[10] As such Monarchists and members of the Church and of the *Movimiento* gave up their ideological and religious convictions in exchange for administrative power and the knowledge that the discord leading up to the Civil War would not be allowed to surface again. Whenever ideological differences did surface, it was always at the bidding of the dictator, who wished to pit one political entity against another.

Against the background of this debate, the current study, which examines the functioning of one of the regime's organs from a gender and social perspective, can contribute greatly to a more subtle understanding of the regime's functioning. General Franco was undoubtedly the supreme arbitrator in many important political issues. It is also clear that he managed to manipulate each of the regime's "political families" so as to create a delicate balance that did not enable the military, the Church or the FET to control the centers of political power for very long. But the dictator did not survive by manipulating and exercising brute force alone. Well into the late 1950s, each of the major sectors within Francoist society still believed that the political construction that emerged from the Civil War constituted the best (even if not the most perfect) means for realizing its political aspirations. In exchange for a long-term commitment to the survival of the regime, both the Church and the FET gained considerable administrative power and a measure of freedom to act on political and social matters.

In my opinion, the amorphous unit that historians have called the "regime" was a bureaucratic apparatus whose policy was formulated through constant negotiation between its different sectors, each with its own ideological perspective and distinct personal and collective interests. The struggle to amend the Civil Code and ratify the Law for Political and

Professional Equality for Women (discussed in chapter 3) provides a good example of the way organs within the "regime" made use of their position in order to legitimize non-consensual forms of activism. The way in which the SF's leadership worked in order to increase the number of working women and improve their working-conditions is an example of the unexpected uses made by agents of the "regime" of the freedom of action accorded them in the public arena.

The current work is based on six years of archival research and a series of personal interviews conducted with ex-SF members. Of these different sources I was able to construct a database containing information about the life histories of 200 members of the SF's national leadership. Members of the national leadership came from several different groups within the organization. To the first group belonged members of *La Nacional*, as the offices of the *Jefe Nacional*, Pilar Primo de Rivera (sister of the Falange's founder José Antonio Primo de Rivera) were called. About 150 women belonged to this group, which headed the organization's political and administrative hierarchy at the national level. The second group included the SF's provincial delegates and secretaries, namely 120 women, who were the organization's political representatives in each of Spain's provincial capitals. Each of the provincial offices was also composed of delegates and secretaries in charge of the SF's professional services (such as Syndicates; Youth; Press and Propaganda; Administration and so forth). This group numbered about 600 additional women. Finally, we must take into account the twenty women who headed the SF's national schools (*Escuelas Nacionales*), where the national leaders themselves, teachers, nurses and youth instructors were trained.

Details concerning the personal lives of these women and their advancement in the organization were collected especially for the purpose of this work. Some of the information existed dispersed through the memoirs of prominent ex-Falangists and SF members such as Pilar Primo de Rivera. Local studies were extremely useful in providing details concerning the provincial delegations in Llerida, Aragon, Valladolid and Almería. The rest of the information was collected from the SF's national archives at the Real Academia de Historia in Madrid and by a series of interviews I conducted with former SF members between the years 2002 and 2005.

The database analysis was conducted paying special attention to the year in which the women concerned entered the organization; their personal and professional background and the type of positions they held within the SF (political versus administrative positions, national versus provincial posts, etc.). Looking first at the women's origin and socio-cultural background and then at the type of positions they held and their geographical location raised important questions concerning the everyday implications of their political affiliation. In Spain of the 1940s and 1950s, what were the economic and social implications of a middle-class single woman's life away from her parents' home, at times within rural and working-class communities? What personal and professional encounters were generated by the constant travels of these women across the Spanish territories? How were their views regarding themselves and other women changed by their work, side by side with men, at the heart of the Francoist administration? Such questions and others later constituted the focal points around which my interviews were conducted.

Looking at the personal histories of a substantial group within the SF's national hierarchy enabled me to reach several conclusions. The first of these had to do with the existence of two distinct generations within the organization's leadership. To the first generation belonged the "Founders" (*Las fundadoras*), the women who joined the ranks of the national leadership prior to 1940. These women came from two main social groups: friends, relatives and fiancés of leading Falangists and professional nurses who joined the SF during the Civil War. The second generation – that of the "Young Sisters" (*Hermanas Pequeñas*) – included the women who joined the SF's hierarchy during the 1950s. The majority of the "Young Sisters" were born during or after the Civil War and became acquainted with the SF during their time at university. While the first generation brought the SF its intimate relations with the men who ran Francoist Spain, the second generation's contribution lay in the formal education and professional training of its members.

Tracing the "Young Sisters" progression within the SF shows that they were fully integrated into both the political and the professional hierarchies. As we shall see, the reason for this had to do with their time of entrance into the SF. During the 1950s, the SF was already starting to show clear signs of "aging." The women who had joined the organization in the 1930s were by then in their forties, and some, like Pilar Primo de Rivera herself, were nearing their fifties. The central event of their lives – the Spanish Civil War – was rapidly loosing its significance in the eyes of young Spaniards. The "Young Sisters" brought with them a more youthful spirit and a common language with the new generation, together with a renewed passion for José Antonio's doctrine.

The interviews I conducted with former SF members were also central to this study. These oral sources added interest and a personal perspective to the research process, but also created some difficulties. When I began my research, only a few members of the SF's founding generation were still alive. Pilar Primo de Rivera herself passed away in 1997, but her good friend (and the last General Secretary of the SF) Teresa Loring was still alive. Two other *jefes* of this generation who were also still alive were Victoria Eiroa and Andresa López Enseñat.[11] I interviewed the first two in their own homes (in Malaga and Madrid respectively). Both interviews assumed the nature of a personal chat, or rather a monologue. Teresa Loring talked at length about her life and work alongside Pilar Primo de Rivera (the two of them had shared an apartment in Madrid in the 1960s), about the *jefe nacional's* shyness, lack of self-confidence and charisma and her terrible taste in clothes. Vicky Eiroa concentrated on the personal significance membership in the SF held for her. Both women expressed bitterness about the way the SF was erased from the collective memory in the years following the transition to democracy. In both cases I encountered strong resistance to answering questions and a no less strong desire to tell the SF's story "in their own words." However, to someone who just weeks before had finished reading the *Crónica de la SF* (which was edited by the Francoist historian Luis Suárez Fernández with the help of ex-SF members), "their own words" bore a suspicious resemblance to the "official version".[12]

These initial interviews raised important questions about the ways in which private memories are formulated. How should one interpret the resemblance between the way in which all three women chose to portray their public activism or the influence the SF and José Antonio's doctrine had on their lives? Was this resemblance due to the shared memories and extensive use of Falangist jargon? To what extent was the project of preserving the SF's legacy (of which the *crónica* was an end result) also a project of reconstruction, which "unified" the personal memories of those who took part in it? Why, in a post-Franco society where entire sectors of the population wished to conceal their relations with the dictatorship, did these women resent any allegation that there were tensions between the Franco regime and the SF? Were their feelings of alienation within the new democracy so great and their need for a sense of belonging so deep that they now preferred to conceal the organization's uniqueness, of which they had been so proud in the past?

The rest of the interviews I conducted were carried out in a somewhat different manner from the first three. To begin with, I was aided in all of the proceeding interviews by a questionnaire.[13] The interviews were carried out in the offices of the *Asociación de Nueva Andadura* (henceforth ANA), an association that grouped veterans of the SF throughout Spain up till May 2006. Any attempt to interview ex-SF members was bound to lead me at one point or another to the central offices of the ANA in Madrid, where the personal information of members still alive was kept. Andresa López, who headed the organization in the capital, agreed to help me schedule the interviews, and, as I later learnt, was to be present in each one. What seemed like a problem to begin with turned out to be quite advantageous. At the ANA's offices there were always additional women who would express their opinion on different issues. So the conversation that flowed between my interviewee and those who became "second-chair interviewees" provided me with unexpected information. Throughout the interviews, Andresa López expressed what I came to identify as the "organizational voice". She attempted to smooth over notes of discord and present the relationship within the SF, between the SF and the regime, and finally between the SF's everyday functioning and José Antonio's doctrine as completely harmonious. López' presence afforded me a better understanding of the points where personal and collective memory came into conflict and the way such conflicts were resolved.

As can be seen from the brief description above, any analysis of the SF's national leadership must take into consideration both temporal and structural elements in the organization's development. These two interrelated lines of inquiry in turn call for the application of two distinct analytical categories: "generation" and "elite." Both categories are no strangers to historical research, however their frequent use can at times conceal quite a bit of confusion. It is often rather difficult to point to the changing nature of the elite in question or to the decisive role that was played by generational turnover in this process. Differentiating between generations can in itself prove to be a difficult task. Should such a distinction be made according to the year in which members of each group were born or according to the time when they gained public prominence as politicians or as intellectuals? There is undoubtedly some degree of overlapping between the two, since people who were born in the same year are likely to reach public "maturity" at approximately the same time, but this is not always the case.

In order to clear up some of this confusion I chose for the purpose of this work to employ Paul Lewis' distinction between "historical generation" and "promotion".[7] Lewis, who researched the ministerial elites of Mussolini's Italy, Franco's Spain and Salazar's Portugal used the term "promotion" in order to describe a group of people who entered the centers of political power at the same time, regardless of their actual age. Historical generation, however, signified for Lewis:

> An age group, whose members share common historical experiences, which influence the way they perceive the world around them . . . Members of the

same generation might hold opposing political positions, but under these apparent disagreements they share a basic agreement concerning the important issues, questions, and facts of life.[14]

Lewis, following the Spanish philosopher José Ortega y Gasset, set the time span of each generation at 15 years. The current work adopts more or less the same lifecycle when referring to the term "generation." Roughly speaking, one can state that the women belonging to the SF's founding generation were born between 1906 and 1915. They spent their childhood years in the shadow of the war in Morocco and the Primo de Rivera dictatorship (1923–1930). Women like Teresa Loring, Mercedes Formica and Vicky Eiroa were in their late teens when the Falange was founded in 1933. The "Young Sisters", on the other hand, included women who were born between 1930 and 1945 and experienced the events of the Second Republic or the Civil War as distant childhood memories, if at all.

On a structural level, a study of the SF's national leadership requires an examination of the concept of an "elite." Works that research the role of women within political and professional elites are relatively few and reflect the fact that, despite the changes in recent decades, relatively few women can be found in the higher echelons of most economic and political organizations. However, when the position of women within professional and political elites has been examined, several conclusions are reached. First, it is obvious that in the majority of cases the presence of women in high-ranking positions was not actively encouraged. Furthermore, their presence was "tolerated" in those cases where they were not perceived as threatening to men who shared or aspired to the same position.[15] The fact that women are often not perceived as a threat stems from another characteristic of their activism within elites. When in the ranks of power, many women opt for "gender appropriate" positions, which are often undervalued by their men counterparts. These included positions within government ministries dealing with education, health or welfare, commissions having a humanitarian basis, the cosmetic and fashion industries, and so forth.

Studies show that women quite often have to find alternative routes to power, employing different patterns of activism and social networks. Some of these alternatives figure prominently in the SF's history, especially the tendency to make use of its leaders' position as the fiancés, widows or sisters of powerful politicians in order to obtain a foothold at the top of the public pyramid. As mentioned, the accepted division of gender roles often pushes women into specific spheres of action. Despite the discriminatory nature of such gender divisions, women often reach exceptionally high positions in "female appropriate" spheres precisely because of the lack of male competition. The fact that such positions are to be found within women's organizations that are often perceived as social rather than political in nature does not diminish their importance and influence. And finally, in times of crisis, especially deep political and social crisis that bring about momentarily suspension of accepted patterns of mobilization and activism, women are sometimes welcomed into the highest echelons of both political and economic power.[16]

As this study shows, the SF's freedom of action within the Francoist regime stemmed, to some degree at least, from Pilar Primo de Rivera's unique political position and from the urgent need for an organization that would oversee the mobilization (and later on the demobilization) of Spanish women. However, I believe that such freedom was also the result of the perception of leading male politicians that the organization dealt mainly with "women's issues" and as such posed no threat to the existing political order. This enabled Primo de Rivera and her *jefes* to directly confront sectors and individual figures within the regime in a manner that might not have been acceptable had they been Falangists, monarchists or military men.

Chapter 1 presents a socio-cultural profile of the two generations of SF's national leadership. It follows the different paths taken by the members of each generation within the organization and the distinct contribution made by each within the organizational structure. The role played by organizational trappings such as uniforms and salaries in setting the national leadership apart from other women within the SF is examined, and the significance of the obligation imposed upon the national and provincial delegates to refrain from marriage is explored in the context of the impact on their personal lives and political activism.

Chapter 2 examines the way the image of the "National Syndicalist Woman" was formed within the SF's rhetoric from the early days of the Civil War until the 1970s. I look at the different cultural models that gave legitimization to this changing image and explore how internally cohesive it was at different points in time. I also try to use the image of the "National Syndicalist Woman" as a key to understanding the everyday experiences and memories of members of the national leadership. The chapter is based on an analysis of the publications issued by the organization for the benefit of its members. The two journals I examined are *Medina* (*Revista para la Mujer Nacional Sindicalista*), which was published during the Civil War and the early 1940s, and *Teresa*, which was published between the years 1954–1977. Other sources for this chapter include interviews, and the protocols and papers presented at the SF-sponsored International Congress on Women (*Congreso Internacional de la Mujer*) that took place in Madrid in June 1970. In my opinion, the papers presented at this congress reflect the enormous flexibility (as well as the limitations) of the SF's discourse regarding women's nature and roles.

Chapter 3 examines the three legislative projects initiated by the SF for the promotion of women's legal, political and professional equality: the 1958 reform of the Civil Code; the 1961 law of Political and Professional Rights for Women; and the 1966 amendments of that law. I focus on the patterns of political activism adopted by members of the SF prior to 1958; the deliberations leading to the acceptance of each of these laws; and the way their implementation was tracked "on the ground" throughout the 1960s by the organization's legal department (*Asesoria Juridica*). By looking at the internal functioning of the SF, I demonstrate the organization's full initiative in promoting innovative legislation long before the economic developments of the early 1960s called for an expansion of women's public role. My claim is that it was the SF's wish to narrow the gap between the unusual patterns of public and political activism exhibited by its own national leadership and the status of wider, non-affiliated female populations that brought about these reforms.

Finally, Chapter 4 deals with one of the central components of the SF's gender policy: namely, the organization's promotion of women's physical education and competitive sports. As in the case of Nazi Germany and Fascist Italy, the SF saw physical education as a tool of indirect indoctrination and a means for creating group discipline. Physical education classes for girls were supposed to help produce healthy future mothers for the fatherland. The organization made an effort to expose as many girls and young women as possible to a minimal level of physical education through compulsory classes within schools, the youth movement, universities and factories. I demonstrate how this policy created a unique space where nurturing the female body, taking pride in it and even exposing it in public were all considered acceptable. The chapter follows the struggle to institute physical education for girls and women against strong objections on the part of the Church, teachers and even parents. It examines the training process of the physical education instructors, who functioned as young, attractive agents of the SF in an occasionally hostile environment. Finally the way the SF used its physical education policy as a recruitment tool for populations that did not necessarily identify with its ideological doctrine and as a way of emphasizing its distinctiveness within the Francoist coalition, is examined.

Dealing with the ideological discourse and political realities of a dictatorship that crushed any sign of opposition, and the basic human liberties of countless people, has at times been a difficult task. More than once, when attending an academic conference, I was approached by a Spanish historian who would tell me that the story, as I tell it, ignores the repressive affects the SF's policy had on the thousands of women who passed through its classes of home economics and political indoctrination or on the girls that had to swear allegiance to nationalist Spain and go to mass every morning in order to receive food and education within its institutions. While in no way dismissing such repressive affects, I feel strongly that the presence of SF members within the centers of Francoist power also had another side to it.

The complexity of the organization's story is perhaps best summed up in the words of the journalist and novelist Antonio Prometeo Moya. In an interview he conducted with Pilar Primo de Rivera in December 1990, Moya reflected on the contradictory legacy of the SF:

> You presented yourselves as ideal women, as women of the future. And in coming into contact with you, my mother, and no doubt countless other housewives like herself, were faced with an existential point of reference that was as valid as the one that could have been provided for them by the institutions of the Second Republic. I am not talking of ideologies, but of the effect of coming into contact with new horizons, horizons that can be accepted or rejected but that are nonetheless there as a point of comparison.[17]

The extent and nature of these horizons, product of the constant interactions between ideology, religion and the everyday experiences of SF members, are at the heart of the chapters to follow.

PROLOGUE

The Birth of a Female Political Elite

Is there a precise moment at which a political elite comes to life? If such a moment indeed exists, it is an intricate task to separate it from the cumbersome and at times dreary, everyday existence of most public entities. For example, let us consider the founding ceremony of the Spanish Falange, which took place at the *Teatro de la Comedia* in Madrid in November 1933. Five young women actively assisted in planning the event. The women were Pilar and Carmen Primo de Rivera (sisters of José Antonio Primo de Rivera), Ines and Doloras Primo de Rivera (the founder's cousins), and María Luisa Aramburu. All five requested to be officially inducted into the new movement on the same day and were rejected out of hand by the founder. José Antonio could not accept female membership in what he envisioned would be the spearhead of a National Syndicalist revolution won by the blood and sacrifice of a chosen few. But captured by the image of a new politics – politics as poetry (*política como poesía*) – and intent on proving their worth, the women insisted. Finally a compromise was reached, and the five women, as well as two other self-identified Falangist students – Mercedes Formica and Josetina Rodríguez de Viguri – joined the Falange Students' Syndicate (SEU).

The entry of women into the SEU did not by any means signify the birth of a female political elite, and it is debatable if it can even be considered the moment when the SF itself was born. As the Spanish historian María Teresa Gallego Méndez noted, at the outset the Falangist leadership did not consider conferring any official status on their female counterparts. However, by mid-1934 this situation started to change. Following the arrest of many senior Falangists and the death and wounding of several others in street fights, the new movement needed all the help it could get. In June that same year, therefore, the Falange's leadership decided to found a separate Women's Section under the supervision of the male leadership.[1]

Although the female political elite with which this book is concerned, came to life within the ranks of SF's national leadership, it did not come into being at the moment of the organization's foundation, but only much later. This distinction does not merely involve playing around with dates, but is essential to our ability to perceive the national leadership as a coherent social group with a distinct political and ideological agenda. The pages of an historical monograph might not be the best place to speculate on "what might have been" but there is no doubt that prior to the eruption of the Spanish Civil War in July 1936, the SF de la Falange was an insignificant organization, regarding both size and ideology.

The outbreak of the Civil War held great significance for the SF. It brought in its wake an overwhelming increase in membership and a sense of political and cultural radicalization brought about by the struggle to impose one specific worldview over another. According to the most conservative estimates, by 1937 the SF had grown from 2,500 to 60,000 members.[2] This process of expansion, which was characteristic of the entire Falange at the time, stemmed from two reasons. First, the Falangist doctrine with its fascist trappings, revolutionary rhetoric and youthful leaders was the preferred means of mobilization for scores of young middle-class men who wished to fight against the government of the Second Republic.[3] An additional reason for the sharp increase in membership was a willingness unusual within the nationalist camp of the Falangist leaders, to open up their movement to former members of the Spanish Left.

Yet despite some similarities, an examination of the process through which new members joined the SF during the war years enables us to point out the first tentative divergence between the organization and its male counterpart. Local studies of the SF in Aragon, Valladolid and Almería show that during the first two years of the war, the majority of its new members arrived from right-wing movements such as the CEDA, Acción Católica, and the ultra-conservative Carlist Comunion Tradicionalista.[4] Former republicans did not begin joining *en masse* until the end of 1938 and grew in numbers once the war had ended. The second difference has to do with the advancement of former left-wing women within the SF. The FET had purged its ranks time and again during 1937 with the intention of revoking the membership of former "leftists". A decree, published on August 4, 1937, stated that only those who had belonged to the Falange prior to the publication of the Decree of Unification in April that year could be considered active members (*militantes*). By 1939, 2,100 members had been forced to leave the movement due to "ideological unreliability". The SF's leadership, on the other hand, sternly opposed internal purges. Furthermore, Pilar Primo de Rivera warned local delegates more than once that former supporters of the Republic must be treated with respect and compassion. In case of discrimination, the local delegates would have to answer directly to the national leadership.

But the precise moment in which the SF, through the actions of its National Delegate, started positioning itself as an independent ideological and political entity within Francoist Spain is no doubt April 1937. Of all the events of the Civil War, none had a greater effect on the Falange than the publication of the Decree of Unification on April 24th, 1937. The decree merged all the political forces of Nationalist Spain into the Falange Española Tradicionalista y de las JONs and transferred control over all militia forces into the hands of the nationalist army. While retaining the name of the Falange, this action in effect accomplished what José Antonio Primo de Rivera had warned against in a letter from his Alicante jail cell on the eve of the war. By the stroke of a pen, General Franco, with the assistance of his brother Nicolas, emptied José Antonio's movement of all ideological content, turning it instead into the largest source of manpower for the newly formed nationalist administration.

In his memoirs, Ramon Serrano Suñer, Franco's brother-in-law and right-hand man until 1942, rather colorfully described Pilar Primo de Rivera's reaction during the 48 hours following the publication of the Decree of Unification:

> In a small apartment in Plazuela San Julian set Pilar Primo de Rivera like a high priestess ready to offer any sacrifice, which might be required, to the memory of her missing brother. Through the apartment passed Falangists from almost every territory in order to express their embitterment and ask for orders. The feelings expressed (there) were presented in their turn before the High Command in an unequivocal manner.[5]

Pilar Primo de Rivera's refusal to accept the Decree of Unification in the days immediately following its publication was only the first step in a long and complex process, which was to establish her position as her brother's ideological successor within Nationalist Spain. This process started when the Falange's leadership first learned of José Antonio's execution in a republican jail, a fact that was kept a secret from most of the rank and file for a long time. In the absence of the founder, Pilar acted in order to consolidate her position as the only legitimate interpreter of José Antonio's doctrine and as a focal point for sentimental identification with the missing leader.[6] Eight months after the unification, at the SF's Second National Congress, Pilar Primo de Rivera called upon members to accept the current political reality in order to enable everyone to continue with the colossal project at hand – winning the war and building a New Spain. But her words also carried a heavy note of criticism:

> Only the military and the Falange should have the right of veto in this difficult hour for the Fatherland . . . It is women most of all who must preserve the Falangist spirit and faith, since the others who understood this spirit are no longer amongst the living. We, who did not go to the front, we, who stayed alive, are obliged to teach Spain what is the meaning of a Falangist existence.[7]

These words constituted harsh criticism that was aimed at new and old Falangists alike, who, in Primo de Rivera's view, adopted the political label but not the true essence of José Antonio's doctrine. However, at the same time, the National Delegation was aware of the fact that in the power struggle taking place within the nationalist coalition, the SF's survival and its leadership's ability to keep alive its own distinct interpretation of Falangism depended on their political usefulness and the number of affiliates they could master. As opposed to the Falange, then, the SF's leadership welcomed all new affiliates, as can be seen from the following instruction of Primo de Rivera to her delegates: "We must accept into our ranks all those Spaniards who are not condemned for all to see. We must teach them the Falangist doctrine, which they attacked in the past for lack of knowledge". [8]

Pilar Primo de Rivera did not hide her reservations concerning the unification; she harshly criticized both Ramon Serrano Suñer, who promoted it, and Manuel Hedilla, the FET's acting General Secretary, who could not prevent it. But as an organizational unit, the SF stood to gain much from the formal recognition of its standing within the new FET. From a small and relatively insignificant women's organization, the SF overnight became the official women's organization of Nationalist Spain. This was the organization that was to deal with every major aspect relating to women's standing, including education and professional training; health and welfare; and even political and professional representation.

If the publication of the Decree of Unification can be seen as the moment at which the SF's national leadership was born as a political elite, it was the 1947 publication of the Law of Succession that symbolized the final consolidation of its status. Within ten years the national leadership had shifted the SF's role from that of an advocate of José Antonio's National Syndicalist revolution, and a faithful tool of the regime, to the champion of women's rights within the Francoist political system. According to one former national delegate, the law, which declared Spain a monarchy and General Franco a regent for life, generated more fears and debates within the SF than the collapse of the fascist powers and the end of the Second World War.[9] The decision to turn Spain into a monarchy, even if only symbolically, stood in stark contrast to the Falangist worldview and highlighted the regime's total lack of commitment to José Antonio's doctrine. Therefore, the shift in the SF's policies caused by the law was a conscious one, and its implications were debated within the national leadership throughout most of 1947.

When the new law was finally submitted for public approval of sorts by means of a referendum, the SF's leadership decided to call upon its members to vote in its favor. Several reasons influenced Pilar Primo de Rivera's decision not to oppose the law publicly. On a psychological level, the experiences of the Civil War were too vivid in the minds of SF members to allow them to act against the regime that, in their view, had saved Spain from the chaos of those years. On an organizational level, everyone within the SF understood that they had no chance of survival outside the regime. Many of the organization's programs were financed by government ministries, including over 50% of the organization's general budget.[10]

From an ideological perspective, there were many within the SF who saw in the events of 1947 a chance for a healthy change of perspective. By attempting to make itself indispensable to the new regime, the Falange lost its distinct identity. A certain degree of distance and independence offered the possibility of examining the latter in a more critical manner. Some leaders were becoming aware that professional and local pressure groups – all of them smaller and more selective than the FET – were efficiently taking over its role as mediators between the regime and different sectors of the population. This understanding made the SF's leadership decide to adopt new patterns of activism and cast the organization less in the role of the regime's representative within different target populations and more in the role of those populations' representative within the regime.

Pilar Primo de Rivera's speech at the SF's Twelfth National Congress in January 1948 reflected this decision. Throughout the years, Primo de Rivera had emphasized the duty of SF members to act "silently" (*hacer callar*), without drawing attention to their public activism. This demand resulted from a feeling that "being a Falangist" was more about actions than words. It was reinforced by the SF's constant need to maneuver between the many dictates of a political system that did not favor autonomous action and the concentration of too much power in the hands of women, even if they were agents of the regime itself.[11] But with the changes undergone by the SF, working "silently" had become a limitation. If the SF was to become the champion of women's rights, it needed to publicize its agenda and highlight its achievements in order to establish itself as an effective mediator between different female populations and the regime. Or in the words of Primo de Rivera:

> In the past we talked of the need to work in silence. . . . This year we have decided that our work would not be so silent anymore. Therefore you must listen to all the reports, not because we wish to brag, but because a better understanding of our activities will bring with in increased financing, which we can not afford to underestimate. And more importantly, it could enlist the understanding of sectors that so far were not really aware of our existence and work.[12]

As we shall see later on, the change undergone by the SF in and around 1947 had far-reaching implications for the organization's development and policies, so far- reaching indeed that the entire history of the SF can be divided into two periods – prior to 1947 and from 1947 onwards. During the first period, the organization was concerned with implementing the regime's policies. This was mainly accomplished by assisting in the consolidation of an autarkic economy and in repairing the demographic ravages of the Civil War by decreasing infant mortality and raising the birth rate of Spanish families. During the second period, however, the SF became involved with wider female populations through exploring their legal and professional needs, and initiating legislative, social and professional projects that would facilitate these needs.

Dividing the SF's history into two major periods according to the organization's different fields of interest and target populations is not a new notion. Spanish historians María del Carmen Agulló Díaz and Aurora Morcillo chose to position the shift in the organization's interests and activities at the end of the 1950s.[13] They claimed that the intense industrialization and urbanization undergone by Spanish society during the 1950s did not leave the SF any choice but to turn its energy to better-trained and more educated populations, or run the risk of becoming irrelevant both to the regime and to Spanish women. If, however, we locate the turning point in the organization's evolution over a decade earlier, this clarifies the SF's investment of effort in the promotion of an entire array of gender-oriented initiatives long before the shift to a market economy, the renewal of Spain's diplomatic relations with the US and its acceptance into the UN. It is only in light of the SF's specific historiography that the policies and legal and associative initiatives explored in the chapters to follow make sense within the larger political and social context of Nationalist Spain.

1

Nurses and Students
Education, Professional Training and the Civil War Experience in the Shaping of Two Generations of Leadership

A woman with a strong personality, the ability to command others, and a strong sense of commitment. Religious but not prudish. Permanently dressed in a severe-looking uniform.[1]

This is how the Spanish historian María del Carmen Agulló Díaz described what she considered to be a typical high-ranking member of the SF. But who were the women behind the severe-looking uniforms? What social and professional life cycles had fostered in them the ability to command others, so rare in Spanish women of their generation? What familial and educational background gave rise to such strong personalities? I shall try to answer these questions by outlining a social and professional profile of two generations of SF national leadership. To the first generation belonged the *fundadoras* – the women who had joined the national leadership from the SF's foundation up until the end of the Civil War. To the second generation belonged the *hermanas pequeñas* (Young Sisters), who entered the ranks of the national leadership in the 1950s, chiefly from the Falange's Students Syndicate.[2]

This chapter will analyze the process by which each of the two generations was mobilized and integrated into the ranks of the national leadership. It will investigate some of the reasons why these women joined the SF, as well as the different social and cultural "baggage" (educational background, professional training, personal experiences, and so forth) they brought with them into the organization. I will explore the use of certain status symbols that accompanied a high-ranking position within the SF (mainly uniforms and salaries, and the members' civil status as single women – *solteras*). This will indicate the manner in which the national leadership set itself apart from other women within the SF. Finally, interviews I conducted with two former SF members – one belonging to the Founding Generation and one to that of the "Young Sisters" – will make it possible to examine the way each generation was, and still is, viewed by the other.

The statistical information is drawn from an analysis of the database referred to in the Introduction. The database contains information about the life history and advancement within the SF of about 200 members of the national leadership. Amongst them are members of *la nacional*, heads of the SF's national services, provincial delegates and Members of Parliament.

"Elite" and "Generation": Two Categories in the Analysis of the "National Leadership"

As stated above, any analysis of the SF's national leadership must take into account temporal and structural elements in the organization's development. In their turn, these two inter-related lines of inquiry call for the implementation of two distinct analytical categories: "generation" and "elite". In dealing with the first term, I have chosen to adopt Paul Lewis' distinction between "historical generation" and "promotion".[3] Lewis, who researched the ministerial elites of Mussolini's Italy, Franco's Spain and Salazar's Portugal, used the term "promotion" in order to describe a group of people who entered the centers of political power at the same time, regardless of their actual age. Historical generation, however, signified for Lewis:

> An age group, whose members share common historical experiences, which influence the way they perceive the world around them . . . Members of the same generation might hold opposing political positions, but under these apparent disagreements they share a basic agreement concerning the important issues, questions, and facts of life.[4]

Lewis, following the Spanish philosopher José Ortega y Gasset, set the time span of a generation at fifteen years. The current work adopts more or less the same life-cycle when referring to the term "generation". Roughly speaking, one can establish that the women belonging to the SF's founding generation were born between the years 1906 and 1915. Their childhood took place in the shadow of the war in Morocco and the Primo de Rivera dictatorship (1923–1930). Women like Teresa Loring, Mercedes Formica and Vicky Eiroa were in their late teens in 1933 when the Falange was founded.[5] The "Young Sisters", on the other hand, were women who were born between 1930 and 1945 and experienced the events of the Second Republic or the Civil War as distant childhood memories, if at all.[6]

This distinction between a "promotion" and a "historical generation" brings to mind Karl Mannheim's multi-dimensional definition. Mannheim offered a definition of the term "generation" that took into consideration both biological and cultural factors. For Mannheim a generation was represented not by date of birth but rather by the sum of cultural representations associated with that date. The sense of belonging to a generation was determined by the way in which a place and date of birth interacted with what Mannheim defined as "generational context" – "a joint perception of change that is the direct result of one's exposure, or lack of exposure, to processes of social and spiritual change". But despite the fact that one can indicate similar perceptions concerning historical change amongst members of the same generation, not all of them react to these changes in a similar manner. In order to explain the differences in individual and group reactions within the same generation, Mannheim coined the term "generational unit". The members of such a unit share amongst themselves a common worldview and common intentions and aspirations. According to this scheme of things, the generational context would function as an actual or imagined space within which several generational units struggle to impose their own unique views and aspirations.[7]

If a generation is a cultural unit whose members share the same historical experiences, one must ask to what extent gender perceptions influence generational identification. Historian Abigail Stewart, who examined the formation of generational perceptions amongst white and black youth in the US during the 1960s, analyzed the relationship between generation, race and gender. Stewart speculated that:

> Generations that had lived through extraordinary historical events will manifest little interest in preserving the values of their predecessors. Their members often see themselves as having taken part in a process of social change and are interested in transmitting to future generations their commitment to this process rather than specific past values.[8]

At the same time, Stewart stated that the women who participated in her research, especially black women, had a weaker sense of generational affiliation than the men. The newfound freedom of American youth in the 1960s was not equally experienced. Some women in particular found this freedom threatening and felt that it undermined some aspects of their existing value system.

The unsettling effect of major historical events on generational and gender perceptions was also explored by historians researching the influence of the First and Second World Wars on the formation of women's identities. Many agreed that these times of crisis caused gender identification to be replaced by generational identification. But such changes were neither complete nor free of contradictions.[9] Penny Summerfield, for example, examined the way in which the Second World War subverted the image of the "daughter" within middle-class discourse. Summerfield inquired:

> What was the meaning, then, of undermining this rigid symbolic code? A celebration of released female sensuality? It is my contention that undermining a firmly set 'identity' does not bring about release from the conscious and unconscious limitations inherent in it.[10]

In the case of the SF, it is abundantly clear that the effect of the dramatic events of the Spanish Second Republic and the Civil War, and their contribution to the severing of gender and family affiliations, brought about a new type of generational identification. This is perhaps best understood from the dozens of testimonies of young women who followed their brothers and fiancés into the Falange. This occurred much to the dismay and even horror of their parents, many of them loyal monarchists and long time conservatives. These shifting gender and generation alliances are clearly expressed in the *literatura rosa* of the time – the romantic novels and short stories produced for and by women and reproduced in women's magazines. These literary materials, which will be examined at length in chapter 2, reflect the manner in which Civil War experience cut across class, gender and political alliances, thus creating a series of conflicting identifications.

While the Spanish case demonstrates that the majority of women were rarely accepted on an equal footing with the men whose ideological lead they followed, the mere fact of their presence at the heart of political mobilization significantly changed their lives. However, by claiming that the SF's national leadership constituted a "political elite", the current study also wishes to stress the fact that women's mobilization had an effect not only on their own lives, but also on the evolvement of the Francoist political system in general.

As the present study illustrates, the SF's freedom of action within the Francoist regime stemmed, at least to some degree, from Pilar Primo de Rivera's unique political position and from the urgent need for an organization that would administer the mobilization (and later on the demobilization) of Spanish women. However, I believe that such freedom was also the result of leading male politicians' perceptions that the organization dealt mainly with "women's issues" and as such posed no threat to the existing political order. This enabled Primo de Rivera and her *jefes* to directly confront sectors and individual figures within the regime in a manner that might not have gone unnoticed in the case of Falangists, monarchists or military men.

While some social scientists tend to see individuals' advancement within political and professional elites as more or less predictable, others have claimed that such routes are anything but predictable or well organized.[11] Cynthia Epstein, for example, demonstrated how newcomers sometimes require the assistance of senior members in the organization within which they wish to advance. In such cases, the desire of senior members to advance newcomers is of great significance, since only those deemed "fitting" receive the necessary help. All others will have to struggle independently to "uncover" the key to success.[12] Women quite often have to find alternative routes to power, employing various constellations of activism and social networks. They might make use of their position as the wives, widows or sisters of the men in power in order to obtain a foothold at the top of the public pyramid. As mentioned the recognized division of gender roles often pushes women into specific spheres of action. Despite the discriminatory nature of such gender divisions, women often reach exceptionally high positions in "female appropriate" spheres precisely because of the lack of male competition. The fact that such positions exist within women's organizations that are often perceived as social rather than political in nature does not diminish their importance and influence. And finally, in times of crisis, especially deep political and social crisis that bring about a momentary suspension of accepted patterns of mobilization and activism, women are sometimes welcomed into the highest echelons of both political and economic power.[13]

From the moment of its inception, José Antonio Primo de Rivera envisioned the Falange as the spearhead of a future national-syndicalist revolution. Against the background of what the founder saw as an alienated society in advanced stages of social disintegration, the future revolution depended on:

> A small and selected group of people, who will represent a clearer, purer and more energetic Spain, free from mediocrity and conservatism. Those who will join this group will be like young, fresh branches that take over an old and shriveled trunk. . . . They will have to carry on their duty even when faced with the momentary objections of their fellow revolutionaries and the opposition of the great masses.[14]

The use of adjectives like "young" and "fresh" as opposed to "old" and "shriveled" testifies to the importance of generational perceptions in José Antonio's vision of the future, however in reality, generational unity was heavily threatened by ideological and class divisions. Falangism was an ideology lacking in democratic spirit. In addition, it assumed a paternalistic attitude, which saw the masses (especially the masses of urban workers) as urgently needing political and cultural guidance. The number of aristocrats amongst the founders of the new movement was indeed relatively low, but the Falange did not draw its members from all social classes. Economic means per se may not have been a condition for entry into its leadership ranks, but was no doubt influenced by cultural and educational considerations. Proof of this may be found in the line of novelists, poets and other intellectuals who joined José Antonio's entourage: Rafael Sánchez Mazas, Eugenio Montes, Arnesto Gimínez Caballero and Pedro Mourlane Michelena, being only a few examples of this.[15]

The speeches and writings of Pilar Primo de Rivera throughout her career indicate that she saw the national leadership of the SF as an integral part of the revolutionary elite that was often referred to by her brother. The national leadership numbered approximately 900 women at any given time. Since there is no direct access to membership cards and personal information concerning the affiliates, it is difficult to precisely estimate the turnover within this group. However, the database constructed for the purpose of the present study has enabled me to draw two conclusions. First, of the women known to belong to the founding generation, 18% belonged to the national leadership from the moment they entered the organization up to its disbanding in 1977. Out of the entire group of leaders studied, 30% belonged to the second generation, which entered the SF after 1950.

The SF's Founding Generation: Growing Up in the Shadow of the Second Republic and Coming of Age in the Shadow of the Civil War

The last two decades have witnessed feminist research's growing interest in issues of sacrifice within modern societies, and in the role played by women in what Julia Kristeva called the *sacrificial social contract*.[16] Research conducted in various societies has indicated that for the most part women, especially fertile women, were prevented from taking part in events with sacrificial potential. This has led researchers such as Nancy Jay to speculate that one of the main goals of the sacrificial social contract was to establish and consolidate alternative lines of social and cultural heritage, which for the most part sidestepped women. Their aim was to transfer social, cultural or political legacies from men who were recognized as the mythical fathers (of a nation, society or specific social group) to those who were defined as their "legitimate" heirs. Since men were not only the main participants in such sacrificial events, but also their exclusive interpreters, women suffered from twofold exclusion. Even those who actively participated in the sacrificial social contract often found that their participation was considered illegitimate.[17]

Apart from unleashing a wave of very real terror and death on Spanish society, The Spanish Civil War is a classical example of what Mary Condern calls the "Festival". The Festival is a chaotic moment when all existing social constructions are demolished in order to bring about the formation of a new social order. During the Festival, the participants often identify some sort of mythical order that they wish to destroy through their sacrifice, and of course a mutual enemy who must be expelled if the new social order is to maintain its stability. But the model of the Festival is not only concerned with the moment of actual sacrifice. It also determines the way participation in that moment is later translated into actual social and political capital in post-war society.[18] Thus excluding flesh-and-blood women from the centers of conflict, and presenting the female element as having a destabilizing effect on mobilized society, limits women's ability to enter the centers of power in the post-war period. In light of this, Condern warned:

> Sometimes during the Festival we witness momentary relaxation of rigid gender dichotomies due to the revolutionary movement's wish to be presented as offering women equal opportunities. . . . Women's formal participation in the war might obscure for a moment the true identity of the victim, but in view of our conception of the sacrificial process as a performative one we need to employ a more complex reading of reality . . . .[19]

But a more complex reading should also take into consideration the way the Festival is affected when women not only take an active part in the sacrificial social contract, but also in its interpretation. Precisely because of the performative element, one cannot ignore the implications such an "intrusion" might have on the war and on post-war society.

The story of the SF's founding generation invites us to examine such possible implications:

> From the moment it ended, the Civil War became a turning point, the climax, in a process of rebirth. The rebirth of the Spanish Woman ... At that moment frivolity disappeared and was replaced by a collective responsibility towards the revolutionary project . . . The war was to become the most important reference point for (Spanish) women.[20]

Pilar Primo de Rivera's words quoted above express better than anything else the role played by Civil War experiences in shaping the lives of the SF's first generation of leaders. The active participation of SF members in the war effort as nurses, social workers and even smugglers of arms and intelligence agents, and the death of 59 of them "in the line of duty", all contributed to consolidating the organization's "ideological lineage".[21] More than any other group of women in nationalist Spain, members of the SF were able to "market" their Civil War experiences. They did so in a way that pointed to their commitment not only to the general cultural values of the newly formed society (fatherland, family and Church), but also to a specific political ideology – Falangism. The best proof of the organization's success in this respect was the fact that leading figures within the regime and the *movimiento* often referred to the SF in their memories as the faithful guardian of José Antonio's original doctrine.[22]

The first generation of the SF's leadership drew its members from two groups in particular: relatives, fiancés and childhood friends of leading Falangists on the one hand and professional nurses and students who joined the SF at the outbreak of the war on the other. The social class makeup of the first generation of leaders was somewhat similar to that of other fascist movements across Europe. Similarly to members of the BUF (British Union of Fascists) and the Fasci Femminili in Italy, most were middle-class women.[23] But unlike the Italian case, where at least 20% of the leaders came from an aristocratic background, in Spain this held true only for members of the Primo de Rivera family. Furthermore, in the British and Italian cases, many of the women had prior experience of political activism (within the British Conservative Party, the Suffragist Movement, the Italian Socialist Party or the Futurist Movement). For the majority of Spanish women, however, membership in the SF constituted their first direct encounter with the world of politics.

The five women who assisted in preparing the Falange's founding ceremony were members of the Primo de Rivera family and María Luisa Aramburu – a childhood friend of José Antonio Primo de Rivera. Two members of the Falange's Students Syndicate in Malaga joined them the same month: Mercedes Formica, a law student, and Josefina Rodríguez de Viguri, a student in the Faculty of Humanities. Of the seventeen known women who joined the SF in the following two years, eight were relatives of leading Falangist men and six were university students.[24] Judging from the organizational discourse and biographical writings of its members, it is undoubtedly the first group that burned itself into the collective memory – those women already possessing clear political views, who entered the organization in the footsteps of their brothers and childhood friends. Women like Pilar Primo de Rivera or Cristina Ridruejo were in an influential position regarding the construction of the SF's image and discourse, and their life stories easily captured the imagination of others. They were personally and intimately acquainted with José Antonio, had received a good education and possessed a clear political consciousness. By following the example set by their brothers rather than their parents, they represented a powerful and new generational identification. The way they were remembered is perhaps best exemplified by the testimony of Carmina Montero, who headed the SF's Social Service in Almería in the 1940s:

> Women could have nothing, nothing to do with politics. . . . And then they
> came, for the first ones it was the hardest . . . but they all had their gold and

silver decorations (for service well done). Almost all of them were sisters of the students who belonged to José Antonio's [entourage]. . . . A group of great girls, intellectuals, but they were also influenced by their brothers' idealism, that is clear. They were with José Antonio and his ideas were all over the house, so wonderful, and eventually they captured the girls' hearts.[25]

However, the Civil War brought about change in the SF's composition when overnight the organization became the main channel for mobilizing nationalist women. This change was also reflected in the leadership. Of the 58 known members who joined the national leadership during the war the largest group were professional nurses who had arrived for the most part from the Carlist Movement (Comunión Tradicionalista). Non-Falangist students constituted another group, having joined mainly from the Catholic Students' Syndicate. Another group of considerable importance was comprised of women whose husbands or fiancés were Falange activists, but who had not joined the SF prior to the outbreak of the war. However, the death of their sweethearts in action had caused these women to devote themselves fully to the SF. In post-war society, there were far fewer eligible men than women, and the sacrifice made by the dead soldiers was constantly on the public agenda. Joining the SF was a way of publicly honoring the memory of the fallen men, while offering some sort of compensation for the shattered dream of family life.[26]

Despite the prominent role played in the SF by these women from the moment they enlisted, very little mention was made of their background. This is not surprising if we take into consideration some of the circumstances in which they joined. It is true that many of these delegates were to serve within the SF throughout its existence, becoming staunch Falangists. However, at the actual moment of their enlistment, most were looking for a sufficiently powerful civil organization that would be willing to recruit women, while making allowances for both their heightened nationalism and deep Catholicism. During the war years, the SF was a perfect solution. Such women, then, were mobilized in the name of religion and the Fatherland, but were not necessarily committed to the idea of a national syndicalist revolution. Some were prompted to join by their parents, who being conservatives, monarchists or military men, saw in their daughters' affiliation within the SF a way of declaring their allegiance to the new regime. The extent to which familial ties and fortuitous events influenced the political choices of some of the first-generation *jefes* is perhaps best reflected in the testimony of Gloria Cantero Muñoz, the SF's first Provincial Delegate in Melilla:

I was affiliated to Acción Católica, because I liked very much going to

Church. My father, as a military man, was assigned to different places. In one of those places of service he met Don Miguel Primo de Rivera . . . the two of them liked each other very much, and of course he (admired) José Antonio as well. Since José Antonio founded the Falange and his sister Pilar founded the SF, my father said 'Look, would you like to join them?' And since I had friends who were in the SF, I joined voluntarily. And then I took those courses we had to take, and since I already took the course they appointed me delegate.[27]

Historian Kathleen Richmonds indicates the tendency of SF delegates belonging to the first generation to move among a variety of political or professional positions within the organization. According to her, the post of provincial delegate functioned as a steppingstone on the way to higher positions in *la nacional*. Richmonds claims that the advancement of the "Founders" within the SF was characterized by "changing fields of activity and the willingness to move from one geographical location to another, unlike women in lower ranks who often stuck to one field of activity and to the same geographical area".[28]

Table 1.1 Family, professional and ideological background of the members who had joined the SF's National Leadership between 1934 and 1939[29]

Background	Number	Percentage
Relatives of members of the Falange	13	17.3%
Members of the Carlist Movement	3	4 %
Students, members of the SEU	9	12 %
Students, members of the Catholic Students' Union	2	2.5%
Nurses	8	10.5%
Total	**35**	**44.8%**

My database analysis confirms Richmonds' general conclusions, but indicates differences between women who joined the national leadership prior to the outbreak of the war and those who joined it later on. For those belonging to the first group, the position of provincial delegate was an important step, but not an essential one. Of the seventeen women I know of, eleven reached *la nacional* but only six of them had previously been provincial delegates. Of the 58 women who were known to have joined the national leadership during the war years, fourteen reached *la nacional*. Of these, twelve held prior positions as provincial delegates. The rapid progress of the original members is not surprising if we keep in mind that four of them belonged to the Primo de Rivera family and the rest were recruited directly by Pilar or José Antonio Primo de Rivera. These women, therefore, did not have to prove their personal and ideological commitment. In addition, the SF's weak hold over the provinces prior to July 1936 dictated a disproportionate organizational structure, with the majority of positions being occupied by members in Madrid.

Richmonds' claim about the easy movement of delegates among various political and professional positions is also validated by the life stories of the women I interviewed. The biography of Vicky Eiroa – one of the SF's leading members – is a good example of the stormy professional routes followed by the earliest national delegates. Vicky Eiroa joined the SF in 1935 following a visit by Pilar Primo de Rivera at the University of Santiago de Compustela, where Eiroa was studying for a BA in history. That same year she was appointed Provincial Delegate of Santiago. During the war she headed the SF's teams of mobile social workers and washer-women (*Cátedras Ambulantes y Lavadoras del Frente*). At the end of the war, Eiroa was appointed the head of the National Department for Budget and in 1941 she became the head of the National Service for Administration. With the opening of the SF's National School for General Instructors *Isabel la Católica* in Avila, she became its head administrator, a position she held until 1956. The same year, she came back to Madrid in order to run the National Service for Foreign Relations, a position she held until she became dean of the *Universidad Laboral Femenina* in 1970. Eiroa's restless professional career was not considered unusual. It supports the claim that the *fundadoras'* first and foremost contribution to the SF, apart from their personal connections with leading Falangists, was their unconditional ideological and personal commitment. In the initial stages of the organization's development, this was immeasurably more valuable than any formal training.

The distinction between the delegates who joined the SF prior to the war and those who joined during the war did not disappear with time. At a lecture given by the National Delegate for Personal at the SF's national congress of 1956, the first generation of leaders was divided into the Founders, or "those that had joined the SF in its first moments out of pure ideological commitment", and the women who had joined the organization during and immediately following the Civil War.[30] The latter, according to the speaker, came from two groups in particular:

> First there were those who were abducted (*arrebatadas*) from the Youth Movement, characterized by vague ideological perceptions and over-commitment to outer trappings. Some of them were lacking [in] even the most basic Falangist values. Then there were those who came from the SEU, with an intellectual background and liberal leanings that were the result of the post-war Spanish university. The first group was lacking in Falangist spirit, its members thinking they were beyond reproach. . . . and the second group, with its intellectual profile, was forever trying to change everything.[31]

As far as numbers are concerned, the conclusions set out here refute this analysis completely. The women who were co-opted during those years into the national leadership from the SEU and the youth movement were only a minority. However, the speaker is accurate when referring to their background and its problematic impact on the organization. Many of the young girls who joined the FET's Youth Movement during the war years had done so under the influence of their parents, who considered their enlistment a further sign of loyalty to the new regime. Their ideological commitment was shaky and their adherence to outer trappings such as salutes and uniforms was seen by many in the SF as empty formalism. One can only comprehend the assertion that the students joining the SF had "liberal" leanings by taking into consideration the meaning imparted to the term "liberal" by SF members at that time. The post-war Francoist universities were of course anything but liberal, but the SF considered liberalism the embodiment of all evil. Those who belonged to the conservative Right (especially members of the CEDA and Acción Católica) were labeled "liberal" and accused of capitalist tendencies and a lack of social awareness. It is no wonder, then, that in 1956 – a year of ideological and generational renewal – this problematic minority embodied everything that the SF's national leadership did not wish to emulate.

The Youth of 1956 in Search of an Ideology and a Profession: The Position of the "Young Sisters" within the SF Leadership

During the first half of the 1940s, most of the SF's activity was directed towards women in rural areas and small industrial centers. This policy was supported and financed by the regime, as it corresponded with two of its major projects: the creation of an autarkic economy and the fight against infant mortality. However, the late 1940s gave rise to a new interest in urban populations: female factory workers, workers in the service industries and university students.

At the beginning of 1948, Pilar Primo de Rivera announced the founding of the first "Medina Club" in the city of Madrid. These clubs, which were active all over Spain until 1977, were defined as cultural-political clubs. Their aim was "encouraging women's cultural, scientific and literary initiatives, which were in line with Catholic and National Syndicalist norms".[32] The Medina Clubs had two central functions. First, they provided a meeting place for both the SF's leadership and Falangist intellectuals and artists. In addition, they served as informal recruitment centers for new members. Although the clubs were open to all women the activities were meant to attract educated women who were interested in current political issues. Since most of the activities took place in the afternoon and evening, they were inaccessible to the majority of married women and mothers. The goal of interesting educated professional women in the SF was further emphasized by Pilar Primo de Rivera during the National Congress of 1950. In her speech, she called upon the provincial delegates to continue spreading the Falangist doctrine "which is best reflected in the actions of the SF . . . not only amongst the unruly masses . . . not just amongst the workers, but also amongst the intelligentsia and the students".[33]

From the moment the Falange was founded, its student syndicate – the SEU – was perceived as the source of the movements' future leaders. The university students' educational background and political awareness made José Antonio's idea of *política como poesía* especially attractive to them. The number of students was therefore relatively high throughout the entire *Movimiento*, especially in those circles that were closest to the founder. Yet with the passing of time, it was precisely the students' political awareness that generated tensions between the FET and the SEU. By the summer of 1941, the widening gap between José Antonio's doctrine and Francoist reality led many Falangist students to join the Blue Division, which left Spain to fight Communism on the German – Soviet front. Some, like Enrique Sotomayor, never came back, while others, like Dionisio Ridruejo, returned to public activism in Spain, but had a hard time finding a place within the FET. Only a few of these renewed their association with the SEU.[34]

With the purging of the SEU's leadership in the early 1940s, the latter's relationship with the FET improved considerably. But the friction was renewed in the early 1950s, when a new generation entered the universities. This promotion, which was to be called "The Generation of 1956" due to its involvement in the university riots of that year, included men and women who were born after the end of the Civil War or experienced it as very young children. Ruiz Carnicer, who called these men the "Young Brothers", wrote:

> This generation chose to situate itself politically by criticizing all those things which the first generation (of Falangists) did not want or know how to change . . . Despite the fact that many old-time Falangists could not understand this criticism, and the partial rejection of their legacy, the "Young Brothers" were attempting in effect to save the regime by turning it into something more dynamic.[35]

The socialization process undergone by the students within the SEU led them to study the original writings of José Antonio Primo de Rivera. This encounter with the founder's doctrine led them to conclude that preserving ideology was more important than safeguarding the regime's formal structure. This position, along with their concern for social issues, earned them the label of "leftists" (*izquierdistas*). Consuelo Valcarcel Burgos, who was recruited from the SEU to the ranks of the SF's national leadership in

1956, described how she was affected by the encounter with José Antonio's writings:

The first time I heard anyone talking seriously about José Antonio was during my BA, in a boarding school where I was completing my Social Service. At that time everyone at university was talking of the Generation of '98 so I read everything and the last one I came across was José Antonio. What affected me most of all was the synthesis between everything that was good on the Right and on the Left. Another thing that really influenced me was his vision of Man. It was the first time I came across a political thinker, a philosopher that looked at Man as a whole. At that time I was studying psychology and was immensely drawn to the vision of Man as a being capable of transcending himself.[36]

As a result of their exposure to José Antonio's writings, many students searched for channels of political action that would express their newly discovered political and social identifications. In those years the SEU fostered two initiatives that brought its members into close contact with urban working-class populations. The first was *El Teatro Universitario*, which was founded in the 1950s at the Faculty of Humanities of the University of Madrid. The aim of this project was to put on plays that were directed and performed by the students. The plays were presented free of charge in all parts of the city, especially in low-income neighborhoods where the residents could not afford to buy tickets for cultural events. In 1956 Consuelo Valcarcel Burgos took over the *Teatro Universitario*:

The Dean appointed me delegate in charge of cultural affairs at the Faculty of Humanities. What an experience it was!!! I had to organize everything relating to the theatrical world. I remember this amazing time, amongst other things, because of the sheer number of productions of all ideological shades and colors.[37]

The second initiative was *El Servicio Universitario de Trabajo*, whose aim (similarly to the SF's *Hermandad de Ciudad y Campo*) was to assign students to work in factories and rural areas on a short-term basis. The students' contribution here was also meant to be cultural and educational, namely helping the population to acquire literacy skills and implement more cost-effective production techniques.

Participation in these two projects brought many students face-to-face with the dire existence of many sectors of the Spanish population. As a consequence they realized that José Antonio's revolutionary dream and Francoist reality had very little in common. Paradoxically, those who were supposed to be the faithful representatives of the revolutionary dream – the

Falange's old guard – rejected the students' criticism out of hand. These older men, who still remembered the horrors of the Civil War and who had invested their faith in the regime that resulted from it, had no interest in being told how far they had deviated from the writings of their founder. This resulted in many students drifting further and further away from the regime.

Amongst the female students, on the other hand, the opposite dynamic was in evidence. The relations between the SF's national leadership and the SEU-SF had always been smoother and more intimate.[38] While many young men felt that their voice was not heard within the FET and that they were being prevented from reaching leadership positions, the SEU functioned as a steppingstone for young women to the ranks of the SF's national leadership. Rather than being pushed to the sidelines like the men of their generation, many of the female students were co-opted into the heart of the regime. Consuelo Valcarcel spoke of the role played by the SEU in her joining of the SF:

> At university there was a Students' Syndicate and within it a feminine section called the SEU-SF. I turned to them and said I was interested in joining the Falange, but they told me I would first have to receive some preparation, some sort of a course. I registered for a course in my district and there I met an incredible woman who left a lasting impression on me. Her name was Sierra Manteola. I was captivated and on the 29th October, 1956, in a ceremony in the mountains, I was sworn in.[39]

The fact that Sierra Manteola, the SF's national secretary at the time, took part in preparing and administrating an entry-level district course further emphasizes the importance the SF placed on recruiting students.

Nevertheless, the fact that the SF's leadership wanted to recruit a new generation of future delegates did not mean that their entry into the organization was necessarily a smooth one. The only document providing clues regarding the tensions accompanying the entry of the "Young Sisters" into the SF was the one prepared by the National Service of Personnel for presentation at the 1956 National Congress. The purpose of the document was to alert members to a structural phenomenon that was causing great concern to some senior delegates. During 1955, 270 new appointments were approved within the ranks of the national leadership. By 1956, 167 of the new appointees had already filed requests for a change of position. Considering that at any given time the SF's national leadership included between 900 and 1,000 members, the appointment of 270 new delegates alone is sufficient to mark 1955 as a year of major turnover. Since there were no structural changes that could account for the number of new appointments, one can only assume that many of them were made at the expense of senior delegates. The fact that over 50% of the newly appointed delegates were not satisfied with their positions reflects the new spirit these women brought with them to the organization. Most of the interviews I conducted seem to indicate that appointments within the SF were dictated "from above" – that is, according to recommendations by provincial delegates or heads of national services. From a geographical perspective, an effort was made to take the members' requests and origin into consideration, especially in the case of those who needed the economic support of their families. However, changes were not made easily and personal requests made by the members themselves were not looked upon favorably.

It is no wonder, then, that the massive dissatisfaction expressed by newcomers generated strong feelings and that these should be reflected in the contradictory ways they were described. On the one hand, it was alleged that these young women had enlisted "in order to satisfy their personal needs and express their dissatisfaction with the social, economic and spiritual reality around them". On the other hand, despite an educational background and process of political soul-searching similar to that of the first generation of leaders that had brought them into the SF, their behavior after joining the organization convinced many that they were "of a low human quality":

> Unfortunately today we are faced with the existence of groups, of petty friendships . . . an attempt to rely on personal relations in order to secure a desired stationing or task. Members reach [the national leadership] immediately upon their recruitment or the completion of their Social Service . . . and have no knowledge of the organization or its political ideology. They undergo a training course at a national level, which in four and a half months can not erase their right-wing and materialistic perceptions. This state of affairs is an inversion of good order. In the past leading positions were held by members who first proved their skills through (years) of service. Now we have newcomers who become delegates because of the degrees they hold or their social standing.[40]

The new arrivals, then, generated quite a lot of resentment. Some of them at least did indeed gain advancement at the expense of more senior delegates, who after years of service felt that they were being pushed aside. The informal skills of the latter, on which they had prided themselves in the past, were not valued as before. A further accusation concerned the newcomers' so-called materialistic worldview, expressed in their demand for higher pay that would be commensurate with their formal education and compensate them for the decision not to turn to the private sector. However, it is important to note that the bitter feelings expressed in this report did not influence the SF's actual policy towards the "Young Sisters". It is possible that not all the delegates shared these feelings. In any case, a decision had already been reached in *la nacional* that only the newcomers, with their formal education and innovative work methods, could invigorate the SF at this difficult period.

Of the 200 members of the national leadership whose progress in the organization is known to us, 52 joined the SF after 1950. Eleven of them arrived from the SEU. While some of the newcomers started their careers in the traditional way – as provincial delegates – all the students bypassed this stage and were recruited directly to *la nacional*. Consuelo Valcarcel, for example, was appointed head of the National Department for Professional Training. Adelida del Pozo, another SEU arrival, was appointed in 1955 to head the National Service of Education.

Table 1.2   Positions held by SF members who joined the national leadership in the 1950s[41]

Position	Number	Percentage
Parliament member	6	11.5%
City Council Member	2	4 %
Members of the Parliamentary Commission for the approval of the 1961 Law for Political and Professional Rights for Women	4	7.5%
Members of the SF's Advisory Committee	39	75 %
Total	**51**	**98 %**

Apart from their rapid advancement in the SF, several other facts attest to the importance attributed to the "Young Sisters'" presence in the organization. Of the eight SF members who were also members of parliament, two held life membership (Pilar Primo de Rivera and the SF's General Secretary), while the other six were all members of the 1956 generation. The presence of these women was also strongly felt in the SF's Advisory Committee. This committee was formed in 1964 in order to ensure that in case Pilar Primo de Rivera should suddenly retire, the next National Delegate would be chosen by the SF and not by General Franco or the General Secretary of the FET. Of the 61 members of the Committee known to us, 39 belonged to the second generation of delegates.

The array of positions held by the "Young Sisters" reflects both their higher level of formal education and a change in the focus of the SF's activities. Four of them represented the organization in independent entities: two as members of the City Councils of Barcelona and Seville, one as the SF's representative in the Ministry of Education and one as Spain's representative in UN committees dealing with women-related issues. Five other delegates were active in the committee that had been formed in order to follow up the application of the Law for Political and Professional Rights for Women. Generally speaking, members of this generation did not move as much between different posts; when they did so, they remained within similar fields. Finally, it is important to note that despite their higher level of formal education, which could have opened up more profitable professional opportunities for these women outside the SF, 50% of them held permanent full-time positions within the organization until 1977.

Uniforms and Salaries:
The Status Symbols of an Organizational Elite

Being paid for their services and the extensive use of uniforms were the first status symbols that set the members of the SF's national leadership apart from the other women who took part in its activities. Payment for their work and the unique dress-code to which they adhered were meant to enhance their sense of political commitment and consolidate their position at the head of the wide bureaucratic network that the SF had created across Spain. While using uniforms and fixed salaries as means of creating structural differentiations within an organization seems only logical the National Delegates' severe dress code and fixed yet very low salaries also functioned, in an inverted manner, as class differentiators.

By examining both the structural and class significance of the three attributes that most characterized the SF's national delegates – the use of uniforms, fixed salaries and their civil status as single women – I would like to indicate a characteristic of the organization that has been and is still intentionally ignored by its members. While the SF's social and political discourse strove to create the image of an entity open to all social classes, the everyday behavior of its leaders reveals a more complex story.

The date at which SF members first started making use of uniforms, and the way they were selected, is unknown.[42] In photos taken during the founding ceremony of the Falange in October 1933, there is as yet no sign of the characteristic blue uniform that the movement was to adopt later. A year later, in a photo taken during a meeting of the *Junta Política* in Valladolid, some members were already wearing the official uniform, which consisted of a blue shirt with a collar (with epaulettes and pockets bearing the Falange's emblem) and long black pants. Amongst José Antonio's personal entourage, however, one could see many men in civilian clothes. The use of uniforms became more popular in the course of 1935, but unlike parallel European movements, the Falange's dress code continued to be a rather eclectic one. The Falangist pants had pockets at the front, which made them look as though they could have easily been part of a suit. The men did not wear boots and their belts and shoes were not identical. To all this may be added José Antonio's strong preference for smart suits, which he wore whenever the uniform was not absolutely obligatory. In contrast to the Nazi and Fascist Parties, it is almost impossible to find photos of high-ranking Falangists wearing uniforms during parliamentary sessions or at social gatherings.

The first women who were photographed in Falangist uniform (in 1935) were not Pilar Primo de Rivera and members of her entourage, but rather two of the most prominent Falangist students, namely Mercedes Fromica and Rosario Pereda, the local delegate for Valladolid. If we consider the ambivalent welcome given by the new movement to its first female members, it is perhaps not surprising that the first SF members to publicly wear uniforms were students, whose heightened political awareness was well known.

The Civil War, the death of José Antonio Primo de Rivera and the publication of the Decree of Unification brought about a change in the way the SF viewed the use of uniforms. With the metamorphosis of the SF into a mass organization, and against the background of the ideological tensions generated by the Decree of Unification, the blue uniform became a sign of authentic Falangism. To insiders, the blue shirt and black skirt (which was knee- length and worn with a leather belt whose buckle bore the Falange's emblem) indicated that they were in the presence of high-ranking members of the organization. To outsiders, the uniform signified a specific ideological commitment. The shirt and skirt conferred a severe and modest look to the wearer – a sort of sartorial embodiment of what Pilar Primo de Rivera defined as "Falangist existence". The Spartan look included short or tightly pulled-back hair held by a barrette and the absolute prohibition against the use of jewelry or make-up.

The purpose of this dress code was to hide any sign of female sexuality and reflect seriousness and authority in a society where women's supremacy was repeatedly questioned by both men and women. But the SF's dress code also reflected its members' aesthetic sense, dictated both by their family background and biographies. Knee-length skirts, a lack of make-up and the prohibition against dyeing one's hair were all viewed by middle-class Spain as signs of a woman's moral standing, regardless of political identification. By making a uniform the greatest signifier of the *Falangist Woman* and ensuring that it conform with middle-class aesthetic ideas, the SF managed to neutralize the unsettling effect thousands of uniformed women might have had on a highly conservative and chauvinistic society. By establishing something as basic as a mandatory dress code, the organization also sent out a subtle message to both its affiliates and its opponents regarding the sort of women who would be welcome and could feel comfortable within its ranks.

Table 1.3   Salaries of members of the SF's national leadership[43]

	1946/8	1950	1956	1958	1959	1962/4	1965	1971	1972/4	1975/6
National Delegate	2,200	2,500	3,180	3,180	3,380	—	—	20,000	24,000	30,000
National Secretary	2,000	2,445	3,060	3,060	3,260	—	—	15,000	20,000	—
Heads of National Services	955	1,125	1,860	2,232	2,432	3,125	5,000	—	—	—
Provincial Delegate1	800	1,000	1,440	1,728	1,928	2,610	4,500	10,300	12,000	15,000
Provincial Delegate2	700	850	1,260	1,512	1,712	2,240	4,000	9,200	12,000	15,000
Provincial Delegate3	675	750	1,140	1,368	1,568	1,960	3,500	8,100	12,000	15,000
Provincial Delegate4	550	700	1,050	1,260	1,460	1,960	3,500	—	—	15,000
Provincial Delegate5	500	650	1,000	1,200	1,400	1,980	3,000	—	—	15,000
Local Delegate (city)	600	800	1,200	1,440	1,640	1,960	3,500	—	—	—
Local Delegate (Village)	600	650	660	792	992	1,008	1,500	—	—	—

Like uniforms, salaries also functioned as a status symbol that clearly differentiated among the national leadership and other SF members. Some members of *la nacional* received regular salaries as early as 1939. In the SF's yearly budget reports, compiled by the National Service of Administration, one can only find references to payments made to members of the national leadership starting from the 1943, and in more detail from 1946.

The main difficulty in evaluating the salaries paid to SF members over the years lies in finding information with which to compare them. According to reports of the Department of Statistical Analysis at the Ministry of Labor, there is no specific information concerning average salaries in the Spanish labor market prior to 1995. The report from that year is the first (and thus far also the last) to include detailed information according to industry, formal training and sex.

The only information I located concerning women's salaries relates to the years 1947 and 1957. The information from 1947 concerns the salaries of female workers at the Spanish Telephone Company (*Telefónica*) in the city of Barcelona. The information refers to three main categories: administrative workers, switchboard operators and accompanying staff (mainly secretaries). It is important to note, however, that the female work force of *Telefónica* had undergone a high level of formal training relative to most other Spanish women at the time, and that generally speaking salaries in Barcelona were higher than in other parts of Spain. Within the administrative staff, only one position was allocated to women – Inspector of Service Units. An inspector's monthly salary was 9,600 pesetas. An average switchboard operator earned between 5,100 and 6,600 pesetas a month. The accompanying staff included both men and women. Women's average salary was 4,200 pesetas.[44] From the information available, one can see that in 1948 the national delegate earned a little over half the monthly salary of a secretary at *Telefónica* and salaries were not substantially higher in later years.

The information from 1957 is derived from documents of the SF's National Personnel Service and concerns the salaries of non-affiliated teachers within the organization's schools. The teachers are divided into four categories according to the number of students in their institutions (more than 200 students, 150–200 students, 100–150 students and less than 100 students). However, it is important to note that teachers did a four-hour working day, which was in no way comparable to that of a *Telefónica* worker or of a delegate in the SF. A teacher in an institute with more than 200 students earned 1,666 pesetas a month. Teachers in the second and third categories earned 1,380 and 1,486 pesetas respectively. Teachers who worked in institutions with less than 100 students earned 1,100 pesetas.[45] The salary of a teacher from the first category was about half that of a national delegate and in the last two categories it was much higher than that of a provincial delegate. Relative to their working hours, political status, seniority and formal training, there is no doubt, then, that the salaries of leading SF members were much lower than would be expected.

One can draw several other conclusions from table 1.3. First, the two most significant increases in salaries took place in 1956 and again in 1965. There are two reasons for this. For many years the salaries paid by the SF lagged behind the cost of living index. The demand that salaries be updated appeared in the documents of the National Service of Administration as early as 1948. But a pay raise was authorized only in 1956, following fears that the low salaries would lose the organization its newly-arrived delegates. In 1966, with the approval of the Falange's new Organic Law, the wage status of the SF's national delegates was equated for the first time with that of other functionaries within the *Movimiento*. There was also a further wage increase that came to expression mainly as an increase in social benefits.[46] Even in the SF's final days, salaries never exceeded 34% of the organization's total budget.[47]

If we track the salaries paid to members of *la nacional* (from the first three categories), we can see that an attempt was made to narrow the gap between the wages of the national delegates and secretaries and those of the various heads of national services. This was part of a general process of amalgamation undergone by this group between the years 1948 and 1956. According to Kathleen Richmonds, the low salaries at the top of the pyramid indirectly reflected the social class of the organizational elite. Lacking the economic support of a husband (which they did not have), only a woman who had an independent income or the support of her family could afford to continue working for the SF. Hard work for almost no pay also differentiated the Falangist model from other paid female work.

When addressing her delegates, Pilar Primo de Rivera rarely referred to the issue of payment. When she did, however, it was in an unequivocal way, as indicated by this circular from 1957:

> We, who came to the Falange in order to serve Spain, must not think all the time of economic compensation. . . . Some members, upon their appointment as heads of some of our boarding schools, claimed that they earn less than the cleaning ladies. Those women have no idea of the meaning of Falangist existence. It makes sense that the cleaning ladies and all those who are working for money should be paid more than we are. If those members [who are complaining] leave the Falange, I have no doubt they too will earn more. . . . But they will be robbed of the moral compensation, with which the service of Spain rewarded us.[48]

Another interesting fact supported by table 1.3 concerns the local delegates in the cities, who did not constitute part of the national leadership at any time. However, over the years (except for a certain fluctuation in 1948), their salaries were higher than those of the provincial delegates in the three higher categories. This fact more than reflects their importance within the SF and points to their different socio-economic background. In the higher echelons of the leadership, the low salaries functioned as a class barrier of sorts, ensuring that only middle-class women could apply and "survive" full-time commitment to the SF. In the small towns, however, it was exceedingly hard to find Falangist supporters among middle-class women. The position of local delegate mainly attracted educated lower-middle-class women, who wanted to make their way through the Francoist bureaucracy. In order to utilize their formal training, professional commitment and time, the SF had to compete with the salaries offered these women by private institutions. For many local delegates, membership in the SF offered an unusual opportunity for professional advancement. Despite the fact that this was never stated aloud, the relatively high salaries served to ensure the professional (if not ideological) loyalty of these women, who functioned as intermediaries between the SF's high command and the masses of women who passed through its institutions.

Who Needs a Husband? Spinsterhood and the SF's National Leadership

Alongside the aforementioned status symbols, the most important personal attribute, which distinguished members of the SF's national leadership from other members of the organization and from the countless women who passed through its institution, was the fact that they were unmarried. The concept of spinsterhood as a premeditated choice and a guiding principle in life was of course not unique to the SF. Joining a convent legitimized spinsterhood, in combination with the commitment to celibacy and religious devotion, as a widely accepted choice for upper- and middle-class women. Another version of "accepted" spinsterhood could be observed throughout the Middle Ages and the Early Modern period in women who chose not to marry, supporting themselves economically as merchants, artisans or intellectuals. Despite their small number, such women were perceived as productive members of their community, public activists and bearers of full legal rights. As Michelle Bordeaux has demonstrated, those women did not receive much public attention, not because they were a minority, but rather because their civil, legal and professional status was not considered abnormal.[49] It was the Enlightenment and the Industrial Revolution that adversely affected the status of the "spinster" in western culture. Within the moral and conceptual world of the new bourgeois society, spinsterhood outside convent walls was considered a temporary legal status, which would change as a matter of course when a woman married.

However, a series of studies that explore spinsterhood in European societies and in the United States point to the fact that, starting with the first third of the 19th century, and parallel to the consolidation of the Separate Spheres' discourse, a growing number of middle-class women remained single.[50] Spanish reports indicate that in 1900 for every 1,000 people, the number of those who married was 898, a number that by 1925 had dropped to 608. If in 1900 the percentage of single women within the Spanish population was 22.2%, by 1930 it had risen to 33%.[51] There were several reasons for the increase in the number of single women throughout Europe; however, it is clear that this situation mainly affected middle-class women. The first reason for this phenomenon was demographic. In regions or countries that experienced violent conflicts such as the Napoleonic Wars or the German and Italian Wars of Independence, marriageable women sometimes outnumbered men by a ratio of two to one. Women's windows of opportunity were also significantly fewer than those of men, so women who reached their thirties often had to give up the idea of marriage and motherhood.

Another reason was related to the growing number of working women.

If the working-class family was to survive economically, wives and mothers often had to go out to work. The exceptions to this were domestic workers, whose employment was almost always conditional upon their being child-less (or at least not having any children living with them). In the 19th century, a series of new professions opened up for middle-class women or women of more "humble" origins whose education enabled them to move up to the "lower-middle-class". Nursing and teaching became popular with middle-class women, whereas lower-middle-class women entered a variety of service professions, such as mail clerks and shop assistants in the new department stores that sprang across European cities.[52] For women in both categories, spinsterhood was almost a pre-condition for professional life, since their respectable professional image depended on their ability to adhere to strict gender codes that dictated a complete separation between women's work and family life.

Finally, it is important to note that the growing number of single middle-class women was a result of another long-term process that this social group had undergone. As Miren Llona noted:

> The growing economic difficulties in supporting a familial unit seemed to have influenced many men's decision to refrain from marriage. To notions of domesticity based first and foremost on diligence and intimacy, social ostentation was now added.[53]

Under such conditions more men chose not to marry, fearful of being unable to provide the level of comfort their future wives and children expected of them, thus diminishing the so-called "husband market" even further.

With the foundation of the Suffragist movement, a new category of single women was created – those who chose a life of political commitment. In what seems an ideological antithesis, two of the largest groups of women who belonged to the category of political activists between the two world wars were members of the Fascist Party in Italy and the Nazi Party in Germany. In both cases, remaining single was a common but not obligatory choice for key members. On the one hand, the totalitarian regimes attempted to coerce women into fulfilling their duty to the fatherland by bearing children. On the other hand, the need to indoctrinate and mobilize the masses of female citizens created a paradoxical reality whereby a minority of largely unmarried women went on to become highly active public and political agents. Elizabeth Heinman indicates the relatively high percentage of single women amongst the Feminine Section of the Nazi Party, and the regime's attempts to enlist single women for a variety of teaching and nursing positions.[54] The Nazi Youth Movement (BDM) gener-ated a series of contradictory messages in this respect. While family life was presented as the height of a woman's aspirations, girls were called upon to postpone their own marriages in order to assist the Fatherland. Women learned through a variety of activities to view men as partners in a joint project. Thus a society that praised modesty also generated numerous opportunities for proximity and social interaction between the sexes.

In Spain the percentage of women involved in political activism prior to the days of the Second Republic was very low, but even amongst those who gained recognition in this field, spinsterhood was not very popular. Known leaders of the Spanish Left (such as Dolores Ibarruri, who was a leading figure within the Communist Party) and intellectuals and political activists within the Spanish Right all divided their time between political engagement and active (albeit non-standard) family life.[55]

The status of SF members was different from that of the women mentioned above, since for them spinsterhood was not entirely a personal choice. On 24 June 1938, Pilar Primo de Rivera published Decree No. 99, under the heading "A Letter to our Married Members".[56] The decree stated that in view of the SF's expanding activities and the full dedication required by them, positions from Provincial Delegate upwards would be held by single women or childless widows only. And indeed, except for one known case, this principle was rigorously adhered to.[57]

In a society where married women were legally defined as minors and excluded from the political and professional arena, it is not surprising that SF members felt that their political activism could not be combined with married life. This feeling in turn created a widening gap between the young women of the Civil War generation and those of the preceding generation. One of the clearest expressions of this growing "generation gap" may be found in Pilar Primo de Rivera's autobiography. The first chapters describe how Pilar and her brothers lost their mother at a very young age and how they were brought up by their aunts, one of whom was a widow and the other married without children. According to Primo de Rivera, although both aunts seemed to live under the shadow of the memory of what they lacked (the one a husband and the other children), they led relatively independent and active lives. As far as Pilar's mother is concerned, the most substantial reference is to her death, of which she wrote:

> Hers was a Christian and heroic death, in keeping with the way she lived. She very possibly knew she was going to die if she gave birth to another baby, but she no doubt felt she was abiding by her duty as a married woman, and this is what her conscience as a Christian dictated that she do. . . . She would never have agreed to the legalization of abortions.[58]

Like many of her colleagues, Pilar Primo de Rivera was aware that in the society in which she lived, the only way to be considered both a good wife and a good Christian was to follow her mother's example. But what if there was a way to avoid that life and still be considered a good Christian and a good Spaniard? What if she could find a way to fulfill her "heroic duty" without being married? In this respect, the lifestyle of a high-ranking SF member provided the perfect solution. It committed the women who chose it to serve a higher cause, while also providing them with the ideal pretext for remaining single.

In addition, the harsh implications of the Civil War undoubtedly contributed to this decision. Many of the SF's first generation of leaders had lost their fiancés during the war. Those who were emotionally capable of seeking new partners at the end of combat found themselves in a situation similar to that of many other European women at the time, namely that men were hard to come by.[59] To all of this must be added the women's newfound sense of independence and self-esteem generated by their recent political engagement. Yvonne Knibiehler describes the personality changes undergone by French nurses and social workers during the First World War in a manner that reflects the Spanish experience as well:

> Religious values were important, but those women were not guided by their piousness, but rather by the wish to abandon the family and discover 'the group'. . . . The girls were invested with a new form of spirituality, activism and the wish to serve. They started developing self-confidence, organizational skills and perseverance.[60]

One of the characteristics distinguishing the classical model of the nun from *la soltera* was the latter's ambivalent relationship with the concept of celibacy. High- ranking SF members could not and did not want to distance themselves from men altogether. In fact, the nature of their job brought them into daily contact with members of the opposite sex; such contact was not of a professional nature only. In the *International Congress of Women*, which the SF hosted in Madrid in 1970, a member of the organization explained:

> The fact that a woman might be single does not mean that she has to ignore a man who might be close to her and to whom her heart is drawn. A mature and independent single woman, with enough energies to stick to her way of life and the will to fulfill her vocation, can enjoy the closeness and friendship [of a man]. The only precondition for such a relationship . . . is the purity of intentions.[61]

Friendship with men was perceived as an important component of healthy emotional life, especially in an all-women organization, where the dangers of overly close same-sex friendships were always present.[62] Against this background, it is perhaps not surprising to find evidence that high-ranking SF members, amongst them Pilar Primo de Rivera herself, had life-long male companions. However, such relations were veiled in secrecy even in the years following 1975. In this case as well, the autobiography of Pilar Primo de Rivera provides us with clues to the difficulty of dealing with intimate relationships that totally diverged from the acceptable model of the period. In her autobiography, Primo de Rivera mentions her male companion on one occasion only, and despite the fact that those brief words speak volumes, they might easily escape the eyes of an unsuspecting reader:

> During those times in Burgos, we often used to go to the Hotel Condestable, to get some word on the [progression] of the war. And it was there that we met a group of sailors, an event that, for some of us, was of transcendental importance. Later on we all went our separate ways, but for me at least, that meeting constituted the most important event of my life.[63]

The kind of reading required to understand such a paragraph corresponds to what Dayle Hymes calls "textual architecture" – the art of scrutinizing an author's use of language in order to read between the lines.[64] Primo de Rivera's words were sufficient to indicate to those who are aware of her relationship with Pablo Suansez, a captain of a Spanish submarine, that she did acknowledge it. However, even as late as 1983 she was unable to speak directly about that "most important event" in her life. One can easily see how revealing such a relationship prior to 1975 would have taken its toll on both her public image and political position. But the carefully guarded language she employed in her autobiography implies that such a revelation would have exacted an even higher price, one she was unwilling to pay, even after the regime's collapse. By publicly breaking Francoist gender codes, she would have disqualified herself from other political and cultural affiliations to which she staunchly adhered throughout her life. Unable and unwilling as she was to adopt new affiliations offered her by the transition to democracy, she would have found herself in an impossibly isolated position socially, politically and mentally. It was only in an interview that she gave six months prior to her death to Antonio Prometeo Moya that Primo de Rivera dared break her silence on this issue. In doing so she also indirectly admitted to the immense significance being a single woman held for her:

> Pablo (Suansez) was a widower with four small children, who lived with a sister, whom I suspect he did not really like. We maintained a more or less platonic relationship for five years. And then he gave me an ultimatum – he wanted me to leave the SF so we could get married. I told him no, I told him I preferred the SF.[65]

Affiliation with the SF continued to play an immensely important role in the lives of former delegates and generated a need to establish such an affiliation by specific socio-cultural codes. This might partially explain the ambivalent reactions elicited by my attempts to discuss Decree No. 99 in the interviews I conducted. When confronted by the original text of the decree, many interviewees insisted that it did not exist or that they themselves had never been aware of its existence. They repeatedly presented their choice of remaining single as a personal one having nothing to do with the organization. For example, Consuelo Salvo Guntin, a general instructor in the SF, claimed that she had lost her fiancé during the war and had therefore chosen to remain single – and this despite the fact that in 1939 she was only 12 years old. According to Salvo Guntin, the issue of "spinsterhood" was no issue at all. It was insignificant, and apart from Pilar Primo de Rivera, anyone could marry, given the opportunity or the desire to do so.[66] María Luisa Muñez García explained that her decision not to marry resulted from an awareness that marriage would put a stop to her work in the SF, while at the same time insisting that she was unaware of the existence of such a decree. Consuelo Valcarcel Burgos knew of the decree, but stated that it applied only to delegates of the first generation:

> At that time, in 1938, Spanish housewives did not have at their disposal things like a washing machine or a dishwasher. They had to wash, wash, wash, 24 hours a day. . . . A married woman could not have a career because she did not have time. At that time married women had to put all their energy into the home. And the delegates, the women who did not marry, for them their work was all their lives. Later on things changed significantly, but then members had to be single because they worked 24 hours a day, seven days a week.[67]

The favorite example presented by those who were trying to prove that spinsterhood was not a norm in the SF was María de Miranda, who was the head of the National Service for Physical Education and Sports in the 1940s and a member of the SF's Advisory Committee. Miranda was acclaimed by all to have been happily married. Only a couple of months after hearing De Miranda's story did I discover that the National Delegate for Physical Education had in fact only married in her sixties, a few years before the dismantling of the SF.

Despite SF members' repeated efforts to present their spinsterhood as the result of a harsh reality, they profited in very tangible ways from their unique civil status. Their long working day was not necessarily a disadvantage, but a privilege, as were their constant travels in Spain and elsewhere. Furthermore, these women enjoyed the unique legal status of single women – the ability to own property, sign legal documents, and so forth. However, despite such advantages and the existence of an active population of single women, Francoist society thoroughly disapproved of *la soltera*. In debates on the status and image of the single woman that took place during the International Congress on Women, many participants expressed their opposition to this popular attitude that equated spinsterhood with failure. María Montserrat Castilla Gabriel, an SF member, criticized an educational system that "did not guide young women on their way to personal fulfillment, but rather in a way that emphasized their dependence on their husbands and sons".[68] She went even further, claiming:

> Single women have not been looked upon so far as real, positive human beings. . . . Fortunately enough it is no longer possible to find in Spain today that old spinster, fearful and unprepared for life on the outside, that woman who was easy prey for strangers and a burden on her family. The caricature of the 'old spinster' desperately and embarrassingly looking for a husband is becoming extinct.[69]

But what replaced these stereotypes? Aside from the tangible benefits of spinsterhood, what kind of an image did the SF attempt to confer on *la soltera*? The answer to this question reflects the extent to which the SF's notions of good citizenship and social and political agency had broken with traditional middle-class (male) definitions that equated a person's worth with individualism and a narrow definition of personal fulfillment. In the Introduction I referred to Karen Offen's definition of *relational feminism*, and the extent to which this concept has made it possible to consider the lives and actions of SF members in a new light. As far as the SF's discourse on *la soltera* was concerned, Offen's insistence on the term "relational" feminism, as opposed to "familial" or "maternalist" feminism, is meant to emphasize female nurturing in its broader sense, not only within the confines of the family.

Such an emphasis is especially relevant in the case of the SF and can be found in many of its members' statements. María Montserrat, for example, called "upon everyone to recognize spinsterhood as a vocation resulting from personal motivations, aspirations and skills such as those dictating the choice of marriage or religious vocation". Many women objected to the assumption that their choice to remain single meant that they had renounced femininity or even motherhood. They perceived their role in society as that of spiritual mothers whose task it was to mentor a new generation of better, more independent women, who were committed to the fatherland. Their work within the SF provided them with the opportunity to act as role models for the younger generations and enjoy the satisfaction of nurturing and guiding their younger colleagues or students.[70] The struggle to turn the image of *la soltera* into a positive one reflects self-awareness, self-esteem and confidence in their achievements and contributions to society. This enabled leading SF members to present their life stories as positive models, which other women could emulate out of free choice. In their view, it was a model whose messages should be integrated into the educational system, and was seriously considered by psychologists and sociologists.

One Generation in the Eyes of Another: The Generation Gap as Reflected in the Interviews

I conclude this chapter with an examination of the generation gap, as reflected in an interview I conducted in Spring 2003. The uniqueness of this interview resulted from the fact that it was conducted with two senior delegates, who were in many respects "classic" representatives of the 1936 and 1956 generations respectively. The interview, which was conducted as a free conversation between the two interviewees was based on questions I had presented to them beforehand. The result gave me rare insights into the way each generation perceived the other.

My two interviewees were Andresa López Enseñat and Consuelo Valcarcel Burgos. López, who was born in 1922, joined the national leadership in 1943 from the Falange's Teachers' Syndicate. Between 1944 and 1949, she was the Provincial Delegate in charge of Youth in Teruel and in 1949 was appointed Provincial Delegate to the city, a position she held until 1953. Between 1957 and 1978, Andresa López headed the SF's National School for General Instructors *Isabel la Católica.* She was also a member of the SF's Advisory Committee between the years 1966 and 1972. Consuelo Valcarcel headed the SF's Department for Professional Training for Women and Youth and the SEU-SF. She was also the organization's representative to the Ministry of Education.

It became clear in the course of the interview that despite López' relatively late co-option to the national leadership, both she and Valcarcel considered her part of the 1936 generation. Both also agreed that the Civil War was the key to understanding the distinction between the two generations. Or in Valcarcel's words:

> It is absolutely clear that someone who has gone through the war, someone who had to run and hid, is different from a kid that just came out of university. What was the essential difference? The essential difference was in the way we experienced our existence . . . those who went through the war came out of it differently.[71]

It is, however, not surprising that the interviewees imparted different importance to the war as an historical turning point. Valcarcel observed: ". . . within the SF, starting with my generation, the war did not have such great significance". For López, on the other hand, the war was one of the major *raisons d'être* of the SF. She claimed: "For me the war signified many things. It divided Spain into two, it separated families and caused backwardness and isolation". Overcoming that backwardness was a central focus of the SF's activities for over a decade and a half.

Despite the fact that not all the women who entered the national leadership during the 1950s were enlisted from the SEU, in Valcarcel's eyes this was undoubtedly a generation of students, shaped first and foremost by the universities:

> *They* who lived through the "disaster" joined [the SF] in order to build a New Spain and to change the Spanish Woman as far as possible. *We* arrived from the university. *Then* there were only two or three women at university. *In our time* the presence of women at university was already felt. Not enough, but we were there all the same.[72]

At this stage the two interviewees were requested to choose one or more adjectives that for them best characterized the other's generation. Interestingly enough, and for different reasons, both chose the same adjective to describe the other generation. Valcarcel replied:

> Those of the war were undoubtedly very open (*abiertisimas*). They were open since they lived in a revolutionary period. Do you think that in 1936 women could go out visiting all those villages? Two women driving alone like Pilar [and Dora Maqueda]? They brought about great changes and we walked through the doors they had opened for us.[73]

Andresa López, on the other hand, felt that the younger generation of delegates was characterized by a true openness that in her view was a result of the changing 1960s cultural mentality and economic situation. Whereas during the 1940s, the SF's schools for the high command operated on weekends and holidays, "in 1965 we started feeling the economic change. During the Holy Week, for example, almost no one was left in school. On weekends many students flew to Madrid or Barcelona unaccompanied. This was the meaning of real change".[74]

The correlation between mobility on the one hand and openness and progress on the other came up time and again throughout the interview. Valcarcel mentioned more than once that during her first ten years in the SF, she hardly ever saw Madrid, where her office was situated; even her weekends were spent traveling throughout the country. Moreover, when referring to her parents' objections to her joining the SF, she remembered how shocked they were at the thought of their only daughter spending most of her time traveling around the country by public transportation. Her parents' reaction reflected the double fear inherent in middle-class perceptions of femininity at that the period – the fear of unrestrained mobility and the unsupervised presence of women in public spaces, especially those where class barriers were presumably broken. When her parents finally came to terms with their daughter's professional and ideological choice, they requested that she at least make use of her father's car in order to avoid using public transportation.

Despite the interviewees' attempts to present the SF as an organization that embraced all social classes, the interviews themselves only strengthened the perception that most members were middle-class women. In referring to class differences between the two generations of leadership Valcarcel claimed:

> One can say that the founders, the first members of the SF, came from upper and upper-middle class families. There were also intellectuals, who arrived from the universities. Those were the women who founded the organization and gave it its form. [Later on] women of all classes joined in. In the SF, at least according to my experience, all were called to serve equally. I, for example came from a well-to-do family. An only daughter with God only knows how many servants. When I entered the SF, I became like everyone else. I shared a room with seven other women in a horrifying little pension in the countryside... that is how I learned to appreciate the different, the human.[75]

Citations such as this emphatically attest to the varied class composition of the SF, emphasizing its members' encounters with lower-class women throughout Spain. Sleeping in crowded rooms in the countryside no doubt exposed members to a lifestyle different from that they were used to, but class diversity existed less within the SF and more between its members and the populations with which they interacted.

As we have seen, the "Young Sisters" indeed brought new patterns of activism and decision-making into the organization. In all the interviews I conducted, it was claimed time and again that Pilar Primo de Rivera adopted highly democratic decision-making processes, according to which all the delegates could express their opinions. From the protocols of the SF's Advisory Committee, it appears that generally the position held by the majority, or the most convincing one, was accepted, even when it was different from that held by the National Delegate. However, a part of Consuelo Valcarcel's testimony indicates that not all the delegates approved of Primo de Rivera's approach. At this point the interview was interrupted several times by Andresa López, who insisted on the "anecdotal" nature of the story and its insignificance. Valcarcel, however, continued thus:

Those gatherings [the SF's national congresses] were very typical . . . we talked, discussed, argued and reached decisions and Pilar listened. Let me tell you something . . . I represented a young and somewhat revolutionary generation . . . as a head of one of the national services I used to come up and say everything I had on my mind and nothing ever happened to me. Then Pilar decided to give up the right to chair the congresses and someone else took over. Things that I did not like started happening and since I was used to saying everything on my mind I came up and did so. And you would not believe what that lady, that great democrat, said to me – 'you had better be careful of what you say Cheli, otherwise those things can come back to hurt you' – I do not want to mention names because this lady is already dead, but you can imagine . . . [76]

"That lady" was in all probability Teresa Loring, a member of the national leadership from 1938 onwards and its last national secretary. Valcarcel's insistence on telling the story only shows the extent to which the younger delegates strove to constitute a regenerating and democratizing force within the SF.

When attempting to evaluate the way generation-based differences were expressed in the interviews, it is important to remember that the dismantling of the SF, and the decision to gather its former members within the Nueva Andadura Association, greatly contributed to the suppression of tensions and subversive memories. In view of this, one must not take at face value the almost ideal picture of the relationship between the two leadership generations that emerges from the interviews. However the current chapter has provided us with reliable information concerning the almost complete integration of the "Young Sisters" within the leadership ranks. Such a level of integration could not have been achieved without a considerable commitment on the part of old-time delegates to the recruitment and training of the newcomers. All the interviews I conducted reflect a great deal of mutual appreciation between the two generations, but in my opinion their central importance lies in what was not explicitly stated. Despite differences between the generations, the SF's national leadership remained largely homogeneous regarding social background. Notwithstanding despite changing patterns of formal training and education and the profound changes undergone by Spanish society between 1936 and 1956, the significance given by the women to the terms "freedom" and "openness" remained constant. What linked Pilar Primo de Rivera's 1935 recruitment tours with the university experience of the 1950s and the urban leisure culture of the 1960s was the opportunity for mobility and prominence. Thirty years after the end of the Civil War, these two essential components of a free existence were still unattainable for the majority of Spanish women. The fact that former members of the national leadership constantly referred to these components reflects their awareness of this fact, while simultaneously imparting deeper meaning to organizational affiliation. This embodied not only ideological passion and the collective commitment to a revolutionary project. But also, and perhaps mainly, the ability to live their lives with an unusual degree of public prominence and independence, without isolating themselves from their original ideological and cultural networks. More than anything else, I believe it was this awareness that helped bridge the gap between the two generations and enabled the relatively harmonious integration of the "Young Sisters" into the SF. The fact remains that despite the immense changes undergone by Spanish society, women who were born twenty years apart still sensed that they were fighting for the same goals, and that their chosen lifestyles had turned them into an isolated minority in Spanish society. Such perceptions can provide an explanation for the strong grip the SF had on its members' lives thirty years or more after its dismantling.

2

The National Syndicalist Woman
The Genealogy of a Gender Identity

For us being religious did not signify putting ourselves under the control of the Church. On the other hand, putting some limits on its (the Church's) power did not mean in any way that we had stopped being devout Catholics.

The SF was all about politics. Of course we talked politics. We discussed each step of the Falange, each word spoken by Franco, national and international developments. Some of us wanted to break with the *Movimiento*, but the majority understood that the only way of continuously improving the situation was to remain within the system.[1]

Being a devout Catholic without supporting clericalism, being a fervent nationalist and a faithful follower of José Antonio, while taking issue with both the regime and the FET, being a working woman, a female politician, a mother-figure and a role-model to others. These words of Pilar Primo de Rivera point to some of the perspectives from which the image and discourse regarding the *National Syndicalist Woman* had to be negotiated. The key to understanding this discourse and being able to discern its unifying qualities despite the many internal tensions, lies in the ability to acknowledge the validity of each of its different aspects.

The SF's discourse regarding the identity of the *National Syndicalist Woman*, what was to be expected of her and what she expected of herself and others was at times a baffling mixture of seemingly irreconcilable images and responsibilities. She was committed to caring for others (children, male companions and husbands, aging parents, younger colleagues), but at the same time was called upon to invest time and energy in improving herself physically and intellectually. She was evaluated according to her homemaking skills, but also according to her ambitions to influence society at large. She was called upon to set an example in the workplace, the school and the street. She was expected to be a proud Spaniard and a devout

Catholic while not always abiding by the dictates of National Catholicism. Historians who have acknowledged these contradictions have tried to reconcile them in one of two ways. Some felt that the progressive aspects of the SF's rhetoric and praxis were formulated in the 1960s, resulting from the general liberalization undergone by Spanish society at that time. For those historians the image of the 1960s presented a clear break with the discourse of the previous two decades. Spanish historian Rosario Coca Hernando, for example, when analyzing texts from SF's journal, *Teresa*, which appeared in the late 1950s, claimed:

> If we consider the age of those who were presented as 'modern women' in the pages of *Teresa*, then the publication was no doubt aimed at young women who in no way could see in the 'old fashioned' woman of the 1940s a role model. . . . All the women interviewed were young, successful and modern. The implicit reason for their appearance in *Teresa* was their academic and professional success, while maintaining a specific feminine image.[2]

A second line of explanation made use of the rigid distinction maintained within the SF between the organizational elite and the masses of grass-roots affiliates (temporary and permanent). The French historian Maria Aline Barrachina, for example, in her now classical article *Ideal de la mujer falangista – Ideal falangista de la mujer*, distinguished between the Ideal Falangist Woman and the Falangist Ideal of Woman. To the first category belonged members of the SF's national hierarchy – highly educated women, active wherever they were needed, whether it was at the front or in the political arena. To the second category belonged the rest of the female population, whose main goal in life was to bring up a new generation of national syndicalist men. Barrachina claimed that the progressive elements of the SF's gender discourse applied strictly to its own members. Furthermore, those elements were disguised behind the façade of traditional images of Catholic femininity and motherhood, so as not to antagonize some of the more conservative sectors of the regime, such as the Church and even some male Falangists.

The aim here is to try and offer a more complex reading of the relationship between the progressive and conservative elements in the SF's gender discourse. This will be accomplished by examining the manner in which the image of the "National Syndicalist Woman" was presented in SF rhetoric from the early days of the Civil War until the 1970s. I will examine the different cultural models from which this changing image drew its legitimization and explore its degree of internal cohesiveness at different periods. In my view, any examination of the SF's gender discourse must span all the years of its existence, since only thus can we follow the development of certain rhetorical arguments and point to their early origins.

My contention is that in the SF, it was not a case of "old fashioned" femininity being replaced over the years by a model of "modern" femininity, but rather that of coexistence of modernist and conservative elements, which could be found in the organization's rhetoric from the beginning. My claim is that the tensions between the elements of what was considered traditional feminine vocation and those embodying modernism existed also within the category of "Falangist Femininity" and not only between categories. These tensions were not resolved with the passing of time since the process of liberalization undergone by Francoist society had little effect on accepted gender perceptions. Within this context, "modern" elements took on considerable significance and were defined more or less consistently over time.

An examination of the SF's gender discourse strikingly reveals the constant references to what historian Karen Offen called "the freedom to become", as opposed to "the freedom from imposed restriction". Offen examined the discourse of French Relational Feminists in the second half of the 19th century and their criticism of the prevailing institutional form of marriage and men's legal control over the persons and properties of women. Offen claimed that such criticism was often expressed in terms of the freedom to become. While the freedom from imposed restrictions was "the language of classic economic and political liberalism, transposed to serve the emancipation of women in the world of socially constructed restrictions", the freedom to become "signified a more philosophical, more transcendental, more internalized project in self realization".[3] Similarly, less emphasis was put on the allocation of blame and more on generating the right conditions for the empowerment of Spanish women in ways they themselves saw fit.

Finally, while the SF's discourse was not aimed at a specific population, it was nonetheless significantly influenced by implicit class notions. For the most part, the publications and public presentations analyzed here assumed that their audience had a certain level of formal education and specific professional aspirations. By offering a variety of strategies by which women could strive for self-advancement and combat discrimination (from legal action to the use of mechanized appliances in order to shorten the time needed to run a household), they also assumed a certain level of financial security.

For the purposes of this chapter, I chose to concentrate on two publications issued by the SF, in addition to the papers presented at the International Congress for Women, which the SF held in 1970 in Madrid. This congress, which was sponsored and organized by the SF, brought together representatives of women's organizations from 45 different countries (mostly from Latin America, but also from the US, France, Japan and some Middle Eastern countries), as well as members of twelve organizations within Spain. I chose these papers as source material mainly because they reflect the immense flexibility (as well as the limits) of the SF's discourse regarding the nature and role of women.

The two journals I chose to analyze were defined as "national", that is, they were published and disseminated in all parts of Spain. Internal documents of the SF also demonstrate that the journals were aggressively marketed by the organization. They could not only be found in the SF's centers and traveling libraries, but were also sent free of charge to SF affiliates, who were instructed to distribute copies to their neighbors and friends. The first journal, *Medina* (*Revista para la Mujer Nacional Sindicalista*), was published between the years 1939–1946. It was printed in black and white, and each volume was made up of about 40 A3 pages. The first part of each issue included articles focusing on ideology and religion, as well as features describing the activities of the SF. Other articles in this section dealt with Spain's recovery from the Civil War and with the progress of the Second World War. The second part of each issue was dedicated to fashion, cooking and home economics, while paying special attention to the economic necessities and dictates of an autarkic economy. For the purpose of my study, I had at my disposal the issues of *Medina* for the years 1939–1943.

The second journal, *Teresa*, was published between the years 1954 and 1977. Each volume included about 60 A3 pages, some in color and some in black and white. Several pages each month were devoted to reporting the activities of the SF and also included citations from the writings of José Antonio and the speeches of Pilar Primo de Rivera. About a third of each issue was dedicated to fashion and home economics. Regular columns reported on fluctuations in the Francoist labor market and provided women with information about the availability of jobs, as well as professional training opportunities in the public and private sectors. Additional articles covered international developments and cultural events, mainly in Europe and the US, but also in Asia and the Middle East. For the purpose of the current work, I examined all the volumes of *Teresa*.

Medina: What is Femininity? The Masculine, the Feminine and the Universal

In her book *Fascist Virilities – Rhetoric, Ideology, and Social Fantasy in Italy* historian Barbara Spackman questioned the nature of discourse in general and of the fascist discourse on virility in particular. In the wake of Foucault, Spackman defined a discourse as a series of segments whose meaning is not necessarily unified or stable. According to her, opposition to a specific discourse may quite often be found not outside, but rather inside that discourse.[4] The nature of a discourse, as defined by Spackman, raises a complex question, namely what are the implications when a certain rhetoric (such as the fascist rhetoric on virility) is appropriated by unexpected users (such as women)? Would the rhetoric of virility then collapse entirely, opening the way for an opposing discourse? Or would we see the creation of a hybrid discourse that would maintain its original "logic of exclusion", while incorporating new elements?

When attempting to answer these questions, the materials published by the SF for its own members' use may constitute a useful source.[5] While I have not performed a deep analysis of similar journals published by the Falange for the benefit of its male readers, a quick survey of some of the "national" journals (such as *Arriba, Haz* and *La Hora*) shows them to have been overwhelmingly "masculine". Women were almost never referred to, and while this was not stated explicitly, it was universally assumed that the reader – a Falangist and a Spanish citizen – was male. When women were referred to at all, it was generally in a schematic manner. They were catalogued as either the guardians of the nation, the bearers and nurturers of future generations or the indoctrinators of husbands and sons into the precepts of National Syndicalism. At times it was possible to find some allusions to the *National Syndicalist Woman* who, unlike the conservative "señoritas" of the bourgeoisie, was hard-working and self-sacrificing, and who, in opposition to communist or anarchist women, was also the embodiment of modesty and Catholic devotion. Yet even this seemingly positive image was rendered rigid and somewhat empty, as it totally ignored the life stories and experiences of those it was supposed to represent. While Falangist publications did discuss issues such as demography, the cost of living or the strengths and weaknesses of the Spanish family, these matters were often discussed without stopping to reflect on women's actual experiences as mothers and consumers. It was never acknowledged that women's unique experiences might put them at odds with men (whether husbands, sons, shopkeepers or employers).

Similarly to the Falange's publications, those of the SF gathered together an immense number of writers and styles, whose cohesion and stability over time are doubtful. At the same time, perusing a large number of such texts does enable one to discern two common principles. The first of these was continued subversion of the principle of "separate spheres", according to which the home was a woman's only realm, and the second was an attempt to differentiate socio-cultural attributes of virility from so- called biological ones. In their turn, the socio-cultural elements were presented as universal, or free from gender connotations, and as such could be adopted by women without threatening their femininity.

One of the interesting characteristics of *Medina* was the wealth of historical and contemporary "models" constructed by its writers. Such models, while attempting to offer a somewhat uniform vision of what "femininity" was all about, did so by creating a rather complex picture of the lives of actual flesh-and-blood women. The historical models were presented in a series of articles entitled "Women in Spanish History" or "Women in History".[6] Contemporary models were based on a large array of images: the SF's 59 martyrs, who had died during the Civil War; leading SF members or rank-and-file affiliates; and finally, with the reopening of Spanish universities at the end of the Civil War, Falangist women students.

The female historical figures most often referred to in Francoist Spain were Queen Isabella I and Saint Teresa of Avíla. Appropriating and manipulating the memory of these two women constituted one of many techniques by which the regime erased the dividing line between the sacred and the profane. Such erosion was necessary in order to present the military uprising of July 18, 1936, as a holy crusade, which opened a new chapter in the fulfillment of Spain's historic destiny. The constant worship of and reference to the figure of Teresa of Avila in particular was meant to impart cultural and ideological legitimacy to the new regime.[7] However, Teresa's complex character enabled the SF to emphasize those personality traits and patterns of activism that were not necessarily referred to by the regime and present them to *Medina* readers as possible models to be emulated. Teresa represented a modern model of sanctity relative to her times, based on a life of monasticism and mysticism, which especially emphasized both personal example and copious writings. Teresa of Avila was also known for her unique social perspective, which was universal in religious and racial terms. Immediately following her death, there were many who suggested Teresa of Avila as a possible patron of Spain alongside Santiago of Compustela. However, it is important to note that some of them at least felt that she was worthy of that position not necessarily because she was an exemplary woman, but rather because she exhibited a unique combination of feminine and masculine traits.[8]

A similar combination of the feminine and masculine can also be found in the life story of Isabella la Católica. The queen, who was lauded by the Francoist regime as an exemplary wife and mother, was remembered throughout history as the woman who was the driving force behind the re-conquest of Spain and Christopher Columbus' patron in his travels to the "New World". The contribution of these women to the glorification of the Spanish people (one by religious endeavors and the other by national-religious ones) is what caused the Franco regime to regard them as such powerful symbols. Historian Giulina Di Febo determined that as far as women were concerned, the Francoist racial myth had a very specific function, as protecting the Spanish race has become an integral part of women's identity as the gatekeepers of morality and traditional values. According to di Febo, the life stories of Teresa of Avila and Queen Isabella were reworked and distorted to such an extent that all that was left were simplistic and uniform symbols of feminine vocation.[9]

I contend, however, that the SF employed the idea of women as defenders of the race in a different way and for different purposes. It was precisely Isabella and Teresa's contribution to large- scale political and religious projects that enabled the SF to use their life stories to legitimize new patterns of female activism. In a booklet published in 1941 in memory of SF members who fell "in the line of duty" during the Civil War, the author attempted to explain why Isabella la Católica was a worthy role model for the SF:

> Isabella I, she and no other. Spanish history has been blessed with queens such as Berenguela, mother of Saint Fernando or María Molina, the embodiment of female wisdom. But we are only interested in Isabel . . . Some of the other women were talented monarchs; others proved themselves loving mothers or worthy advisors; and all were exemplary patriots. But only Isabella of Castille, who commanded the re-conquest of the last territory from the infidels, who aided that visionary man Columbus . . . she is an eternal and unequivocal example of the ability of feminine will when acting in the name of true patriotic and Catholic vocation.[10]

This citation is one example of many testifying to the fact that the "logic of exclusion" to which Barbara Spackman referred is irreversibly altered in the movement between the original discourse of virility and that employed by the SF. The organization redrew the boundaries of female activism, utilizing the life story of Isabella la Católica to demonstrate that Spanish women must not limit themselves to merely being the companions and advisors of the men who changed history. Women too could change history, sometimes at the head of a conquering army.

As we shall see, the SF's discourse acknowledged self-fulfillment as a motive for women's activism, but at the same time glorified their commitment to a larger national project. While the regime and the SF chose to make use of the same historical figures as role-models for women it is essential to position their respective discourses in their differentiated contexts. The SF, by exploring more fully the complexity of Teresa and Isabel's lives, far from flattening those into a homogeneous image constructed in fact a discourse much similar to that of 19th century Spanish feminists.[11] Isabella and Teresa were applauded not simply for their religious devotion and heightened sense of "Spanishness", but for their specific interpretations of Catholicism and nationalism in keeping with their personal perceptions of these concepts. A central aspect of "their" Catholicism or nationalism was that it was influenced by their experiences and the possibilities open to them as women. Where women-related issues were concerned, the SF, like the Francoist regime, forged a direct link between the Golden Age of Spain and Francoist Spain. However, it did so by highlighting the importance and legitimacy of women's education and their moral and personal contribution to public life.

Another historical figure often mentioned in *Medina* was the famous scientist, Marie Curie. Using the image of Curie, a foreigner and a scientist, might seem strange at first sight, but "Madame Curie" was no stranger to Spanish women's journals. Her life story presented a model of femininity that many Spanish feminists at the turn of the 20th century could identify with. For these women, who were united in their struggle for better education and equal professional opportunities for women, Curie, the mother and the wife, the scientist who worked alongside her husband, was considered a highly positive model. [12]

The SF made the leap between such appealing yet remote historical models and a more widely applicable and contemporary identity through the elaboration of two popular images. The first image was the product of the chaotic experiences of the Spanish Civil War, while the second originated in the return to relative normality.

The story of the SF's 59 "Martyrs" – the 59 members who had died during the war years – is perhaps one of the best examples of the way the Falangist discourse on virility constituted a starting point for subverting traditional definitions of "femininity".[13] The biographies of the SF's 59 martyrs formed the basis of a carefully constructed narrative that frequently appeared in the organization's publications. Unlike the historical models described above, these young women's lives had been similar to those of thousands of other Spanish women. It was the Civil War more than any other event that forced them to reveal their full potential as "nacional sindicalistas". The message that the SF's leadership wished to convey was that every national-syndicalist woman was just a step away from following their example if she so wished. All she needed to do was be aware of what this entailed and the price she might be required to pay.

The most important issue raised by the "Model of the 59" involved the way in which personality traits and patterns of activism, which were defined as essentially masculine, could be appropriated by women without undermining their femininity. This was done by emphasizing the acquired socio-cultural components of virility. The fact that the term virility (*virilidad*) included mainly socio-cultural attributes enabled a discursive twist that would make them appropriate for women as well. A quick look at three well-known Spanish dictionaries shows the most common characteristics of the term "virilidad" to be courage (*valor*), energy (*energía*), forceful personality (*entereza*), vigor (*esforzado*), determination (*tenacidad*) and intelligence (*inteligencia*).[14] An examination of the texts composed in memory of the SF's 59 martyrs reveals their most frequently referred characteristics to be courage, intelligence, forcefulness, intensity and enthusiasm, determination and heroism. The parallel is suggestive enough

– all the characteristics included under virilidad (and some, which were not but which have clear masculine connotations, such as heroism) appear in almost all of the texts, and in a frequency which rules out the possibility of pure chance. It is important to note that these so-called masculine characteristics did not appear by themselves. They were always accompanied by adjectives describing feminine traits, such as affectionate (*cariñosa*), compassionate (*compasiva*), self-sacrificing (*abnegada*) and gracious (*graciosa*), as well as other less gender-specific traits such as animated (animada), disciplined (disciplinada) and tranquil (tranquila).

I contend that these characteristics were chosen not due to their "virile" nature, but rather because they were considered to be free of gender connotations, and thus could not possibly undermine the femininity of the women they were attributed to. In view of their political and cultural background, members of the SF's leadership had to be extremely careful not to challenge the "manliness" of such characteristics. However, by regularly applying them to women, that is in effect what they did. It is therefore not accidental that they chose not to present an abstract image of the "New Spanish Woman", but rather to cite the life stories of flesh-and-blood women (whether historical or contemporary). Although such stories were carefully adapted, they remained far more complex (and hence easier to identify with) than any one abstract model might have been.

With the reopening of the Spanish universities in 1941, another contemporary image made its appearance in *Medina*. Throughout 1941, the editors published an extensive series of articles dealing with women's right to higher education. All the articles voiced a claim not often heard in the Francoist press – that women's intellectual abilities were equal to those of men. But even after the intellectual ability of women was more or less established, a further question arose: Could femininity and intelligence co-exist without contradictions? Most of the more conservative sectors within Francoist society would answer this question with a resounding "No!". Although they conceded that some women could possibly achieve the almost unattainable goal of completing a university degree, such an achievement could very well cost them their femininity. The SF's leadership refused to accept this claim. For example, Beatriz Blesa Rodríguez, a lawyer by profession and the SF's property registrar, when asked if she felt that certain fields of study could undermine one's femininity, replied: "How absurd! Lack of femininity does not result from studies but rather the opposite. A woman whose femininity is lacking can retrieve it through intellectual endeavors".[15]

The writer of a June 1942 article interviewed several students at the University of Madrid, who expressed their emphatic unwillingness to sacrifice their studies in the name of their femininity or vice versa.[16] Margarita, a third-year criminal law student, was quoted in what sounded like an outright feminist critique:

It seems to me that our aim should be the consolidation of the rights already won and the improvement of the general status of Spanish women. I myself am inclined towards criminal law . . . through my own experiences I hope to prevent others from undergoing those painful moments brought on us by [the actions] of the previous generations.[17]

María Dolores, a student of humanities who was also interviewed in the same article, added:

As women we look here [at the university] for an affirmation to our personality. We wish our intellectual abilities to influence all our other personal attributes – temporal or eternal. Later on, armed with our intelligence we will be able to give the Fatherland sons of superior formation.[18]

The desire for higher education is prominent in both the above citations, as well as the interviewees' perception that their intelligence was an integral part of their personality. Not less manifest was the pride they took in their femininity and the accusation that those who claimed that intellectual achievements could not go hand in hand with femininity were trying to rob them of an important part of their identity.

As has been shown by research concerning other right-wing women's organizations in Spain prior to the Second Republic, the SF was not unique in its efforts to publicly demonstrate women's intellectual abilities and promote their right to higher education and professional opportunities. A similar agenda to the one advanced in *Medina* could be found in publications of the Feminine Section of the lay Catholic organization, Acción Católica, or the nationalist women's organizations that operated across Spain in the 1920s. But the radicalization undergone by such organizations during the years of the Second Republic caused them by the end of the Civil War to support women's exclusion from the public sphere and the adoption of rigid gender dichotomies.[19] Against this background one can say that, while not original, the discourse that appeared on the pages of *Medina* was definitely exceptional in Francoist society.

Amongst other things, the uniqueness of the SF's discourse on women's role and position in nationalist society resulted from a sense of alienation in face of men and other women outside the organization. The Civil War signified a break in inter-generational affiliations. Nowhere was this break better exemplified than in the serialized novels and short stories that abounded in *Medina*. One such serial, *The Ball* (*El Baile*), appeared through the first half of 1941. *The Ball*, by the German writer Irene Nemirovsky, told the story of the Kempf family (that made its fortune through speculation on the stock exchange in the early Weimar years) through the eyes of 14-year-old Antonieta. The entire tale unfolds around the preparations for the family's

The Genealogy of a Gender Identity

first ball, which both Kempf parents consider the final step in their acceptance into the ranks of German high society. Antonieta, intelligent, graceless and unimpressed by social conventions, disappoints her mother by failing to meet up to her expectations of how a young woman of "good standing" should comport herself. As the story progresses, Antonieta's desperate attempts to please her mother are replaced by a deep contempt for everything her parents represent and a conscious choice to be different – a new woman. The following citation, published in *Medina* in April 1941, simultaneously expresses the empowerment achieved by breaking with corrupting past conventions and the extent to which this choice was influenced by a painful sense of alienation and an inability to fit in:

> Idiots, blind idiots – she thought – I am a thousand times more intelligent, more profound. [I] am worth more than all of them put together. And these people dare to try and educate me, show me what is what – these roughnecks, uneducated, newly-made rich.
>
> Never before had she seen in those maternal eyes that cold look of a female enemy. Egoists, evil – she thought – I want to live, I am young. And they are robbing me of every bit of happiness on this earth.[20]

The burning hate for a generation of conservative parents, greatly attached to their worldly goods; the humiliation resulting from an inability to live up to restricting middle-class expectations turned into an encompassing ideology of being different and the desperate wish to grasp life not by "coming out", courting, finding a husband, but rather through study and travels. These feelings, which characterized an entire generation of women in inter-war Europe, were often voiced in women's romance novels, or *literatura rosa*.[21]

One interesting example was the novel *Cristina Guzmán, profesora de idiomas* by Carmen de Icaza – a novelist and former head of the SF's *Auxilio Social*. This work, which was published in 1936, was widely read by Falangist women prisoners and was considered a favorite of the Primo de Rivera sisters. It was also serialized, along with many of Icaza's short stories, on the pages of the SF's journals. The novel tells the story of a young mother who earns a living by teaching languages. From the outset, we know that Cristina, although living in a modest apartment, must come from a wealthy family, since her home is furnished with elegant antiques and her clothes, though simple, are described as well-made and stylish. Due to her uncanny resemblance to his missing daughter-in-law, Gary Prynce-Valmore, an American millionaire, asks Cristina to fill in for her. His son, Joe, is deathly ill and asks for nothing more than the return of his wife, Fifí, who turns out to be Cristina's long-lost sister. While nursing Joe, Cristina falls in love with Gary and reveals to him that she is actually the duchess of Monterreal – his social equal and not just "una maestrita". After Joe's death, Gary and Cristina decide to marry, and the heroine is rewarded for her years of self-sacrifice and poverty by her new advantageous connection.

While the novel culminates in a conventional "happy end", as Cristina's marriage provides her child with a father and a "traditional" nuclear family and frees her from the need to work, up to that point the novel is far from straightforward regarding gender. It is true that Cristina's profession as a foreign language teacher and her role as Joe's nurse in his last days are both typically accepted feminine positions. Yet, her position as a single mother, which is never fully explored or explained, and as a woman who supports herself financially, is far from traditional. The novel is replete with allusions to the fact that Cristina's way of life represents a break with the conventions of former generations and that she identifies with "the modern women . . . who strive to create a new modus vivendi that will permit them to emancipate themselves of the absurd law that decrees that a woman can only exist maintained by a man".[22]

What is emphasized most strongly is the struggle between Cristina's constant need to give to others and the wish to consider herself, which brings Cristina to cry in despair at one point "Always giving, and never, NEVER, receiving anything!"[23] Literary critic Catherine Bourland Ross highlights the fact that "throughout the novel various indications of feminist awareness are debated and denied".[24] According to Ross, such debates must be read in the context of the cultural and practical limitations imposed on Icaza in the context of Nationalist Spain. The debates are Icaza's way of exploring a new female perspective, whereas the denial allows the author to avert the threat of censorship. However, when considered within the larger context of the stories, interviews and article published in *Medina*, one becomes aware that the internal deliberations and personal conflicts experienced by Cristina Guzmán are in fact a reflection of the personal experiences of countless nationalist women. These women were engaged in a constant struggle to reconcile their religious and political beliefs with a growing sense of personal empowerment and the desire to live autonomously.[25]

In the ultra-conservative mood that characterized nationalist society in the early 1940s, harsh, inter-generational criticism such as that expressed in *El baile* and epitomized by personal conflicts such as those of *Cristina Guzmán*, was rarely heard. A more typical strategy employed by those discussing the *National Syndicalist Woman* was to construct a commonly acceptable "other" with which she could be compared. The negative "other" that conferred legitimacy on the *new nationalist woman* was *la miliciana* or *la roja*. The image of *la miliciana* (who was not only a communist, but one who actively fought against nationalist forces) was endowed with all the qualities that were emphatically rejected by the SF. The extent to which this image was burnt into the collective memory can be seen in the words of

Isabel Escobar Toresano, a former SF member from Almería and the daughter of a Francoist politician:

> People, who set fire to Churches and got into fights with others. The militia-women were for the most part women of low quality, who did not know how to read. You couldn't find middle-class people of this sort, much less women. The evils of the war . . . the evil people . . . lacking in intelligence, lacking in talent.[26]

The Falangist "martyrs" were described as heroic and determined, while at the same time compassionate and self-sacrificing. The Falangist students were declared to be intelligent and talented and like Isabel la Católica and Teresa of Avila, all were good Catholics and committed to the glorification of the nation. *La mujer roja*, on the other hand, was either lacking in the right qualities (uneducated and lacking in talent) or carried them to the extreme (i.e., she was belligerent rather than heroic or forceful). Left-wing women were actually rarely expelled from the post Civil War SF, but at a time when communism was considered the root of all evil, the image of *la roja* was a useful rhetorical tool. It enabled those who wrote for *Medina* to present their own model of femininity as acceptably moderate, restrained and balanced.

Teresa: The Women We are, the Women We Wish to Be

While the journal *Medina* was the SF members' companion throughout the Spanish Civil War and the Second World War, *Teresa* served as the organization's mouthpiece in its struggle for women's political and professional equality. *Teresa* therefore constitutes one of the most important sources for examining the SF's gender discourse from the 1950s onwards. *Teresa's* editor throughout the years was Elisa (Lola) de Lara, a journalist and writer from the SF's founding generation, who for many years headed the SF's National Service for Culture. De Lara, whose most striking traits were her sense of humor and biting tongue, strongly influenced the journal's choice of writers and articles. But she primarily exerted her influence through her highly critical and cynical editorials that appeared under the headings of "Teresa" and "A Letter to . . . ".

Numerous messages from over a decade before made their way into the pages of *Teresa*: the importance of higher education for women; considering women's careers as their vocation; and of course women's potential unique contribution to Spanish public life through increased activism. Women's role within her family was still discussed on *Teresa's* pages. But whereas a decade earlier the tensions between women's role within the family and their wish for professional fulfillment remained unresolved, the writers now attempted to suggest strategies for coping with the conflicting demands of both professional and family life. Some of these strategies were generated by Spanish society's recovering economic situation and went hand in hand with the regime's attempt to turn middle-class housewives into pillars of a new consumerist economy. The automation process undergone by Spanish households in the 1960s no doubt made middle-class women's lives easier. Washing machines, refrigerators and cars not only shortened the time needed to take care of the children and the household, but also made it possible to plan ahead regarding food preparation and laundry. But technological innovations paled in comparison to much more complex strategies, which subverted acceptable Francoist perceptions of both women's vocation and the nature of the nuclear family.

The distinction between the socio-cultural and the so-called biological attributes of femininity, which were explored above, also received much attention from *Teresa*'s contributors. Countless articles analyzed women's inferior position within the labor market and claimed that women's poor professional and educational achievements were not the result of inherent inferiority, but rather of hundreds of years of discrimination. Some writers even went so far as to claim that men's superiority in the academic and labor market enabled them to institutionalize aggressive and competitive work patterns that made the integration of women – who supposedly tended towards cooperation and mutual support – difficult.[27]

As part of the campaign to improve the working woman's image, while acknowledging the role of the spoken and written word in shaping reality, some writers criticized the chauvinist way in which many Spaniards used their language. In an article published in 1960 under the heading "Think, Write and Talk Properly", the writer claimed:

> How shall we call a woman who holds a medical degree or a Ph.D. and who has legal authorization to practice her profession? Médico or médica? There is no doubt that the feminization of certain professional adjectives is in line with grammatical norms. But the Academy of the Spanish Language does not even try to feminize professional titles such as engineer, architect or judge . . . no doubt since the number of women in those professions is low. Everything eventually comes down to grammatical habits . . . and the final decision is not in the hands of the Academy but of the public. It is the public that chooses to use these titles for better or worse.[28]

As mentioned above, two of the central goals of *Teresa* were facilitating women's access to the labor market and supporting them in their struggle for professional equality. Although the attention paid to the way grammatical constructions shaped popular perceptions concerning women's work was impressive, the journal's main contribution in this field lay in providing women with practical information. This included details concerning the different training schemes available to women; the positions open to them within the SF and government agencies, as well as in the private sector; and finally, the working conditions and remuneration they should expect. In November 1955, the newspaper began publishing a new column entitled "Women Want to Work", whose aim was "to urgently assist women to become conscious of their role and position. To assist each woman . . . in finding the job best suited to her true destiny".[29] While about a third of all the professions examined in this column were practiced within SF institutions, others included a variety of non-traditional professional fields for women, such as law, architecture and the police, the air force and even the bullfighting ring.[30]

Women's wish for mobility and visibility was also referred to frequently on *Teresa*'s pages. In an editorial opening the first issue of the journal, Elisa de Lara wrote:

> Teresa is anxious to roam the world as she always did. She is determined to go where the road will take her. Just like in the past, only this time Teresa is motorized, driving a Vespa. She speaks a bit of English and smokes. And nothing is going to happen to her, since none of those things constitutes a sin. Teresa's wide world is now half a universe.[31]

Five months later, somewhat humorously, somewhat seriously, de Lara referred to her wish to be considered "one of the guys" in the world of journalism. This was epitomized by her ambition to enter the world of *tartulias* – the intellectual social gatherings that characterized Spanish intellectual life. Women never had easy entry into this world, but were almost completely excluded from it in the post-1939 years. De Lara wrote:

> Today I will share with you something very personal that Teresa can not go on hiding due to the happiness it brings her. Today my friends, Teresa, to her great surprise, found herself the object of praise. Young journalists – all of them graduates of the National School for Journalism – headed by Don Juan Aparicio, expressed their admiration towards the wonderful things taking place within its pages. Teresa was offered an 'editors' coffee' and this is an event of great importance. Teresa is a young woman and therefore knows how to appreciate the compliments showered on her today over cups of coffee in Madrid's Journalist Club.[32]

In 1972, with the Francoist regime nearing its end, De Lara addressed "An Open Letter to Auntie Mercedes", her grandmother's older sister who had since died. The letter constituted yet another attempt to settle some of the scores the women of her generation had with a series of biological and spiritual mothers and grandmothers. Despite the liberalization Spanish society had undergone in the 20 years since the publication of *Teresa's* first issue, it remained clear that women's ability to move freely in a masculine world was still considered a "declaration of independence" not to be taken for granted by everyone:

> How was I supposed to know that one day I would feel the need to talk to you. . . . And all of this is the fault of an Italian reporter that explained [to his readers] that in Madrid, today, a girl dumped by her boyfriend is still perceived as someone whose honor was violated. A bit like I was in your eyes that day when you surprised me coming out of *El Aguilar* where I was drinking a double beer all by myself. 'What would people say?' you asked in a terrifying voice. And guess what? People didn't really have that much to say.[33]

Despite some similarities and a certain degree of consistency between *Medina* and *Teresa*, the latter was no doubt characterized by a growing degree of self-confidence on the part of its contributors. This new attitude was expressed in a variety of ways throughout the years. One expression was the more critical and cynical style of writing employed in the portrayal of "others", which now included not only older women and communist militia fighters, but also men. Men were frequently presented as responsible for women's grim social and professional conditions and as those who prevented them from leaving the house and advancing themselves. In a 1955 article written by Isabel Cajide, a journalist and a member of the SF, men were presented as a collective whose demands were so ridiculous that a healthy dose of cynicism was the only possible antidote against them:

> The men who took part in the interview answered our questions so promptly, that we have no choice but to take them with an equal amount of seriousness. All but one felt that women should work at home, and in all probability they are right. The problem is that in order to satisfy them we have to greatly reform the structure of Spanish society, something which is beyond our ability. In any case we are grateful to men for trying to make our lives more comfortable than their own.[34]

Another accusation leveled against men was that their expectations were often responsible for women being flirtatious, frivolous and ostentatious.[35]

While presenting the Spanish man as corrupting and somewhat ridiculous, women were presented as empowering and positive. This was especially the case when dealing with political issues that had a direct effect on Spanish national pride. In 1966, for example, at the height of renewed tensions with Great Britain concerning Gibraltar, Elisa de Lara wrote an "Open Letter to the Spanish Women who refuse to Work in Gibraltar". In a two-pronged argument expressing class criticism and national sensitivities, Spanish housekeepers, who were exasperated by Spanish passivity in this matter, decided to express their protest in an effective and unusual way: by refusing to work in British households:

> What can I tell you but well done!!! If they, the British housewives in Gibraltar, do not want to be Spanish nor to evacuate a land that is not theirs ... let them wash their own dishes. Hundreds of years the housewives of this British colony – those who are now making sounds of independence – dumped every manual task on you – simple, modest women who came from the 'other side of the tracks' each morning in order to earn a living ... No more!!![36]

Writers in *Teresa* also dug their teeth (or rather their pens) into two issues which earlier writers had not dared to tackle: the division of labor between men and women within the Spanish family and the feminist movement. The SF's attitude towards the feminist movement, be it in Spain or elsewhere, was always ambivalent. On the one hand, the SF's "model of femininity" was based primarily on women like Concepción Arenal, who were well known for their feminist agendas. But in most cases the feminist movement constituted not only a social movement, but also a political one that was generally closely identified with the Left. To the aversion created by this political affiliation was added the fact that some Anglo-Saxon feminists, by highlighting issues such as the right of divorce or reproductive freedom, undermined some of the basic values with which SF members identified. It is thus perhaps not surprising that time and again SF members rejected any attempt to "accuse" them of feminism. But the need to repeatedly refute such accusations only emphasizes the extent to which their lifestyles were at odds with the prevailing norms within Francoist society.

Despite a certain ambivalence, the SF's publications paid close attention to the evolvement of the Second Wave of Feminism, especially in the US and across the border in France. Key books such as Betty Friedan's *The Feminine Mystique* or Simone de Beauvoir's *Le Deuxiéme Sex* were often referred to in *Teresa* and were recommended to readers as "thought-provoking".[37] In 1959 one of the writers, Matilda Medina, declared: "British Suffragists were not at all as (people) portray them. They were beautiful women and good mothers and their legacy is inspiring".[38] This citation and the entire article attest to the problem faced by the SF in this respect. The citation expresses an almost desperate attempt to "rescue" the image of the British Suffragist by insisting on her femininity and her being a worthy mother and companion. This was done in order for Spanish women to be allowed to publicly acknowledge the debt they owed to those who had fought long before them to obtain professional and political equality. In 1959 the SF leadership was deeply involved in the struggle to get the Law for Political and Professional Equality for Women ratified, and its members were desperately looking for "acceptable" precedents that would prove that such equality would in no way destabilize Spanish society. However, they had to be careful in choosing precedents that would not undermine the law's chances of being approved by Parliament. It was impossible to totally ignore the negative image that the Spanish Right had conferred on British and American feminists for so many decades. The "rude, tasteless . . . and some-what masculine" woman could not be obliterated, but was claimed to constitute a minority within the Movement. In her defense it was asked: "How else can women who are faced with such a hostile environment behave and dress?"[39]

Teresa's position on gender roles and the division of labor within the Spanish family was also prey to many tensions and internal contradictions. On the issue of divorce, for example, an anonymous writer commented in a 1968 article: " . . . it is difficult to accept the fact that one should continue to suffer in a failed marriage for the rest of one's life". On the other hand, she claimed that this sort of sacrifice was precisely what was required of devout Catholics, since the dismantling of a marriage was a sin.[40] However, in a presentation given by Dr. Alberto Combarros at the International Congress of Women: it was stated: "It will be absurd to maintain a legal relationship empty of all emotional content. In such a case one could say that the marriage was done for anyway. The continued maintenance of an outer legality only helps in hiding the true emptiness".[41]

On July 1968 the Vatican published its official position concerning the use of contraception. The SF's leadership was adamant in its opposition to abortions, but as far as the use of contraception was concerned, many members were aware that they were fighting a losing battle. In an article, which appeared in *Teresa* two months after the publication of the Papal Bull, the writer stated:

> I feel sorry for the man on the street that reached the simplistic conclusion that the Pope said no, that the Church continues in its old way and says a complete no to the Pill. This last Papal publication did not completely block the way, but one must understand that in essential issues the Church cannot afford to compromise. Christianity acknowledges the fact that compromises do exist, but its own way cannot constitute a compromise. It acknowledges the fact that there are indeed sad caricatures of love, but it is not the Church's place to draw the believers' attention to them.[42]

In light of the perceived deterioration in the status of the "Spanish

Family", the editor of *Teresa* invited contributors to suggest strategies that would improve the stability of family life. Such stability was no longer taken for granted and was in no way seen as women's responsibility alone. In a series of articles published in 1954, Mercedes Formica, a lawyer and a senior member of the SF, called upon parents to accept responsibility for their married daughters' welfare. Formica warned against a situation where 90% of marriage contracts did not provide for an equitable division of family assets and left women with no economic means in case of separation. Formica also resented the fact that every Spanish family strove to ensure that daughters would reach their marriage day in perfect health. On the other hand, no one protected them from physical abuse once they were married or ensured that the prospective husband was not carrying diseases that could harm his wife or future children.[43] A male writer, Enrique Warleta Fernández, pursued another line of criticism in his column "The Family Corner". Fernández was enraged by Spanish fathers' total lack of involvement in the lives of their children. The family should no longer be left in the exclusive charge of the mother, and fathers had further duties than just to put food on the table or discipline their children. It was their responsibility to create a positive emotional relationship with them – a relationship that must be reflected in daily periods of communal play and study.[44]

The greater emphasis put on the nuclear family and the need for both parents' active contribution to it was no doubt the result of the demographic changes undergone by Spanish society in the 1960s. Acute unemployment in the countryside alongside developing industry and a booming housing market brought about massive internal migration to urban areas (especially Madrid and Barcelona). This in its turn caused the splitting up of many extended families and the breakdown of traditional support networks. Such processes had special significance for the raising of children, leaving the main burden in the hands of the parents. *Teresa*'s writers, however, did not limit themselves to pointing out the price exacted by these socio-economic trends. They attempted to shape their readers' response to change by advocating a new division of labor within the family, one that undermined the last bastion of masculinity – the assumption that providing nurture love and warmth were qualities inherent in women only.

The International Congress of Women: The Practical and Theoretical Limits of the Discussion of Femininity and Women's Experience

The International Congress of Women was held in Madrid in summer 1970. Formally the purpose of the congress (that took almost two years to prepare) was to provide an opportunity to explore the status and experiences of women in different societies. Its goal was to foster the discussion and development of strategies for women's political, professional and cultural promotion. In addition, the event was viewed by many members of the SF's national leadership as an opportunity to initiate and consolidate working relationships with different women's organizations across Europe and Latin America. Furthermore, the congress was seen as an opportunity to discuss and facilitate joint projects (preferably under the supervision of the SF) with other women's organizations within Spain, twelve of which took part in the proceedings.

The congress, then, while directly dealing with issues concerning women's status within the family, their political and professional rights and their social and cultural contribution to society at large, can also be seen as the SF's reaction to larger political changes undergone by Spanish society. In 1964 the Franco regime published its new Association Law (*Ley de asociaciones*) that for the first time since 1939 authorized the formation of new civil associations of a social and cultural nature. The new associations could be established outside the FET, but under the supervision of its General Secretary. In the following decade, 11,000 such new entities were registered in Spain. Some of them, like the Housewives' Association (*Asociación de Amas de Casa*) or the Organization of University Women (*Amistad Universitaria*), were national women's organizations.

The associations created under the auspices of the 1964 law generated a process of structural change within the SF. For the first time since 1939, the organization had to face the fact that it no longer held a monopoly over women's organizational life. It now began searching for ways to establish and maintain working relations with the variety of new entities that addressed women-related issues. A document presented at the SF's 1974 National Congress specified 97 local and national associations with which the organization was in touch.[45] Some of those entities (such as the Medina Clubs or the folklore association, *Coros y Danzas*) originated from former departments of the SF. Such associations were partially financed by the organization and headed by its members.

The aim behind their registration as independent entities was to make use of their cultural activities in order to attract populations that were not otherwise identified with the SF. Other associations (such as the Housewives' Association) were completely independent, but held similar (albeit not identical) positions to the SF on gender issues, and it was common to find members of the SF within those associations. The third group was made up of associations with no prior attachment to the SF, whose members at times were of both sexes (such as the Neighborhood Associations). Maintaining everyday contact with such groups was important to the SF precisely because of their distinct social and political agenda, and in order to show that the organization still had a hand in each and every entity that addressed itself to women.

In 1967, in order to co-ordinate its contacts with the new associations, the SF formed the Department for Participation (*departamento de participación*), whose task it was "to encourage, direct and supervise the associations in which women took part".[46] Another way of keeping in touch with the variety of cultural and social positions promoted by the new entities was by holding national and provincial events in which different views could be expressed and debated. One such event was the International Congress of Women.

Over 300 papers, which were divided into four major panels, were presented at the congress: Women in the Family; Women in the Workplace; Women's place within Social and Civil Community; and Women in Education and Culture. All four panels raised issues, which even in the final years of the regime still generated heated debate. Some – such as women's equal professional rights, the right to vote or run for public office had already been made law through the efforts of the SF, although, as we shall see in the following chapter, they were by no means universally implemented. However, other issues were publicly voiced for the first time by women of the Spanish Right.

The panel on *Women in the Workplace* was comprised of papers which, having accepted women's work outside the home as a given reality, discussed the need for a system that would more successfully monitor salaries and social benefits to ensure the application of the equal work – equal pay principle. One of the central debates of this panel revolved around the need to find new means to encourage women to enter technological institutes from which they had previously been conspicuously absent.

In the panel dedicated to *Education and Culture*, the papers dealing with co-education and sexual education for girls best exemplified the extent to which the SF's discourse on women and femininity encompassed some of the major feminist concerns of the time. Elena Catena, an SF member, declared: "Education must be identical for men and women, we must educate the person and not the sex – a proposition, which the [results] of coeducation in schools and colleges surely reinforce".[47] Marta Portal went further in stating: "Instilling a sense of equal efficiency and blindness to sexual differentiation at an early school age would encourage intellectual equality and help improve the mediocre performance [of girls] at pre-university levels".[48]

Portal, who was not a member of the SF, also took a firm stand on the need for sexual education in its broadest sense: practical advice alongside consideration of the emotional implications of becoming sexually active. According to her "A young, economically independent woman, who finds a worthy man, and is well aware of the joys and servitude of sexual relations, can in complete liberty embark on a life of full sexual realization".[49] In their talks both Portal and Catena directly confronted the subtle socio-cultural mechanisms that made it possible to subjugate women. They both continued to assert that women were unique in their potential role as either biological or spiritual mothers. At the same time, they advocated economic independence and sexual awareness as tools for overcoming women's subjugation, which was grounded in ignorance and isolation.

Of the congress's four panels, the one dealing with women within the social and civil community conveyed the most radical message. María Dolores de Asis, for example, analyzed points of continuity and rupture between Simone de Beauvoir's critique of patriarchy and that of the Catholic school of thought which she and other participants advocated. Asis and others opened the way for a constructive dialogue with De Beauvoir's work by emphasizing its existentialist dimensions at the expense of its Marxist ones. Asis accepted the claim that "the world in which feminine subjectivity floats is not a world constructed by women but rather one created and imposed on [women] by men". She felt, however, that "by privileging existence over essence . . . the way was paved for a rejection of the rationalist and empiricist traditions, which viewed women's nature as an unvarying".[50] Existentialism for Asis embodied the acknowledgment of one's experiences and the validity of the personal interpretations given to those experiences. While not embracing all aspects of Existentialism, Asis nonetheless found enough in common with this school of thought to enable a critical discourse. Since she prioritized existentialist experience above biological make-up but in no way dismissed the latter altogether, Asis could not accept De Beauvoir's conclusion that femininity was just a myth totally devoid of meaningful content. However, she did insist that each woman's personal perspective could be detrimental to the way her femininity was expressed and perceived.

Another paper meriting attention on the same panel was that given by María Teresa Arias de Recio and entitled "Promoción de la mujer en la Iglesia". Arias de Recio, who belonged to the International Union of Feminine Catholic Organizations, pushed the conceptual revolution of the Second Vatican Concilium almost to its limit in her discussion of feminist claims concerning the role of Christianity in the subjugation of women. She pointed to the "Jewish, apostolic and patrician roots of Christianity, as the possible [reason] for its seemingly anti-feminine outlook" and warned:

> We all know that the Church is a divine institution, but being controlled by . . . men it also has its faults. Despite the words of the Pope the Church maintains within it some anachronistic traditions . . . concerning the position of women.[51]

In an attempt to abolish such traditions, the Union requested that all canonical texts calling for discrimination be erased; that discriminatory interpretations of biblical texts be censored; and that the term *"laico"* be used to refer to both men and women, guaranteeing equality in all fields where lay action was required.

Spiritual motherhood, with its connotations of social and political commitment, was discussed throughout the congress as an acceptable, and at times even a preferable, replacement for biological motherhood. However, many of the papers that were given demonstrated awareness of the fact that the traditional patterns of marriage and motherhood were changing as well. The massive entry of new technologies into the Spanish household left housewives with more time on their hands. Some chose to work part-time, others to study, and some were rapidly becoming consumers of a new leisure culture. All of these women were "invading" territories from which their marriage had excluded them in the past, but despite considerable improvement, social reality was slow to change. Legislation was a possible way of bridging the gap between women's changing self-perceptions and the reality surrounding them, while an additional way to accomplish this was to change the traditional behavior patterns of within the family. As Elsa Velasquez Zamudio claimed, women had to take responsibility for that part of the process:

> Through our everyday routines and lack of attention . . . we, as mothers, teach our sons and relatives the unconceivable: that there is one morality for men and another for women. Sons maintain unthinkable privileges within the familial unit through the insistence of the mother and other women. Only coeducation [within the family] will teach children of both sexes learn to live side by side as friends.[52]

The 1970 congress exposed the fact that ultimately Spanish women at the heart of the Francoist establishment shared many of the theoretical and practical concerns raised by Second Wave Feminists. But they could only adopt the solutions offered by activists and theoreticians like Simon De Beauvoir or Betty Friedan on condition that such solutions could be reconciled with their religious and ideological beliefs. Nevertheless, it seems to me that the refusal to abandon their original political and religious affiliations should not be perceived as a simple rejection of women's promotion and empowerment. Their struggle to constantly reconcile Falangism, Catholicism and female consciousness attests to the fact that these women possessed a highly critical and personalized view of femininity and of gender relations in general. Such a view took into consideration not only the personal history and experiences of nationalist women, but also the entire spectrum of values they claimed as their own. In refusing to "give up" on

Catholicism and Spanish nationalism and in struggling to invest these with a somewhat different meaning, Falangist women in fact demonstrated as much autonomous thinking and personal empowerment as could be expected from women intent on changing their social and political reality.

The writers and activists who shaped the SF's discourse on gender recognized and validated the interpretations given by women to their own experiences and acknowledged the values they claimed as their own. Furthermore, they did so while taking into consideration women's shifting self-perceptions when fulfilling various roles (as mothers, professionals or companions) and facing different significant others (such as children, parents, husbands or co-workers). While men were targeted by the SF's discourse as responsible for women's victimization and their position within society, they shared company with older women, ideological enemies and the liberal and/or working class culture. Alongside men all of these either actively worked to discriminate against women or had corrupted them to such an extent so as to undermine their struggle for autonomy. This shared allocation of blame resulted from the incorporation (either implicit or explicit) of class, religious and ideological concerns into the SF's discourse on gender. The more subtle feminist critic of the last three decades could have easily demonstrated the way in which male privilege had in fact acted "behind the scenes" to generate those same ideological and class considerations. However, one must keep in mind that the notion of self-realization as an individual project freed from national and/or group affiliations, such as those exhibited by Falangist women, is ideologically constructed as well.

It is only by focusing on women's experiences as they themselves relate and analyze them and by taking into consideration the implications of the relational perspective, that one can discern the way self-advancement and autonomous thinking operate within a discourse laden with nationalism and Catholicism. The writers in *Medina* and *Teresa* and the speakers at the International Congress of Women all exhibited conscious discomfort and even anger over institutionalized injustice towards women as a group. Chapter 4 and the Conclusion will explore the extent to which the SF as a political elite advocated the elimination of this injustice by challenging the authority that perpetuated it.

3

Bridging the Gap between Elitist and Mass Politics
Gender Legislation and the Sección Femenina de la FET

Throughout the centuries, men did not face any competition from women
. . . and then came a woman like myself . . . I always took the time in order
to study things thoroughly. I always came well-prepared there was no chance
anyone was going to surprise me, because everything I did had its logic.[1]

Until recently, research on the SF tended to ignore the organization's role
in shaping Spanish legislation concerning women's civic and labor standing.
The SF's close cooperation with the Franco regime, and the latter's constant
attempts to silence and exclude women from the political, legal and
economic arenas, helped in many cases portray the organization itself as one
which to a large degree ignored the needs and issues concerning the
country's female population – a simple vehicle used by the Franco regime
in order to carry out its policies within a specific target population. As seen
in chapter 2 such a view of the SF cannot be reconciled with the organization's own rhetoric on women's rights and work or, as the current chapter
will demonstrate, with its legislative initiatives.

When faced with the contradiction between the organization's supposed
image and actual policies, some historians claim that the SF's legislation –
most notably its 1961 *Law of Political and Professional Rights* (*Ley de
Derechos Politícos, Profesionales de Trabajo de la Mujer*) – must not be viewed
as an effort to provide women with more political and professional freedom
in order to improve their general status. Rather, they argue, such legislation
should be viewed as an attempt to adjust the role of women to the changing
needs of the Spanish economy.[2] In its transition from autarky to a free
market economy, the regime needed women to gradually enter the public
sphere (from which they were so far excluded) both as consumers and as

workers. The SF, therefore, had no choice but to initiate a legal project that would facilitate such a change or run the risk of becoming irrelevant both to the regime and to Spanish women.

This claim has been reiterated since the 1980s, but in 1998 a first study was published that examined in depth the economic assumptions upon which it was based. The article, written by Spanish historian Cilia Valiente Fernández, demonstrated that Spain's economic situation on the eve of the approval of the *Law of Political and Professional Rights* did not require an expansion of the workforce. Had there been such a need, Fernández further argued, it would have been easily satisfied by the thousands of unemployed men who had lost their jobs as a result of the *Economic Stabilization Plan*.[3] In addition, if these men were not sufficient, the Spanish economy could have relied on many single women who had already completed their professional training.[4] The article demonstrates that under the economic conditions existing at the time, it was more profitable for the state to continue employing women who were already trained in a limited number of professional fields and who were paid below-average salaries, rather than improving women's working conditions or relaxing the ban on married women's work.

In view of these findings, Fernández speculated that the reason behind the new legislation might have been political rather than economic. Following the renewal of diplomatic relations with the US in 1954, and especially with Spain's entry into the UN in 1955, the regime had to initiate certain reforms in order to present a more democratic façade to the world. According to Fernández, therefore, it was only a matter of time before it promoted some sort of change in Spanish women's legal status. According to this line of reasoning as well, the SF's leadership had no choice but to support a reform that it did not initiate.

I would like to offer a different interpretation of the motives behind the legislative efforts of the SF. Such an interpretation is based not only on an evaluation of the three central laws promoted by the organization (the 1958 reform of the Civil Code; the 1961 *Law of Political and Professional Rights*; and the 1966 amendments to that law), and their progress through the Spanish Cortes. I chose rather to focus on the deliberations within the SF concerning each of these laws (as well as other more specific initiatives aimed at improving women's working conditions) and the way their implementation was followed up "on the ground" throughout the 1960s by the organization's legal department (Asesoria Juridica). A long-term examination of the inner functioning of the SF makes it possible to discern how the organization worked to promote innovative legislation long before the economic developments of the early 1960s required an expansion of women's public role. My claim is that the reform was brought about by the SF desire to narrow the gap between the unique patterns of public and political activism exhibited by its own national leadership, and the formal status of wider non-affiliated female populations. The first evidence of this process can be seen as early as 1949, but the political and economic conditions were ripe for its culmination only a decade later.

The Politics of Personal Relations: The "Falangist Woman" and the Francoist Political System

Before examining the SF's legislative projects and their implementation, it is necessary to investigate the nature of the public, especially the political, activism of SF members in the years prior to 1958. This will provide a better understanding of the way in which the legal reform discussed here indeed bridge the gap between the life experiences of a handful of women and that of larger sectors of Spain's female population.

The first generation of SF national leadership had come to realize the rigid distinction between itself and the masses of Spanish women as a precondition for its ability to continue its public work within the Francoist political system of the early 1940s. Throughout the organization's existence, its members maneuvered between their wish to improve the political and professional reality of Spanish women and the fear that such a change might irreparably undermine the stability of the regime. A change in women's status was often tied rhetorically to the success of the National-Syndicalist Revolution, but could never be allowed to gain precedence over it. As long as the Franco regime was seen to provide the best guarantee for the implementation of national-syndicalism, the SF continued to see itself as a faithful tool in the hands of the regime, even when it did not see eye to eye with some of the latter's policies.

As mentioned in the Prologue, the approval of the 1947 *Law of Succession* marked an end of an era for the SF and initiated a major shift in the position of its members regarding their role within the regime. It was at this stage that the national leadership began giving priority to gender-related initiatives in an attempt to legitimize new patterns of political and professional activism for women. Such initiatives were modeled on the experiences of SF members within the Francoist system and on the aspiration to make such experiences available to larger female populations. But what exactly were the political and professional experiences of SF members starting from the early 1940s? How were they able to penetrate the centers of political power and affect decision-making processes? And even more importantly – under what conditions and in relation to what issues did they do so?

Judging from the internal correspondence of the SF, it appears that there was a clear distinction between the patterns of activism adopted by the heads of the organization's National Services and those adopted by the SF's

Provincial Delegates. Within the higher echelons of the SF, one could see significant reliance on personal connections, preference for informal negotiations and attempts to avoid overt conflicts. Pilar Primo de Rivera's preferred channels of intervention included private appeals to the FET's General Secretary and intimate conversations with ministers' wives over afternoon tea. The correspondence with the Movement's General Secretaries, who were considered loyal Falangists "of the first hour" (such as Reimundo Fernández Cuesta or José Luis Arrese), as well as with late arrivals whose ideological loyalty might have been doubted (such as José Luis Solís), were always personal, direct and firm. Meetings with ministers' wives and with Carmen de Polo Franco were viewed as a last resort when all other attempts to get through to the men had failed.[5] Official receptions presented countless opportunities for solving problems (from budgetary issues to confrontations with ministers and Provincial Delegates of the FET), so the National Delegate carefully chose the ones she attended. Primo de Rivera would arrive accompanied by the delegate who was concerned with the problem in hand. Her personal secretary, Icha de Cuesta, testified that she often referred to such social events as "part of the working day" and used to joke about the need "to go through life begging and learning to live off charity".[6]

Amongst Pilar Primo de Rivera's correspondence, one can find long and frequent letters addressed to General Franco on a variety of issues. The National Delegate did not hesitate to approach the Caudillo as a final arbitrator when she felt that the SF was being discriminated against, even when the source of such discrimination was the General Secretary of the FET himself. In a letter to Franco dated March 23 1948, for example, she complained of the relatively small budget allocated to the SF's Youth Movement in comparison to that of the FET. Referring to José Antonio Elola, who headed the FET's Youth Movement, she wrote:

> I do not know if Elola is better gifted in asking for donations, or maybe there are some who feel he runs his organizations better than we do. . . . I am aware of the economic limitations faced by the Spanish State and if there is a need we are, of course, willing to save and skimp. But we want to see the demand [to save] addressed at everyone equally. Right now we are called upon to make use of our 'skills' as women to work miracles with a meager budget, something no one else in the *Movimiento* is asked to do.[7]

Private appeals and interventions were made possible first and foremost due to the numerous personal connections of members of the national leadership with the men who headed Spain's political system. As seen in Chapter 1, these personal relations were perhaps the most important contribution of the SF's founding generation to the organization. While Pilar Primo de

Rivera is the best-known example, a long list of other Falangist women did not hesitate to make use of their standing as sisters, childhood friends and fiancés of leading members of the original Falange, who in time became prominent members of the regime.[8]

On the other hand, on the provincial level, relations between SF and FET delegates were characterized by considerable tension. The first cause of this state of affairs concerned the delegates' personal background. Many of the SF's provincial delegates, who were appointed during the war, were the relatives of local Falangist activists. While many of these women continued to hold office after 1939, there was a major personal turnover within the FET at the end of the war. Old-time Falangists were replaced by new arrivals of monarchist persuasion, who were placed under the supervision of the civil governors. This different ideological background generated many tensions that only worsened as a result of the lack of direct communication between the two organizations. Another source of conflict was the nature of the SF's provincial delegates' activities. As part of their role as local representatives of the organization, the delegates were involved in daily power struggles with local Church authorities, educational institutions and the syndicate system. Complaints from physical education instructors who were expelled from Catholic schools under various pretexts poured into the offices of the provincial delegate, in addition to those of female syndicate representatives who were not allowed to voice their position on labor disputes and of youth instructors who had to manage with inferior financing and installations.

Under such conditions, it is not surprising that there was endless correspondence between the FET's General Secretary and the SF's National Delegate, in which Primo de Rivera was called upon to restrain, and sometimes even dismiss, her loud and forceful provincial delegates. Two extreme examples occurred in 1939 and 1964. On February 17, 1939, following direct and well-publicized confrontations between the SF's Provincial Delegate in Guadalajara and the FET's Provincial Chief in the area, the General Secretary addressed the following demand to Pilar Primo de Rivera:

The national hierarchy of the SF must calm down (*frene su favor*) the Provincial Delegate of Guadalajara and make sure that she obeys the FET's provincial chief, whom we consider as the highest political authority in the territory and the *Movimiento*'s only representative.[9]

I have not been able to locate Pilar Primo de Rivera's response, but the SF's delegate, Antonia Gimmenez González, continued to fill her post until the end of 1941, with great public visibility, to which the local papers colorfully attest.

In May 1964, the Civil Governor of Albacete, Miguel Cruz Hernández, demanded the immediate dismissal of the SF's Provincial Delegate, María

Mercedes Tabernero Garrido. The reason was Tabernero Garrido's refusal to instruct members of the SF to vote for the governor's favored candidate in the imminent parliamentary elections and her insistence on publicly endorsing a different candidate. As in many other cases, the Provincial Delegate received Pilar Primo de Rivera's full backing, reflected in the following letter addressed to the FET's Provincial Chief:

> I will be grateful if you instruct the Civil Governor to revoke his demand for the dismissal of my Provincial Delegate since I have no intention of agreeing to it. I do not think that members [of the SF] have to vote according to the instructions of the governor, who has no other reason to ask for my delegate's replacement than her refusal to act on this matter.[10]

The complex relations between the SF (as an independent organization with its own ideological and gender-based agenda) and the FET (with its array of political and social perspectives) generated conflicts that in their most extreme form were even brought up to debate in *La nacional*. Primo de Rivera's willingness to back up her delegates reflected her strong sense of gender and organizational solidarity, as well as her commitment to letting them run their own territories with a large measure of freedom.

An analysis of the SF's internal documentation demonstrates that with the passing of the years, there was a significant change in the issues that its delegates chose to challenge directly and energetically. Until the end of the 1940s such interventions had to do mainly with matters of salaries and financing. The SF's economic situation at that time was extremely bad and most of the conflicts with the FET's leadership focused on demands for equal funding and the *Movimiento*'s assistance in financing the salaries of the SF's local representatives.[11]

By the 1950s, the national leadership was becoming involved in more general political conflicts. In 1953, for example, one of the parliamentary seats allocated to the FET fell vacant. The SF was the only organ of the *Movimiento* whose National Secretary was not also a Member of Parliament. At that time Pilar Primo de Rivera was not only the sole SF representative in Parliament, but also the only woman appointed to that body. In a series of private meetings with the FET's General Secretary, Primo de Rivera attempted to convince him to allocate the vacant seat to the SF's National Secretary, Sierra Manteola. However, the SF did not receive a second parliamentary seat until 1963 (by which time it was Teresa Loring who received the appointment), when female parliamentary representation was finally expanded, it only through much personal pressure exercised by the SF leadership.

With the expansion of the SF's activities, the tensions accompanying its relations with different government agencies and branches of the FET increased as well. In 1954 Pilar Primo de Rivera asked the General Secretary to intervene with the Minister of Education on behalf of the SF on account of "constant attempts of (his) middle-level functionaries, especially certain general inspectors, to paralyze the SF's activities".[12] During January 1955, the protocols of the meetings of the Heads of SF's National Services all centered on the crisis developing with representatives of the National Syndicates. The National Syndicate of Paramedical Workers prevented female nurses from forming an independent all-woman syndicate under the auspices of the SF.[13] This crisis was resolved (this time in favor of the SF) only after a series of private meetings between Pilar Primo de Rivera and the head of the National Service for Sanitation with the National Delegate for Syndicates and the General Secretary for Social Services.

Leaders of the SF did not hesitate to interfere in a variety of ideologically-oriented matters as well, but their involvement in these was much more discreet. The reason for this seems clear: despite the reservations evoked by the SF's gender policies, when it was acting in regard to legal or professional questions concerning women, the organization's involvement was easily justified. However, when it came to issues concerning the Falange's political status or the validity of different interpretations of José Antonio's doctrine, members of the SF found themselves on shakier ground. Despite Primo de Rivera's personal standing, and the fact that her position was employed by the regime to demonstrate its commitment to José Antonio's doctrine, her involvement in "men's politics" generated considerable resentment. Thus when dealing with such issues, the SF had to exercise utmost discretion.

In 1964 Franco called for parliamentary elections. While the National Delegate publicly urged members to vote to ensure the election of "true Falangists," she expressed her true opinion privately in a letter sent to the FET's General Secretary:

We are suffering all of a sudden from the need to prove our liberal nature and our participation in democratic procedures and this will be the end of us – an end to all the positive things which the Falange is fighting for. You, like all of us and like everyone who takes part in this process, should be aware of the hypocrisy characterizing these elections.[14]

Pilar Primo de Rivera's position in this matter reflects the traditional Falangist view, which saw the party system and free elections in general as a hotbed of subversion and divisiveness. However, it also reflected the fear that in a truly free election (which was in no way the case in 1964) the *Movimiento* and the regime in general would find themselves lacking in public support.

The new generation of Spanish politicians and activists that came into the fore in the late 1950s also engaged the SF's attention, eliciting many ambivalent reactions from its leadership. On the one hand, Primo de Rivera and other leading delegates did not hesitate to mobilize their personal connections in order to fight for the future of old-time Falangists such as Julian Pemartín and Jesus Muro. On the other hand, they also protected young Falangists who publicly criticized the regime and even Franco himself.[15]

The public and political involvement of members of the national leadership was very intense from the start. Whether they chose to act through official political channels or make use of their personal connections deep within the Francoist system, they demonstrated an excellent understanding of the issues at hand and the personal and institutional interests involved. Furthermore, they proved determined to protect what they perceived to be their own political agenda. The first step on the organization's way to increasing female professional and political participation was to cause other women to be just as "visible" as they were within the system. In order to do so, they had to struggle against a number of attempts to ignore women by erasing them from the existing legislation, robbing them of associated representation, and depriving them of the information regarding their few existing rights.

Becoming Visible: New Associative Initiatives for Women and the SF's Legislative Reform

The legal framework against which any examination of the labor and civic legislation promoted by the SF must be conducted is that of the Franco regime. The great achievements of the Second Republic in this respect constitute a necessary point of comparison in order to understand the extent of exclusion and discrimination forced upon women by the new regime.[16] Such achievements can also provide a framework for understanding the extent of the reform to which many women aspired during the Franco years in contrast to which the SF's legislative projects may at times have seemed rather limited. However, one must remember that for many right-wing Spanish women, the 1931 constitution represented a threat to core values which were at times more important to them than formal political and legal equality. The legalization of both divorce and abortions was viewed as an unprecedented threat to family life. The abolition of church-sponsored schools and the advocacy of co-education were felt to undermine such values as freedom of religion, modesty and the division of social and gender roles. Many women, therefore, wholeheartedly supported the military uprising and the regime that resulted from it. Some, like the members of the SF, made a considerable effort to make themselves indispensable to the new political order. However, their identification with the Franco regime did not necessarily mean that they identified with each and every aspect of its rhetoric and legislation. One must therefore acknowledge and understand the cultural dictates and legal constraints within which the SF's national leadership operated. Furthermore, one should not assume *a priori* that these constraints were automatically accepted or rejected by SF members. In its capacity as a political elite, the SF had to constantly negotiate with deeply engrained cultural values and the dictates of the legal system, reinforcing some values and negating others.

As part of the Franco regime's attempts to reestablish some of the rigid gender codes held by sectors of the Spanish society prior to the Second Republic, in August 1939 it hastily reenacted the 1808 Napoleonic Civil Code. The code, while granting single women some professional and financial freedom, reduced married women to the status of a legal minority. Married women were barred from appearing before the courts; from taking independent decisions concerning the future of their children; and from making use of family assets without the explicit permission of their husbands. A 1947 law forced women to take an involuntary leave of absence (*excedencia forzosa*) of their jobs after marriage while a 1957 law forbade them from "dangerous" or "morally jeopardizing" work.[17] Women's problems and the discrimination against them did not end upon their entry into the workplace. Despite the fact that women were entitled by law to equal pay for equal work, in reality their salaries were significantly lower than those of men, an "oversight" consistently ignored by the regime. A woman's workday was also significantly shorter than that of a man. While men could work up to ten hours with the possibility of unlimited overtime, women worked an eight-hour day and their overtime could not exceed two hours.[18] This law, which was ratified during the days of the Second Republic, was supposed to protect women; in reality, it made employers reluctant to hire them.

One of the benefits provided by the regime to all workers was a family subsidy, which was part of a general policy to encourage increased birthrates. The family subsidy included a progressive payment made by the state for each child, starting from the second one. While a family of four children received 40 pesetas a month, a family of twelve children received 1,080 pesetas. The payment was added to the salary of the head of the household; however, in families where both parents worked, it was payable to the husband only. Even in cases where a woman was acknowledged to be the head of the household, a special committee had to approve her eligibility for the family subsidy.

Despite this discriminatory legislation, Spanish sociologist Cristina Borderias has demonstrated that the years 1940–1960 nonetheless brought about the most significant increase in the number of Spanish working women.[19] If in 1940 the percentage of gainfully employed women was 8.8%, by 1960 (even prior to the full impact of Spain's economic recovery), it rose to 15.13%. While in 1950 women made up 23.3% of Spain's working population, by 1960 their presence increased to 28%. The newly acquired visibility of Spain's working women in the years covered by the present study was partially the result of the country's expanding industry and changing demographic conditions. In the post-Civil War period, the immense struggle for survival experienced by many Spanish households meant that women had no choice but to go out to work if they wished to support their children. Furthermore, the migration of many Spanish families from rural to urban areas provided women with more opportunities to take on paid work outside the home. By doing so, they "moved" into the category of the "gainfully employed," becoming "visible" to the official census. However, another less widely discussed aspect of the increased presence of women within the Spanish labor force of those years concerned the SF's efforts to create professional frameworks that would cater to women and disseminate information concerning their legal and professional rights.

In order to pierce the thick screen of invisibility and discrimination affecting Spanish women, the SF first had to make government agencies and private employers aware of the rights of their female employees and cause them to respect these rights. The first step in this long battle included founding departments within the SF that could reach and instruct both employers and employees. In May 1938, in a letter to her provincial delegates, Pilar Primo de Rivera announced the signing of an agreement with the Ministry for Syndical Action (*Ministerio de Acción Sindical*), which created the position of SF syndical coordinator (*enlaces sindicales*). The syndical coordinators were to act as the organization's representatives in each syndicate that included female members. In the first years the coordinators were required to be SF members as well as members of the syndicate within which they acted. The provincial delegates were called upon to look for members between the ages of 20–35 who exhibited "social awareness, a minimal cultural background [and were] disciplined and friendly".[20] The coordinators' first task was to make a list of all the female members in the syndicate in order to allow the SF to campaign in matters concerning their working conditions. Another aim was to "increase the knowledge of the women on general, intellectual and domestic issues".[21] This demand reflected the SF's ambivalent attitude towards working-class women. On the one hand, women's paid labor was understood as essential to the survival of their families. On the other hand, since reproducing a family (in the biological sense) and ensuring its survival (in the economic sense) were perceived at times as two mutually exclusive tasks, the SF was apprehensive that the one would interfere with the other. One way of solving this conflict was to establish day care centers for working-class children.[22] Another was to ensure that working-class women were constantly reminded of and instructed in their double obligation as workers, but also as mothers and wives.

The coordinators' work was not an easy one, and despite their contribution to both the SF and the Ministry of Labor, they were not paid by either. Their involvement in matters relating to the syndicate's functioning often put them in a difficult position both socially and professionally, especially due to the fact that they were not elected by either the workers or the employers, and were often regarded suspiciously by both. In an interview I conducted with María Nieves Sunyer, the SF's former Provincial Labor Delegate in Madrid, she reflected on some of the tensions that were inherent in the job of the syndical coordinators:

> The syndical coordinators were recognized by the Ministry of Labor. Therefore, when we had a problem we did not have to go through the syndicate, but rather approached the Ministry directly. We had to say that so and so happened in a certain factory and the problem would be resolved. And that girl, who was not elected by the workers, and who was known as the Ministry's collaborator, was the one who notified us of problems. I remember one girl named Mercedes, a great person and an excellent worker, who was a production supervisor. In her factory they were making steel pitchers and she noticed that the quality of the materials was low and refused to use them. They decided to fire her. She called me and told me what had taken place and I called the human resources director and made it clear to him that Mercedes was working for the Ministry of Labor and could not be fired. And she came back to work.[23]

As Nieves Sunyer's words imply, the SF managed to situate its coordinators at the problematic point of contact between the FET and the Ministry of Labor. Thus by providing important information to the Ministry, the coordinators found a powerful ally in their struggle for recognition and equal representation within the syndicates.

In order to ensure working relations and open communications with the National Syndicates, a second agreement was signed in April 1940, according to which the SF's department *Hermandad de Ciudad y Campo* was to coordinate efforts on that front. To this complex web of representatives were also added the *vocals*, women who were not SF members but who managed, as a result of their work in a specific industry, to be elected independently as workers' representatives. Such representatives were elected locally, provincially and nationally. Theoretically women were not prevented from applying for the position of *vocal*, but the relatively small number of women in mixed industries often prevented them from actually being elected. During the 1940s and the 1950s, the role played by the *vocals* was purely representational, since working conditions were exclusively determined by the Ministry of Labor. At the beginning of the 1960s however, this situation changed, when collective working contracts (*convenios*) started being raised for negotiation once every two years. Initially the female *vocales* and SF representatives were allowed to take part in the negotiations as observers only, but by the mid-1960s, most of them were awarded a vote as well. The negotiations were extremely limited, since workers did not have the right to strike, and pay increases were often determined beforehand. However, within this unfavorable system, the SF's representatives tried to secure specific benefits for women. Or in the words of Nieves Sunyer:

> The role of the SF's representatives was to raise before the syndicate's central committee particular problems relating to women: their working hours, maternity leave. . . . They also had to take part in the discussions that took place when working contracts were reopened and advocate our position. If the last contract stated that maternity leave would be a month long, we managed to secure a two-month-long leave, and so forth.[24]

Sunyer attempted to present a harmonious system where changes took place through negotiations and mutual consideration between employers and employees. However, her own testimony only emphasizes the fact that women's rights were not considered a weighty issue and that the small number of working women made it difficult for them to be heard. Despite the fact that the SF's representatives didn't always promote an agenda that was acceptable to all female workers, the organization undoubtedly managed to increase an awareness of women's specific needs and to bring about an improvement in their working conditions.

Nurses comprised one sector of the female working population that constantly engaged the SF's attention. The prominence of nurses amongst the SF's first-generation affiliates was discussed in Chapter 1. The fact that nursing was probably the most culturally acceptable female profession at the time and essential to war-stricken Europe of the 1930s and 1940s turned it into a perfect arena for the SF's first labor battle. In 1943 a new law was approved which regulated workers' social security rights. In its capacity as the body responsible for the provision of social security benefits, the Ministry of Labor decreed that all medical services necessary to prove eligibility for such benefits would be provided by the FET. The new legislation had major organizational implications, since previous legislation had already stated that the SF's nurses would provide all medical services required by the FET. In February of that year, Pilar Primo de Rivera addressed a letter to her provincial delegates demanding that they organize a series of courses for the training of new nurses and refresher courses for those already registered with the SF.[25] This was to ensure that the SF could provide enough nurses so as to prevent the Ministry of Labor from hiring women trained elsewhere.

The decree concerning the provision of nursing services was of immense importance to the organization for several reasons. First, despite the fact that during the Civil War the SF managed to create a de facto situation where all professional nurses in nationalist territory had to be affiliated with the organization, after the war many nurses secured private employment. In addition to the Ministry of Health, the Ministry of Labor was the major employer of nurses in the public sector and its decision had thus turned the SF into the biggest provider of nursing services in Spain. Another reason had to do with the fact that nurses, like other service providers within the SF, did not receive regular salaries prior to 1944. The Ministry's decision to employ them constituted an indirect contribution to the SF's budget. But even more importantly, as Primo de Rivera indicated "salaries will enable us to confer an official status on the nurses and to obligate them to combine their professional work with social work conducted within and for the SF".[26] The National Delegate emphasized the fact that the salary payable to each nurse (500 pesetas a month) constituted a privilege. She therefore demanded that when choosing the nurses to be sent to the Ministry of Labor, those who had worked voluntarily within the SF in previous years were to be given priority.

This circumstance demonstrates that the SF promoted women's professional advancement primarily for the benefit of its own affiliates and within its own institutions, and only in cases when this was not possible did it work to support other associative frameworks. Similarly to the promotion of recreational culture (to be discussed in Chapter 4), women's professional advancement had both ideological and organizational significance. The championing of such issues by the SF was considered a powerful means of bolstering its own political and organizational strength.

In 1951 the SF began to take an active interest in the professional status of female domestic workers. The SF was not the first organization within the Spanish Right to take an interest in this sector. As early as 1931, the Syndicates of Catholic Workers, promoted by the Catholic Church and Acción Católica, founded the Syndicate of House Servants (*Sindicato de sirvientas*) that united young domestic workers who served as cooks, maids and nannies. This syndicate was concerned with improving the economic conditions of these women, but mainly with ensuring them "a moral and professional environment in accordance with the dictates of the Church". The SF, on the other hand, while acknowledging the specific "personal and moral" position of domestic workers, was more concerned with securing their professional and economic rights.[27]

The exact number of women employed in domestic service in the early 1950s is not known. We do know, however, that female domestic workers were the largest group within the "service industries" sector. It is estimated that domestic workers made up the third largest category of Spanish working women in the second half of the 20th century. According to a statute from 1944, a domestic employee was anyone who worked on a regular basis in a private household that was not owned by his or her immediate family. Domestic employees were usually entitled to accommodation as well as a salary. Sometimes, however, they worked in exchange for food and accommodation only. In her study of domestic workers in Chile, historian Nora Milanich established that in the first half of the 20th century, the discourse regarding working women completely ignored those concerned with domestic work. This was true despite the fact that over 40% of the working women in Chile at that time were domestic employees.[28] Milanich showed that domestic servants were not acknowledged by the labor legislation of those years, and a census carried out in the 1930s classified female domestic servants as economically inactive. Historian María Rosa Capel demonstrated that the same held true for Spain, and the big question was: if domestic work was not a form of employment, what was it? Milanich defined female domestic workers as having "a social status with specific familial and moral connotations". Life in their master's household, side by side with the middle-class family for which they worked all day long, was seen by some as the best way of safeguarding these women's moral conduct. Yet it was precisely the employee's acceptance into the household and her intimate standing as part of the family that made her professional position so problematic.

The 1944 statute regarding domestic workers indicated the need to formalize the working conditions of female employees and declared them entitled to all social benefits required by law, but in reality nothing was done in this respect. The difficulty in dealing with this sector is reflected in a document issued in 1950 by Carmen Warner, the SF's Head of the Department of Social Assistance and Sanitation. The document, which was presented to the SF's Heads of the National Services, stated:

> In the cities and villages there will always be a certain percentage of women, who due to their conditions or the lack of means available to them will prefer domestic work. . . . Today there is a large number of women who are working without any legal protection, without health insurance or a pension fund. On the other hand, we have people of the higher classes who sternly oppose the idea of granting professional status and social benefits to women who, in most cases, have no formal training.[29]

Warner's document reflects the SF's desire to secure certain rights for female domestic employees, while at the same time acknowledging the uniqueness of their situation. The attitude towards domestic workers was grounded in the accepted image of the middle-class family at the time. As Warner put it: "Domestic work is inseparable from the family as an institution, and it is (the family) that must vouch for the servants' morality and at the same time provide solutions to their lodging problems".[30] In the eyes of the SF's leadership, the bourgeois family provided a substitute for the familial networks left behind by many women when they went to work in the cities. These women were perceived to be in need of guidance and supervision in order not to fall prey to the corrupting temptations of the city. In this respect, middle-class families were at times seen as the most appropriate substitute for the women's original families. The relationship between the master or mistress of the household and their domestic employees was considered to be different from the standard employer-employee relations, and the SF had no wish to bring about its total regulation. In light of this, Warner recommended that domestic employees' working contracts should not be standardized by law, but that the length of their working day and their salaries should. The organization also demanded that each employer provide health and accident insurance, and create a pension fund. All employers were also required to provide their female domestic workers with accommodation.

In order to ensure those rights, the SF demanded the formation of a syndicate uniting all female domestic workers. This demand was brought up at several meetings with the Minister of Labor between the years 1953–1954, but to no avail. Finally in 1959, the SF's leadership decided to form the "Domestic Workers Mutual Fund". The status of a public "mutual fund" was defined by Francoist legislation of the years 1941–1943, according to which a mutual fund was any non-profit association that was formed in order to provide its members with mutual aid and social benefits. Social benefits were financed through payments made by the members and by any organizations that supported the fund, as well as through regular social security payments, which employers were legally required to pay . Individuals, formal associations and syndical organizations could all establish mutual funds; in cases where a fund was formed by an existing association, it had to prove structural independence. However, later on it was recognized that when the founding association contributed more than 25% of the fund's budget, it was entitled to appoint representatives to the board of directors.[31] This legal clause ensured that the SF would be actively involved in the everyday running of the Domestic Workers Mutual Fund.

According to the concept of vertical representation, the "Domestic Workers Mutual Fund" was meant to include both employers and employees. The membership fee was 40 pesetas a month and despite the fact that it was stated that 75% of the fee would be paid by employers, it was not clear how, if at all, they could be forced to do so. According to the SF's estimates, the salary of a maid in Madrid in 1956 was 300 pesetas a month plus accommodation. The membership fees, then, constituted 11% of an average maid's salary. Under such conditions, it was unclear how most maids could indeed afford to pay the sum without the help of their employers. In January 1961, elections were held for the fund's directing committee, which was to be made up of four workers and two employers from each province. The committee's first move was to declare that, starting from January 1962, each member of the fund would be entitled, on top of the benefits mentioned above, to a marriage grant of 1,500 pesetas.[32] However, it was only in the 1970s that the formal professional status of all female domestic workers in Spain would finally be regulated. Nevertheless, the history of the fund is a good example of the way in which the SF did not hesitate to challenge popular socio-cultural notions when such a challenge was in line with its social and political agenda. By unionizing domestic female employees, the organization not only guaranteed some of their basic rights but also turned them into a visible sector of the Spanish economy.

In 1951 Pilar Primo de Rivera asked Mercedes Formica – a lawyer by profession and a member of the Falange's Students Syndicate since 1933 – to produce a general report on the situation of women's employment in Spain, and to enumerate the reforms required in order to improve this situation. Formica assembled a team of eleven women who, with the aid of the Institute for Political Studies (*Instituto de Estudios Políticos*), worked to produce the report. The document was supposed to be presented at the International Hispano-American Congress for Women, which the SF organized in Madrid in June of that year, but the session where it was to be discussed was cancelled at the last minute. As it turned out, Formica's report was never published by the SF, probably due to the author's insistence on a lengthy discussion regarding the situation of women in the liberal professions, a topic that Primo de Rivera refused to address formally at that stage.[33] Yet, unknown to Mercedes Formica, the contents of her report were used in a series of position papers compiled by the SF and addressed to the Office of National Works (*Dirección Nacional de Trabajos*) as early as 1952.[34] The main concern of the SF at the time was the abolition of *excedencia forzosa*. Certain sectors within the regime sincerely believed that an increase in the number of working women might have devastating repercussions for the Spanish family, so the SF chose not to employ the argument of women's right to professional equality. Rather, the notion of *excedencia forzosa* was opposed due to what the SF defined as its "unhealthy moral effects," namely the fact that it caused many women to refrain from marriage for fear of losing their jobs.[35]

The steps taken by the SF to increase women's political professional representation prior to 1958 improved the conditions of very specific groups of working women, but in no way affected a more general change in women's labor rights or in the attitudes towards female paid employment.

The SF was ultimately motivated to publicly propose an alternative legislative project by this realization and in hope that the progressive social and cultural changes experienced by Spanish society in the late 1950s would make it more open to a major change.

The 1958 amendment to the Spanish Civil Code was proposed by Mercedes Fromica (who by then had already left the SF, but continued cooperating with the organization) and endorsed by Primo de Rivera. The reform included 66 articles, most of them concerning the legal status of married women. Article 168 of the Civil Code according to which widowed women who remarried were to lose custody of their children by their first marriage was amended so as to state that "a second marriage of neither father nor mother would affect their parental rights".[36] Article 1.882 of the Civil Judgment Act (Enjuiciamiento Civil) that defined the family home as the property of the husband (casa de marido), therefore depriving a woman who filed for legal separation with justified cause of the right to keep on there, was also amended. The reformed article defined the family home as just that – *la casa de la familia* – thereby requiring a husband to seek his wife's permission before any transaction involving family property. Article 105, which treated adultery as a crime resulting in separation only when committed by the wife, and made the killing of an adulterous wife by her husband punishable by up to six months in prison or an eviction of the killer from his hometown, was also amended. Adultery now became just cause for separation on both sides. Yet, alongside such amendments, the civil code still retained some serious limitations, such as a married wife's need to seek her husband's permission to participate in legal proceedings (article 60); to accept or reject any kind of inheritance (article 995); or to function as a legal executor of any kind (article 893).

Once these changes had been achieved in the civic status of women, the SF was now free to begin working on what was to become its single most important legacy to Spanish women – the Law for Political and Professional Rights for Women. Lidia Falcón, a leading Spanish feminist and the founder of the women's group *Partida Feminista*, admitted about the law: " . . . it was a notable effort . . . to arrange such conflicting criteria and interests. Therefore it is essential to forget, for the moment, the many failures that it contained on account of the good intentions with which they were committed".[37] Presenting the law, and achieving its approval by the Cortes, can be seen as the culmination of a long process in which the SF acted as both the initiator and the subject of extensive cultural and social change.

The 1961 law included five articles only, the first abolishing " . . . any limitations on the political, professional or labor rights of women apart from those established by the present law".[38] This article was of special importance in view of the tendency by employers to use the Spanish Work Charter as their reference when rejecting women applicants out of hand. The charter, like all other legal documents of the time, was written in masculine language and employers and lawyers made use of this document in a way that was doubly discriminating. One the one hand, the use of masculine language was perceived as "natural" and did not diverge from the legal norm of the time. On the other hand, the fact that the document explicitly addressed itself to men only was grounds for depriving women of their most basic labor rights. Articles 2 & 3 of the new 1961 law, therefore, explicitly stipulated that women could vote and be elected to any public post, including positions of state and local administration, and should have free access to all levels of education. Article 4 also affirmed the right of all women to independently sign labor contracts. The final article of the law stated that in cases where marital permission was still required, a woman who was denied such permission could challenge her husband in a court of law. If it was proved that a husband's refusal was given in bad faith (*mala fe o con abuso de derecho*), his decision could be overruled. In such instances, the courts were instructed to render their decision within ten days, so as to prevent spouses from using legal proceeding to stall for time. However, the 1961 law still barred women from some posts. These included: military positions; posts requiring the use of arms; positions of judges and magistrates (except in labor and children's courts); and positions in the Spanish merchants' fleet (apart from those relating to health and sanitation).

The Law for Political and Professional Rights for Women was approved by the Cortes and put into effect starting January 1, 1962. However, according to the testimony of Teresa Loring, former National Secretary of the SF, it soon became clear that it had been a mistake to accept some of the limitations imposed by Article 3.[39] Pilar Primo de Rivera approached the Minister of Justice and suggested that his office be the one to suppress the section prohibiting women from holding posts of judges or magistrates, but he refused, claiming that there was no Spanish precedent for women to positions in the judicial system. When both Primo de Rivera and Loring insisted that they would present an amendment of the law before the Cortes, they were told that it would be impossible to approve such an amendment without the assistance of the Ministry of Justice. Once it was presented, however, the proposed amendment was approved [and the decree, signed by Franco] on 28 December 1966.[40]

Women as Agents in the Legal Arena: Petitioners and Legal Advisors

As numerous documents of the SF's legal department show, the approval of the 1961 and 1966 laws by the Spanish Cortes was in no way a guarantee of their implementation. It was the SF's *asesoria juridica*, which had to find the means of turning legislation into reality.[41] In a letter addressed to Pilar Primo de Rivera on December 6, 1961, the Head of the National Welfare Institute (*Instituto Nacional de Previsión*) at the Labor Ministry, Francisco Labadie Otermin, warned against the stern opposition that any attempt to implement the new legislation would encounter. His recommendation was that the SF create "a special office whose sole function will be clarifying doubts and preparing periodical press releases (concerning the laws)". Labadie Otermin did not consider that a legal background was necessary for fulfilling this role and his advice to Primo de Rivera was to look for "an energetic, amiable and intelligent SF member, who along with a secretary, will suffice for the job".[42]

The task was assigned to the SF's legal department, which was headed at the time by Aurora Huber. Huber was joined by Carmen Salinas Alfonso de Villagomes , who was to head the department in later years, and Belen Landaburu Gonzalez, who in 1967 was to become one of the first female members of the Spanish Cortes. All three belonged to the younger generation of the SF and all were to serve on its most important advisory committee – the Central Committee for National Services (*Junta de Regidoras Centrales*). True to Labadie Otermin's recommendation, none of the three had any kind of legal background, but this was not necessarily a disadvantage when dealing with institutions within the Francoist political system. With the blessing of Primo de Rivera, members of the Legal Department did not hesitate to render their services, in many cases relating to the legal, political and professional standing of women. This held true even when their appeals ran a clear risk of antagonizing powerful sectors within the regime or undermining cultural or moral norms.

A case in point is a request made in 1958 by Julia Hernandez Fernández (SF member from Valencia), which was referred to Aurora Huber by the Provincial Delegate of Valencia, María Pilar Gracía Latorre. Hernandez Fernández was involved in a failed legal proceeding to have herself declared the lawful daughter of one Felix Jimenez.[43] There is no documentation of the outcome of Huber's intervention or the form it took, but undoubtedly she agreed to act in Fernández' name. If Julia Hernandez Fernández was indeed the daughter of Felix Jimenez, it can only be speculated why her standing was not recognized legally. But whether the reason was the annulment of her mother's marriage to Jimenez or her being born out of wedlock, legal recognition of her claim would have gone against the dictates of the local Catholic hierarchy, something which did not deter either Gracía Latorre or Huber.

Another case, this time indicating the SF's willingness to take on matters relating to local administration clearly out of its jurisdiction, has to do with a petition referred to the legal department by Primo de Rivera in 1966.[44] The original petition was written by Maria Cegarra Salcedo (local delegate of the

SF in La Union, Murcia, and a representative of the SF in the Village Council) on behalf of the population of the entire village. Cegarra Salcedo's goal was to enlist the SF's help in fighting the decision to suppress the activities of the local court (*juzgado de primer instancia*) following a reform aimed at centralizing the legal system. Cegarra Salcedo's letter is an illuminating example of how the population and its grass-root activists perceived the legal department and the SF's leadership in general. The petition did not contest the rationality of the legal reform in general or the decision concerning La Union. The population was clearly aware of the fact that "numbers, statistics, necessity and developmental problems" were precisely what brought about the reform.[45] But in the villagers' view, all of these should have had no bearing on the case, since they had "earned" their rights in the "New Spain", not on the basis of current reality, but rather due to their actions during the Spanish Civil War the primary event in the founding of Francoist Spain. When other mining communities around Murcia had rebelled against the advancing nationalist forces the miners in La Union:

> Did not cause any social problems, but rather occupied themselves with the preparations for the Mining Folklore Festival, thus expressing their pain and love through the good and sincere art and the deepest and most honest sentiments.[46]

The letter went on to express the miners' total lack of comprehension of the way their loyalty was rewarded at this "great hour for Spain," since all their petitions to the municipal authorities had been rejected. Furthermore, in the same paragraph in which Cegarra Salcedo described the men's despair, she also laid the ground for her own petition:

> But we, the women, are only starting. Your voice, Pilar, was not yet heard. You have made me councilor of this village and, you have to join in our justified petition. If they had suppressed our court let them reconstitute it, for there is still work to be done.[47]

Within the tight net of personal connections that characterized the Francoist administration, the SF managed, so it seems, to create its own semi-official network of favoritism, which the people of La Union summoned to their aid. In order to do so, they constructed a discourse that would emphasize their historical loyalty not only to the regime, but also to the national-syndicalist rhetoric of work and hierarchy. The men failed to do so vis-á-vis the Falange, so now it was the women's turn to call upon the help of the SF. Within such a system, it was indeed almost irrelevant whether members of the SF's legal department had any formal training in the field, since it was not the legal system that they were challenging. The suppression of La Union's court was debated rationally and legally at the municipal level, and was presumably found valid. What was required now was the sort of political intervention Pilar Primo de Rivera had exercised in the past by meeting privately with ministers and administrators, only this time it took place at the provincial level.[48]

With an endless flow of petitions concerning the 1961 and 1966 laws flooding the SF's legal department, Aurora Huber, Carmen Salinas and Belen Landaburu used the same combination of private audiences, cajoling and exerting thinly veiled pressures to try and effect the implementation of the laws.

Despite the wide diversity of petitions and petitioners, it is striking that they seem to have certain common characteristics. One attribute that is prominent in most of the letters is the sense of intimacy in the writers' manner of addressing members of the SF's national hierarchy. None of the petitions I read were directly addressed to the Legal Department, but rather to members of *La Nacional* – mainly to Pilar Primo de Rivera or the SF's national secretary Teresa Loring. Petitioners not only felt they could address these women directly, but did so using the second person singular, which would have been a highly unusual choice for any formal correspondence at the time. This is especially striking, since all the letters manage to convey a great sense of respect. Exercised not through the use of formal grammatical constructions, but rather by praising the work of the SF and invoking its leaders (especially Pilar) as the petitioner's personal protectors. Such invocations are not unusual in themselves, but combined with the direct and personal effect of the second person singular, they typify the ideal of Falangist writing rigorously adopted by the SF's leadership.

Another striking characteristic is the total honesty of the writers. Many of the letters describe the brutal (and in formal Francoist standards, also far from moral) reality of women fighting to balance their economic needs and professional aspirations with the dictates of family life. For example, a large number of petitioners admit to "living in sin," due to postponing their marriages until the 1961 law was implemented so as not to lose their jobs.[49] Whatever the private views of Primo de Rivera and others on such matters, their responses clearly show that they did not feel it was the SF's duty to intervene in the private choices of their petitioners, but rather to create a situation in which they would not have to choose between work and family life.

Finally, as the work of the SF's legal department gained some publicity, the petitioners' backgrounds diversified to include not only non-affiliated women, but also men. Petitions by men rarely had anything to do with the Law for Professional and Political Rights, but are highly interesting because they seem to indicate those areas in which the SF's intervention was perceived to be more effective than that of the Falange.[50] Some petitioners asked for the SF's help in obtaining special decorations awarded by the Falange (an indication that people did not always differentiate between the two organizations), while others attempted to enlist the organization's aid in family matters.[51] Even more interesting are attempts to involve prominent SF members in political power struggles, especially at the local level. One such example is a letter sent to Pilar Primo de Rivera by Juan Pablo Martinez de Salinas, the Barcelona Teachers' Syndicate's candidate to the parliamentary elections of 1967.[52] Pablo Martinez' letter to Primo de Rivera is a declaration of personal allegiance, and it is precisely on the basis of his loyal representation of the SF's interests within the syndicate that he called upon her for help:

> When the Barcelona syndicate was first formed, it gathered to its ranks several SF members, later on obtaining for some of them positions at a national level. . . . Now, that I am running for parliament, many are the women who would vote for me.[53]

Yet Pablo Martinez' problem was that one such potential voter, a general instructor of the SF, and a member of the national teachers' syndicate, was in Germany at the time and could not vote. He therefore attached a list of the eleven female members of his syndicate, some of which were SF members, informing Pilar how important their votes would be for his election and virtually asking her to make sure the women voted the "right way". Martinez signed his letter by citing Montserrat Tey, the SF's Provincial Delegate in Barcelona, as a character witness. As the historian Antonio Cazorta Sánchez indicates, the very existence of petitions such as Pablo Martinez' shows that the Franco regime had initiated a national web of *clientelismo* of unprecedented proportions. The SF, then, was perceived as an organization powerful enough to take part in such a political game.[54] Moreover it is clear that many viewed the SF as both promoter and arbitrator of female activism.

Going back to those documents of the SF's Legal Department relating directly to the 1961 law, one can detect a clear discrepancy between the public interest in the law and the reaction to it of the various government agencies. In December 1960, six months before the law was debated in the Cortes, the Legal Department started receiving letters inquiring about its nature and the date at which it would come into affect. Women had heard of this new legislative project through a campaign sponsored by the SF on *Radio Nacional* and on the pages of the organization's magazines. From some of the letters, however, it becomes clear that this was perceived at first as a piece of legislation aimed at SF members only – something constructed by the organization's leadership in order to free its own members for full-time work under better conditions.[55] Such misconceptions were only natural in view of the minimal exposure, if any, given to the law by government offices and other state institutions. One example of the way the regime's formal legal discourse chose to ignore the SF's legislative projects is a 1966 letter addressed to Primo de Rivera from the Institute for Political Studies. This institute, which kept in close contact with the SF and even assisted with the preparation of the 1958 reform of the Civil Code, was in charge of periodically publishing a volume entitled "Political Laws of Spain". Yet only in 1966 did the head of the institute find it necessary to ask for the SF's "organic law" (*normas organicas*) and a copy of the 1961 legislation, so they could be incorporated into the substantial subsection dedicated to the *Movimiento*, which had never previously mentioned the Sección Femenina.[56]

In a society where few women had the economic means or legal knowledge needed to challenge labor decisions in a court of law, ignoring the new legislation was an employer's best means of not implementing it. As a result, many women were simply told that the law did not hold in their case; it was at this stage that they turned to the SF's legal department in order to verify whether their claim was valid and to seek practical help. The majority of cases that came before the department had to do with married women's right to continue working. In this category, the only cases rejected out of hand were those relating to women who had been married prior to June 1961, and who were therefore not protected by the new law.

The dates on both petitions and replies indicate that a sincere effort was made to resolve matters far more rapidly than any legal proceedings would have allowed. One such example is the case of María de los Angeles Fontao de la Vega, a nurse by profession. She was informed by her employers that the new law did not apply in the case of nurses working for the National Welfare Institute and that she would therefore have to resign her post once married.[57] Fontao de la Vega's petition to the legal department is dated March 25 March 1963. Belen Landaburu's reply is dated April 2, 1963. In it she already informed the petitioner that her employers had been contacted. They had assured Landaburu that not only would they apply the new law fully in the future, but that Fontao de la Vega's case had been resolved favorably and that an official confirmation to that effect was on its way to her.

Another case was that of Julia Escribano Sales, who in 1963 applied for the post of administrative assistant (*auxiliar administrativo*) at the Ministry of Housing in Bilbao. Escribano Sales received the highest possible mark on the official exam, but was later told she could not be appointed to the post because she was married. Carmen Salinas, who dealt with Escribano Sales' case, did not bother to approach the Bilbao office, but addressed herself directly to Enrique Salgado, the minister in charge. Her letter, indicating Pilar Primo de Rivera's interest in the case, was a mixture of pretended innocence and veiled pressure: "I am sure this can not be but a mistake since, as you well know, starting January 1962 no woman applying for a job can be discriminated against on the basis of her marital status".[58] Salinas went on to urge the minister to do everything necessary to secure the post for Julia Escribano Sales.

The more "masculine" (i.e. public and high ranking) the position in question, the more entrenched was the institutionalized opposition to the appointment of women to it. Women such as Florinda Sánchez (who in 1962 applied for the position of Deputy Director of the Women's Prison in Valencia), or Aurelia de la Sierra del Río (who in 1967 presented her candidacy to the Cortes on behalf of the Barcelona Lawyers' Syndicate), threatened to break with every traditional feminine stereotype.[59] Yet this did not deter the Legal Department from arguing their cases before the Minister of Justice and the *Consejo General de la Abogacia* respectively.

The Falangist ideologist Dionisio Ridruejo briefly explored the role and nature of different pressure groups within the Francoist political system in *España 1963 – examen de una situación*,[60] his analysis of how the regime was functioning. According to Ridruejo, such groups came for the most part from the "heart" of the system, their secure political (if not ideological) position being the only guarantee of their relative freedom of action. Such groups could exist only on condition that their interests intermeshed with those of the regime and that this symbiotic relationship functioned on two levels. On the one hand, within a system where very little, if any, public pressure could be exercised, their strength rested entirely on their members' ability to capitalize on their personal standing with the regime in order to bring about change. On the other hand, it was precisely this vested interest in the existence of the regime that inspired Franco's confidence that the pressure exercised by such groups would stop short of seriously undermining his position; thus he allowed their continued activity.

The SF came very close to Ridruejo's definition of a pressure group. While the organization undeniably owed its very existence on a national level, as well as a major part of its budget, to the Franco regime its members were far from simple instruments in the implementation of the regime's gender policies. As recent works published about the different political "families" of the Franco era have shown, the amorphous unit historians have called the "regime" was far from being monolithic in either structure or ideological outlook.[61] The unity imposed on such groups within Spanish society, such as the *Movimiento*, the different sectors of the Catholic Church and the military, was a result of the Civil War and the urgent need to overthrow the government of the Second Republic. Such unity was maintained since all the sectors involved understood that the system put in place by

General Franco represented the best guarantee of their political survival. However, underneath a heavy curtain of propaganda lay a reality of power struggles and contested policies, which were only strengthened with the passing of time and the different evolutionary paths taken by each sector of the regime.

Yet unlike some groups within the *Movimiento* and the Church, the SF's evolution did not necessarily mean a break with past ideologies and practices. From the start, the political and professional opportunities opened before high-ranking SF members were undeniably at odds with the gender model, which the regime tried to impose on Spain's female population. The legislative projects discussed in this chapter reflected the SF's attempt to make such practices accessible not only to the women who shared the educational and professional background and aspirations of its affiliates, such a lawyers, nurses and public servants, but also to others such as domestic employees and factory workers. But the SF's new legislative discourse and the work of the SF's legal department "on the ground" did more than just champion the rights of specific women. For the first time within the Francoist labor market and court system they made women as a collective entity visible.

The fact that such a project could only gain support in the early 1960s, in synchronization with Spain's economic progress and the changing balance of power within the regime, should not obscure its early origins. By examining the relations between elite and mass politics within the SF over time, one is made aware of the extent to which the gap between the *ideal falangist woman* and the *falangist ideal of women* was narrowed. Even more importantly, this was done by retaining the central attributes of the former while changing the latter. When analyzed against the background of the general social and economic developments in Franco's Spain, the goals and rate of this process indicate that the SF's leadership had in fact carved out a place for itself to which many objected strongly – namely, that of a political elite intent on bringing about political and social change for the benefit of large segments of Spain's female population.

4

Am I That Body?
Sección Femenina de la FET and the Struggle for the Institution of Physical Education and Competitive Sports for Women

> One must fight against preexisting mentalities based on backward and all too theoretical ideas and mistaken concepts. We must also fight against the attitude of women, who found themselves isolated and inactive . . . and of the Ibero-Celtic man.[1]

> The activity of physical education instructors and professors in the discussed period played a decisive role in eradicating the taboos imposed on women who wished to participate in sporting activities.[2]

Women's physical education was a field over which the SF gained almost exclusive control starting in the late 1930s (both within the school system and as a leisure activity), and which it considered, and used, as a powerful recruitment tool throughout its existence. The interest in physical activities and body perceptions as part of a general effort to shape and supervise gender relations was not specific to Spanish society under Franco. Processes similar to the ones I will discuss here took place under most of the authoritarian and totalitarian regimes of the 20th century, and to a lesser degree in democratic societies.[3] The interest of the Franco regime, and that of the SF specifically, in issues concerning gender and the female body far exceeded the field of physical education. Such an interest manifested itself in a long list of family laws, relentless references to demographic problems, and the attempt to create popular models of female beauty and aesthetics. But of all these issues, that of women's physical education is the most prominent due to the tensions it generated within the different sectors of the regime. In her book *Mujeres en el Franquismo*, the journalist and feminist activist Carmen Alcalde emphasized the degree to which the attention paid by the SF to female physical education was perceived by many as no less than a "National Catholic scandal." Such a position was championed by the Catholic Church, whose representative, Cardinal Segura, considered the mere concept of women's physical education to be "scandalous and lewd".[4]

The decision to examine this aspect of the SF's policy, then, results not only from the immense importance accorded to it by the organization's leadership, but also because it can be singled out as an important crossroads in a heated public debate over sexuality, social class, political ideology and religious perceptions. It is important to emphasis that this debate did not take place outside or on the fringes of the regime, but rather raged within its institutions and between the different sectors that helped shape its policy. Both the Labor and Education Ministries issued decrees establishing mandatory physical education classes for schoolgirls and industrial workers. But as we shall see, this did not deter schoolmistresses and employers from banishing the SF's instructors from their institutions. Furthermore, those instructors who did manage to get their foot in the door soon discovered that they had to struggle with educators, parents, and at times even with civil governors, in order to carry out certain sporting activities and impose discipline. In this respect, an examination of the SF's policies, set within a wider context of the period's social and cultural history, can provide fresh insights regarding the regime's functioning and evolution through time.

In recent years scholars have drawn attention to the ongoing tensions between the main ideological forces operating within the Franco regime. However, for the most part historians have tended to see it as monolithic and hierarchical, emphasizing policy making as a one-sided, repressive process. Legislation and formal rhetoric were seen as a reflection of the regime's entire spectrum of political, social and cultural positions. A gender-based and social perspective such as that of the current work and an examination of everyday practices and the implementation of formal policies, can highlight not only the gap between rhetoric and praxis, but also the non-linear nature of the regime's evolution[5].

An examination of the SF's physical education and sports policy exposes a paradox: While the Franco regime was less inclined than its German or Italian counterparts to invest time and funds in organized leisure culture for the masses, it did see sports as a powerful recruiting tool. The institution of compulsory physical education and the promotion of certain competitive sports (such as football) were viewed by historian Victoria de Grazia as a "culture of consent" and in the case of Spain, by Arnd Krüger as "the culture of evasion".[6] Such activities were implemented to create spaces where discipline and state supervision acquired a somewhat more positive image and to bring both young people and workers into the orbit of the *Movimiento*. Like the thriving cinematic industry, popular sports such as football were also used by the regime as diversions that were to assist in the maintenance of a much desired politically apathetic population, while generating a vague sense of nationalism. However, in a highly conservative society where there was hardly any sporting tradition to begin with, any attempt to relate to women's bodies in a more progressive way encountered stern opposition. The institution of female physical education might have been one of the regime's declared goals, but on the ground the process was slow and problematic with little support being offered by government agencies other than the SF.

Like in Fascist Italy, the promotion of sports in Spain was entrusted not to the government, but to the party.[7] Yet unlike the German and the Italian case, the SF's officially declared position was that most efforts and funds should be directed towards non-competitive activities with little public exposure. In reality, however, one can find documents describing competitions for women and girls at the provincial and national levels. There is also much information about the participation of women athletes in large open-air demonstrations before a mixed audience. In the first rally organized by the Falange's Youth Movement in Seville in October 1938, for example, 1,600 girls and adolescents participated in public displays of gymnastics and regional dancing. A year later, in front of an audience of 100,000 people, amongst them General Franco himself, 1,450 girls (between the ages of eight and twelve) participated in a gymnastics performance and another 750 in mixed exercises with boys of the same age.

In the immediate post-war years, the number of such displays decreased for two reasons. The general climate of demobilization that reigned in Spanish society at that period did not favor mass public displays of any kind. Furthermore, the years that followed the regime's progressive distancing from the Fascist powers also saw the consolidation of the vague Francoist ideology of National Catholicism. Those were years of heightened presence of the Catholic Church and its officials in the public and political life, and as such a time of great conservatism, especially from a gender perspective. Under such conditions any policy that supported the nurturing and public exposure of the female body met with great opposition, as we shall see. However, when mass sporting events were renewed in the second half of the 1950s, the presence of girls and women was again in evidence.[8]

The complex nature of the SF's policy regarding physical education is further made clear when one considers the internal division between the different sporting activities the organization chose to sponsor. Some (such as swimming, tennis or gymnastics) clearly fit the definition of "beauty sports", that is, sports that developed refined patterns of physical activity while maintaining harmony, posture and a supposedly minimal level of effort, and were considered appropriate for women. However, in the post-World War II years, there was a heated public debate (not only in Spain, but in the English-speaking world as well) surrounding the participation of women in other sports such as handball, hockey or athletics, due to their "masculine" nature.

The SF's objection to the commercialization of women's sports also raised questions regarding class issues. Such objections resulted for the most part from the fear that by relying on the backing of private enterprises, the organization would lose some control over the sports practiced, how they would be practiced and the implicit social and cultural messages that this would convey. Historian Mary Hall pointed out the role played by commercial sponsorship in widening the circle of participants in sporting activities in western societies.[9] Women of the upper- and upper-middle classes (who were exposed to sporting activities in private schools and universities) could afford to avoid participating in competitive and commercialized sporting events. For most working-class women, on the other hand, commercialized sports offered unique opportunities, as sponsors were prepared to provide not only uniforms and equipment, but also traveling and training expenses.

In the Spanish case one can point to two interrelated processes: At the heart of the SF's sporting ethos was a middle-class perception of women's physical being, which emphasized refinement, self-control and modesty. In order to control the nature of women's physical education in Spain, the organization opposed the commercialization of this field. Yet it did try to make up for the loss of private funding by creating a nationwide network of sports teams open to all women (especially urban workers). The SF provided the women and girls who participated in sports activities within its institutions with free uniforms, equipment, coaches and travel expenses, all at a considerable cost and at times even at the expense of more "ideologically"-oriented activities. Such a policy only makes sense if we consider that the network of sports teams served as a powerful recruitment tool in the struggle to bring some of the more "problematic" populations in Francoist society under the SF's control.

Keeping these contradictions in mind, I shall attempt to answer the following questions: Which populations were targeted by the SF's sporting policies? To what extent was the promotion of women's physical education used in order to bring women who would have otherwise preferred to avoid any contact with the regime's official organs under the SF's influence? Who were the SF's physical education instructors, and how did they perceive their role within the Francoist education system? Were their everyday working experiences a reflection of the organization's compliance with the coercive and regulatory role assigned to it by the regime? To what extent were the SF's more subversive messages concerning the female body evident in its representatives' activities "in the field"? And finally, how did the SF's physical education policy affect its political standing and relations with other sectors within the Franco regime?

The Legal and Theoretical Framework: Physical Education in Francoist Legislation and Teaching Manuals

The first reference by the Francoist regime to the issue of physical education in schools was made in May–September, 1938, as part of a more general effort to legally codify the changes undergone by the Spanish education system in the nationalist territory. As part of this reform, it was declared on September 20, 1938 that all Spanish students would be entitled to six weekly hours of physical education, music, arts and crafts.[10] In order to ensure that these activities took place, it was decided in 1941 to form the National Department for Sorts and Physical Education that was to be supervised by the FET's General Secretary. The SF, which a year earlier had gained control over the Feminine Section of the FET's Youth Movement, now also entered the school system when it was decided that all physical education classes for girls would be administered by its instructors.[11]

In 1944 the SF's mandate in this field was further expanded when a decree published by the Ministry for National Education stated that attendance at physical education classes was mandatory for the completion of a university degree.[12] Under the supervision of the SF, women students were required to successfully complete at least one gymnastics or folk dancing course, as well as a course in basketball, handball, hockey or tennis.

From mid-1944, Francoist legislation concerning physical education reflected a conscious attempt by both the Ministry of Education and the SF to create a new profession. On July 20 a General Supervisor for Physical Education was appointed. Numerous provincial delegates of both the FET and the SF worked under the General Supervisor, whose job it was to ensure the maintenance of sporting facilities and the organizing of competitions. Until 1961 physical education instructors were trained at one of two institutions: The National Institute for Physical Education (that operated under the supervision of the Ministry of Education) or the FET schools (*Isabel la Católica* for women and *José Antonio* for men). A 1945 law standardized the status of the certificates issued by the FET schools, equating them with those granted by the Ministry of Education.[13] In 1961 the newly formed National Council for Physical Education and Sport canceled the FET's authority over sporting activities, with one exception. The SF's National School, *Ruiz de Alda*, continued to be recognized as the only institution for the training of female physical education instructors. The SF, which offered a comprehensive training scheme under reasonable conditions and at a low cost, managed to maintain its monopoly over this field until 1975.

The theoretical framework at the basis the SF's physical education and sporting policies was developed by one man in particular – Dr. Luis Agosti, the SF's National Advisor for Physical Education. Agosti was a doctor by profession and a world-class javelin-throwing champion. During the Civil War, Agosti served in the nationalist army and was injured on the Northern Front in 1938. While he was hospitalized at Santander, he met Elisa de Lara, who was then the Head of the National Service for Culture, and she introduced him to Pilar Primo de Rivera.[14]

Agosti's theoretical approach was based on what is often referred to as the "Swedish School" of physical education. The Swedish and German schools, which originated at the end of the 18th century, reflected two opposing approached that dominated the sports world and affected its development well into the 20th century. The German school, which was developed by J. S. P. Gutz Muth and L. Jahn, emphasized the importance of physical strength in gymnastics and exhibited a clear preference for marching and the use of apparatus (such as ropes, parallel bars, etc.). This school was highly popular with military instructors, who by the last quarter of the 19th century also introduced it into many of the national youth movements.

On the other hand, the Swedish School, which was developed by Father Enrique Ling, saw physical activity as a way of combating disease and promoting the harmonious development of the human body. This school emphasized accuracy and style. Ling saw the body and mind as an integral unit and on the basis of physical and anatomical information, attempted to develop "a system of movements that will lead to a new physical culture that will contribute to the gymnasts' health and morality".[15] This model necessitated a high level of discipline and complete attunement between the individual and the group in order to reach an exact and harmonious execution of the movements. Professionals who promoted physical education for and amongst women preferred the Swedish school first and foremost because of its emphasis on refinement rather than on activities that called for sweaty physical proximity, and were therefore deemed masculine.[16] Ling's perception of physical education as promoting discipline was a powerful argument in the hands of those who wished to see more women involved in sports, since one of the main arguments against the latter's ability to engage in sports had to do with their perceived lack of discipline.

Luis Agosti saw physical education as a form of personal expression, with its very own national and gender characteristics. While emphasizing women's role as potential mothers and workers, Agosti felt that physical activities were beneficial to women of all ages, especially when they were carried out in the open air and in suitable clothing (that was not too heavy or confining).[17] In a book published in 1948, the doctor called upon physical education instructors to divide their target populations into groups: babies (0–3 years old); young girls (3–7 and 7–11 years old); adolescents

(11–16 years old) and women from the age of 16 and up. Agosti took the special needs of pregnant and menstruating women into consideration, but stated:

> Avoiding physical activity while menstruating is a mistake, however, one must refrain from activities that might cause hemorrhaging or extreme excitement. Pregnant women should avoid extreme positions, but our general opinion is that physical activities are essential during pregnancy and in preparation for parenthood.[18]

In a book edited by Dr. María Jesus Inchausti and Carlos Guttiérez Salgado for the SF's instructors, it was stated that a balanced model of women's physical education should include Ling's gymnastics combined with folk and classical dance, as well as some team sports (such as handball, volleyball, hockey, tennis or swimming).[19]

In their research on the manuals of physical education produced under the Franco regime, historians C. Carbajosa Menéndez and E. Fernández Bustillo summarized Luis Agosti's influence thus:

> He was an educated and clever man, in love with his work and the research he conducted. The tragedy was that for many years he was no more than a lonely preacher in the desert. His books were the Bible of physical education, but most of the instructors were not intelligent enough to enjoy his contributions. Instructors with superficial training found his explanations too complex. Those who are interested in knowing something about the Francoist sporting project only have to look at the period's manuals, which speak more of morality and spirituality than of (physical education).[20]

While this judgment is certainly true to some extent, it would be a mistake to view the manuals of the Francoist period as the only evidence for the nature of women's physical education at the time. Nor would it be justified to lay the entire blame for poor performance on the shoulders of physical education instructors. As we shall see, the training schemes and requirements for the position of SF physical education instructor were on a relatively high level. A high school diploma was required for entry and the women's studies were on a par with those in the more advanced European institutions of general and physical education. However, the lack of sufficient funding and the struggle to continue their work in what generally proved to be a hostile educational system made the instructors' task a difficult one.

Moral Sports and Sporting Morality:
Values, Sporting Fields and Uniforms

It is necessary to clarify a number of working definitions for this chapter. The term "sports" serves here in its strict definition as organized sports, or: "The learning of game skills . . . institutionalized through teaching and systematic preparation [by] organizations . . . (clubs, schools and national sport organizations) whose purpose is to prepare competitors and regulate the competitions".[21] It is not my intention to examine spontaneous sporting activities or initiatives carried out in private clubs that were not under the supervision of the National Board for Physical Education (*Junta Nacional de Educación Física*). The term "physical education", on the other hand, refers to the ongoing teaching and sporting activities carried-out within the official school system. This sort of teaching was non-competitive by definition and was aimed at exposing the largest number of girls possible to a basic level of physical activities over time.

Most historians agree that the appearance of sports as an organized, widespread, cultural phenomenon followed the consolidation of an urban middle class, "to whom fell the pleasures and problems of using the free time, which accompanied their growing affluence, in a manner that was both enjoyable and respectable".[22] In light of this, it is not surprising that the sporting ethos common to many western societies up to the 1950s was one that reflected and duplicated a bourgeois value system. Opening the world of sports to new audiences was a highly selective process; women achieved access to it only insofar as they did not subvert the refined image of respectable femininity. Workers were encouraged to take part in organized sports as an alternative to the popular and supposedly illegitimate culture of the pub, the billiard hall and of political meetings. But the ideological and practical control exercised over the introduction of such populations to the world of sports was always a partial one. The growth of women's sports all over the world was marked by a dialectical process between the need to conserve old social patterns and the development of new ones, and this is especially evident in the case of Spain.

The first Falangist correspondence concerning physical education was based to a large degree on a small number of references made to it by José Antonio Primo de Rivera. Physical education and moral teachings were defined as the two central components of human integration. Physical education had a social goal, namely the strengthening of group discipline, the body and through it the spirit. At the same time, all the texts attempted to clarify that the Falange did not see physical education as an end in itself. Falangist ideology stressed time and again the Christian value of sport – physical activity as a way of bringing man closer to God.[23]

At the end of the Spanish Civil War, the SF's leadership began reorganizing its different departments, amongst them the Department for Sports and Physical Education, which was to be headed by María de Miranda. On August 24, 1939, de Miranda published a document outlining the goals of the new department and defining its scope of authority and different fields of action:

> The aim of this national department is to create strong, healthy women, capable of bringing forth a race of titans. . . . Women's physical education must be brought under our total control. We wish to be the official organization [in charge of this issue] and create a national school for physical education.[24]

At the opening ceremony of the National Sporting Championships for Youth held in Barcelona in 1939, Pilar Primo de Rivera called upon the participants:

> You, the youngest amongst us, can perhaps serve the SF best by demonstrating to Spain that the Falange is new, clean and agile like yourselves. . . . Furthermore you must remember that nothing is achieved in life by accident, those who win are always the best.[25]

However, such a complete adaptation of the discourse concerning the greatness of youth, and the goal of being considered equal representatives of the Falange were all short-lived. Even those Falangists who proposed a more modern attitude towards the human body frowned upon any adaptation of these concepts to the female population, and they certainly had no place within the discourse of the newly formulated ideology of "National Catholicism". As a result, the SF's leadership had no choice but to reestablish women's physical education within its "proper" context. In order to fend off accusations of ostentation, it was decided that the majority of funds and efforts would not be channeled towards competitive sports, but rather towards the construction of a widely based teaching apparatus, which would attempt to reach as many girls and women as possible.

The aversion to professional sports was perhaps best expressed by the SF's leadership's contemptuous attitude towards the "professional woman athlete", who earned her living through participation in competitive sports. One would be hard pressed to find any examples of professional women athletes in Franco's Spain prior to the 1960s. Thus this fictitious figure (which official rhetoric called into play every so often) was no doubt inspired by the American and Russian athletes of the post-World War II period. Surprisingly enough, a lack of femininity was not one of the insults heaped on this figure by the SF. They rather focused on the fact that such women were well paid for their participation and that a large budget was required to train them, which was described as unjustified and unprofessional.[26]

The claim concerning the right of each woman to physical education and the need to reach large populations may sound impressively egalitarian, but one must not forget that the model of sports as a non-sponsored and free leisure activity was first and foremost a middle-class construction. The assumption that the only barrier stopping a woman from engaging in sports was a lack of facilities ignored the double workload of countless women, who after spending many hours at the factory or workshop had to go home and take care of their families. Without the employers' cooperation, any attempt to expose such women to the wonders of physical education within the different SF syndicates was doomed from the start. If employers refused to set aside time for sporting activities during the workday, only a few very determined women could be expected to take advantage of the facilities the organization offered them.

In the 1940s the discourse concerning female physical education had a pronounced moralistic tone. In order to win legitimatization and establish its standing in the post-Civil War political arena, the SF was forced to frame any discussion concerning the female body on at least a partial use of the acceptable images and values of the period. An internal document written by María de Miranda in 1941 reflects the rhetorical acrobatics that were necessary in order to reconcile the contradictions between a totalizing political ideology, such as Falangism, and its Catholic worldview:

> In giving us this marvelous body, God provided us with an immeasurable gift. Abandoning such a gift, not taking care of it using the best measures offered to us by science, constitutes ingratitude. And while the mission we are called to fulfill is not solely a moral one ... we are obliged to comply with our Christian duty ... [since] the essence of Falangism is religion and militia, spirituality and discipline.[27]

Another document by de Miranda from the same period claimed that the religious prohibition against suicide also implied a need to strive vigorously for the continued improvement of one's health[28]. The SF's declared view, therefore, was that participating in physical education activities was tantamount to a moral obligation.

During the 1950s and early 1960s, the SF's rhetoric on women's physical education underwent some changes. The new tone called to mind the organization's earlier rhetoric from the war years and it was part of the more general realignment of the SF's discourse on gender identity and women's role in society, as already discussed in previous chapters. The way this was translated into the field of physical education can be seen in a 1965 lecture given by the new Head of the National Department for Sports and Physical

Education, Concepción Sierra y Gil de la Cuesta. She indicated the partial improvement in women's standing in Spanish society, which in her opinion manifested itself mainly in the area of women's work. In analyzing the conditions that might allow for further gender equality, Gil de la Cuesta presented the SF's view on the social conditions necessary for long-term change:

> The process of social promotion we see today does not push women to exhaust their potential to its fullest. Such a process is limited to institutional and structural aspects. We need to act on the [following fronts] as well: the judicial, educational, economic and social . . . [29]

Encouraging women to enter the field of physical education was presented as an integral part of their general advancement in society. Quoting a research study, Sierra y Gil de la Cuesta pointed to a high correlation between women's level of institutionalized physical activities all across Spain and the level of their integration into public life.[30] Two exceptions to this were the Balearic Islands, where a high level of women's involvement in public life was reported, despite the scarcity of institutionalized sports activities. In Granada, on the other hand, where women's sports activity was well developed, there was a relatively minor female presence in public life. Gil de la Cuesta concluded that in the first case the lack of correlation was due to the existence of a developed tourist industry, which brought an unusual number of women into the labor force, regardless of other social and cultural conditions. In Granada, however, a complex web of "customs and worldviews typical to the South" rendered women's social and professional advancement extremely difficult.

As interesting as Gil de la Cuesta's conclusions are, they ignore an important question. Why did the SF find it so difficult to develop a sustained sports culture in an area exposed to diverse cultural and gender-based influences, whereas in the South, with its "problematic" mentality it was largely successful in this? One possible answer might be that like in other fields, here too the SF's policies interacted with a complex web of existing local traditions, gender perceptions and broader economic and social processes. Only a localized research study would be capable of providing us with answers regarding the influence of the SF's physical education policy on different female populations in both Granada and Balearic Islands. One question such a research study would have to answer would be the continuity between women's mobilization patterns within those regions prior to the arrival of the SF and that organization's success in mobilizing different social classes and age groups. Another line of questioning would need to analyze the different perceptions such communities might have had of "public life", especially in relation to women's activism. As part of its engagement with different rural communities, the SF did focus on the importance of women's work in the home and as part of familial units (be it in agriculture or the local crafts industry), but such work was not equated with "progressiveness". In a cultural context where considerable emphasis was placed on women's paid labor as an indication of their public involvement, Andalusia, with its high level of female illiteracy and low level of paid employment had to be considered a failure by the SF on all counts. Finally, I would hazard a guess that the exposure of the Balearic women to "liberalizing" foreign influences through the tourist industry only made them more aware of the contradictory and problematic nature of "female promotion" as defined by the SF.

Having glossed over such perplexing questions as the ones raised above, the SF's National Delegate nonetheless made a strong case for the relationship between physical education and women's changing patterns of public activism:

> The timidity and passivity exhibited by some women in high positions is at times nothing more than a pattern of behavior resulting from social conditioning. . . . There is no doubt that the sporting world . . . provides people with the strength to protect the essence of their personality. We therefore see in the [qualities] of leadership, initiative and decision making required in sports a perfect channel for promoting women's role in society.[31]

Quotations such as this explain the theoretical importance imparted by the SF to female physical education. However, in order to examine the way this was translated into everyday practices, I now turn to the different sports activities sponsored by the organization and at the different populations that took part in these activities.

One of the most heated debates between the SF leadership and the Church hierarchy, from bishops and all the way down to heads of convents, centered on the issue of which fields of physical education were appropriate for women. Similarly to other issues, the liberating effects of the Civil War may be discerned here as well. For example, a document from 1938 enumerated the branches of sports in which the SF's physical education instructors were to be trained. The list included gymnastics, athletics, swimming, tennis, hockey, football and basketball. A further document from 1939 specified those fields to be included in the physical education curriculum in schools. Amongst these one can find gymnastics, athletics, regional dancing and singing.[32] At the same time, the organization also endorsed mountaineering and ski, but stated that being expensive (in terms of the equipment needed), these sports could not be given priority. Despite such declarations, it was precisely these two activities that became the most popular at the SF's boarding schools. Amongst university students, on the other hand, swimming and athletics were the two most popular sports.[33]

However, the SF's leadership had to quickly come to terms with the fact that at least three of the above-mentioned sports were viewed as highly inappropriate for women by different sectors of the Francoist coalition. Women's athletics, which in the eyes of many resulted in women becoming "mannish", was banned by Spanish law from 1940 to 1963. As a result, the SF dispensed with athletics in schools and within its Youth Movement, but continued to provide its own members and physical education instructors with athletics activities. Early in 1961, the National Department for Sports and Physical Education instructed all provincial delegates to reintroduce athletics into their installations. When the official ban was finally lifted two years later, fourteen Spanish women athletes participated in the mixed athletic championships in Madrid.[34]

Gymnastics was another field destined to cause many problems. Carlos Guttiérez Salgdo, the SF's National Advisor in this area, testified that Pilar Primo de Rivera had shown him more than one letter accusing the organization's instructors of morally corrupting the girls entrusted to their care. The bishop of Tarragona, for example, was shocked to discover that girls were told to exercise their abdominal muscles. The bishop of Galicia demanded that girls be instructed to exercise only their arms, claming that exercising the abdomen and buttocks was a highly immoral activity.[35] The reaction to such accusations was always the same. The instructors were told not to argue back for fear of worsening the situation, but neither were they instructed to change their program. All complaints had to be referred to the national hierarchy, so that they could be handled with the appropriate authority and tact.

Finally, the most problematic of all sporting activities proved to be swimming. The only bathing suit approved by the Church had to include "a skirt reaching the middle of the thigh, with short pants underneath and sleeves".[36] Under such conditions, Pilar Primo de Rivera instructed all SF teams to train in inside pools and only when these were not being used by anyone else. Instructors were called upon to make sure that the girls were bathrobes outside the pool, yet the SF's official bathing suit was sleeveless and had a short skirt with no pants underneath.

In urban centers and private schools, moral issues such as the length of uniforms and type of exercises served as a barrier to the full implementation of the SF's physical education policies. However, in rural and working-class areas, the problems were of an economic nature. The SF's documents do not reveal differences in the budget and sporting ethos for different populations; yet, the interviews I conducted paint a very different picture. It seems that, at least until the late 1950s, physical education classes in many rural areas were administered by local priests, as part of their role as village teachers. The official reason for this was a lack of qualified SF instructors. It is certainly true that there were not enough instructors, and even in schools where there was a qualified physical education instructor, she was often in charge of teaching the entire school population – from kindergarten to the senior class. However, one cannot ignore the fact that despite its egalitarian rhetoric, in many cases the organization chose to solve its human resources problem by cutting down on instructors in the most backward areas, where physical education classes at school were the only form of sports activity available to most children. Girls who came from such areas only arrived in the city in their senior year in order to be examined by qualified SF instructors. M.J., a physical education instructor from La Rioja, told me about physical education classes in the villages and the final exam that was carried out in Logroño:

> In the mountains around La Rioja there were physical education classes, but they were carried out by the local priest. The SF ordered physical education manuals for high school students. The manuals included tables and sketches of the exercises to be given by the priest. [For] those girls who came from the sierra, it's clear that there was no [relation] between what was written down and what they actually did. But what could you do? You couldn't tell them [that]. You had to let them pass. Even if the exercises came out real bad we gave them a good grade. We didn't fail anyone.[37]

During the 1940s, the SF attempted to bridge such gaps by accepting a certain number of students from rural areas as external students (*externas*) in city colleges. According to the testimony of Andresa López, who headed the SF's National School for General Instructors, *Isabel la Católica*, this situation gradually changed in the 1950s:

> In later, more advanced years, the SF recognized that there was a problem in the rural areas and this recognition brought about the creation of colegios menores. The SF gave out many scholarships, which enabled girls from the villages to receive a more comprehensive education. During the day they went to regular schools and in the afternoons they came to centers where there was a qualified physical education teacher. Such centers were active from at least 1956.[38]

At the beginning of the 1960s, a new system of special schools – *los San Benitos* – was formed. *Los San Benitos*, which functioned to a large extent like the *colegios menores*, were operated by the SF in working-class neighborhoods and rural areas. But while the *colegios* were private institutions, *los San Benitos* were also authorized by the Ministry of Education to issue matriculation certificates. Each of the schools had an extensive physical education program supervised by a qualified SF instructor.

Regarding the number of girls and women who participated in each sporting activity sponsored by the SF, the only statistics I have been able to find were published by the organization itself in reply to inquiries by the Ministry of Education. Such statistics are highly inaccurate (different documents from the same period present different numbers) and problematic, especially if we take into consideration that they were compiled in order to convince the Ministry of Education of the success of the SF's physical education programs and the need for further funding. However, they are worthy of note, since they do outline some general tendencies.

An internal document published in 1943 and again a year later indicated the number of women in the SF's sporting teams to be 7,514. Of these, 4,000 were SF members (that is, slightly over 2% of the organization's members at the time)[39]. One could see a clear preference amongst SF members for gymnastics and basketball. Third and fourth in terms of size were the hockey and handball teams respectively. Swimming and skiing, on the other hand, attracted the lowest number of participants[40].

Undoubtedly, such preferences were at least partly the result of financial dictates. Sports such as basketball and handball were team sports characterized by a ratio of many participants to every coach. They developed qualities such as coordination, cooperation and discipline and the cost of facilities and equipment was relatively low. Despite the opposition of Church leaders, gymnastics were considered by many to be a "beauty sport" appropriate for women, and here too the cost of facilities was very reasonable. Hockey, on the other hand, was a fast-moving, intensive-contact sport, which was seen as somewhat "mannish". It was also more expensive than the previous ones. However, because it became so popular amongst women, it underwent modifications at the beginning of the 20th century (mainly concerning the amount of violence and physical contact allowed), which made it more gender-appropriate. Unlike athletics, hockey was not banned by Spanish law and the SF made an effort to find ways of financing the required facilities, at least for its own members. Swimming was not only an expensive sport, but as we have seen, also a controversial one. The SF's leadership therefore decided to make it obligatory only in coastal areas or in provinces where the organization's provincial delegate specifically demanded it.[41]

In 1948 the number of women participating in SF sports teams increased drastically, reaching 94,605.[42] Of these, almost 74% were not SF affiliates.[43] In 1952 the number of non-affiliated women almost doubled, and in 1954 it increased again.[44] These numbers are illuminating, since by then SF recruitment levels were dropping drastically. The regime was fast approaching a phase where brute political repression was at an all-time low (although this would reemerge in the late 1960s) and a growing emphasis was put on indirect supervision through cultural enterprises. Hence the majority of women and girls who took part in the SF's sporting activities were not SF affiliates, but rather members of subordinate organizations such as the syndicates. Membership in these organizations did not necessarily imply an ideological commitment and in many cases stemmed from a wish to enjoy the SF's recreational, educational and leisure services. Under such conditions, the organization's physical education and sporting policy did indeed play a central role in widening the SF's contacts with different female populations.

However, by the mid-1960s the situation had changed. By 1965 the number of non-affiliated women participating in the SF's physical education activities had dropped by 39%. Internal documents from that time describe the growing resistance of many women to take part in sporting activities imposed upon them by different institutions. In a letter written by María de Miranda following a series of visits to physical education classes at the University of Madrid, the National Delegate stated that the deteriorating condition of the facilities were the reason for the lack of discipline:

> The majority of gymnastic classes are conducted in deplorable conditions, when they are carried out at all. It often happens that the professor faced with a great number of students and the inadequacy of the spaces allotted decides to cancel the class, limiting herself to taking the names of those present.[45]

But the same document demonstrates that it was not necessarily the general conditions, but rather many students' lack of interest, which caused difficulties. According to de Miranda, it was often "impossible to have silence and the instructor had to yell in order to be heard – something which jeopardized her health".[46] This lack of interest was compounded by newly found alternatives to the SF's courses and activities. By the 1960s, the general improvement in the economic situation brought about the founding of private sporting clubs in urban centers. Furthermore, the new Law of Association (1964) widened the choice of legal associations available to women, bringing with them new cultural alternatives. New discourses on the female body and the role of women in society had to wait for the death of General Franco in order to gain a public voice, but that of the SF was already losing ground.

The issue of sports uniforms also generated friction with the Church authorities. The severe dress code imposed on Spanish women in the years following the Civil War was incompatible with most types of physical activity. At the beginning of the 1940s, Enrique Pla y Daniel, the archbishop of Toledo, summarized women's dress requirements as follows:

> Clothes should be long enough in order to cover most of the leg, something

reaching the knee is not sufficient. An exposed neck is an immoral [sight] due to the intentions it conveys and the scandal it might cause. Sleeves which do not cover the elbows should be considered immoral as well.[47]

The main problems encountered by the SF with respect to uniforms concerned their length and the inclusion or exclusion of pants. Pants were considered mannish and immoral because they were fastened at the front and accentuated the waistline. The struggle to incorporate pants as part of women's sports uniforms lasted almost twenty years and necessitated every bit of diplomacy the SF could muster. The first sporting activities in which pants were already worn in 1941 were skiing and mountaineering. This was not so much due to the impossibility of practicing such sports in a skirt, but rather because the majority of women who indulged in them were SF members. Pilar Primo de Rivera was better able to dictate the use of uniforms as she saw fit within the organization's own sports facilities. Perhaps even more important is the fact that the SF's leadership perceived its own members as less susceptible to possible "moral corruption" as a result of wearing pants or bathing suits or participating in athletics events or hockey games.

In the field of gymnastics, the situation was more complex. In order to turn it into a popular sport and incorporate its instruction in as many schools as possible, the organization had to compromise. The result of this compromise was the famous Spanish *bombacho*. But those puffed-out pants, which were supposed to look like a skirt and were zipped at the side, did very little to alleviate the Church's fears, especially when Decree No. 492 (which regulated the SF's sports uniforms) stated that a minimum-length *bombacho* could reach mid-thigh.[48]

The difficulties encountered by physical education instructors are reflected in the decrees published by the Department for Sport and Physical Education during those years. The need to make students dispense with unnecessary clothing items (such as scarves and undershirts) was emphasized time and again. Other documents dealt with the demand that despite the objections of some headmistresses, students had to take off belts and corsets during class for fear of blood circulation problems.[49] The opposition of teachers, parents, and at times even the students themselves only emphasizes Primo de Rivera's assertion regarding the need to fight not only old-fashioned theories, but also (and perhaps mainly) the collective mentality of both men and women.

The relative political and economic stabilization, which characterized the late 1950s and 1960s, and the slow but steady penetration of new cultural influences into Spain, brought about a process of socio-cultural liberalization. This process influenced women's dress codes as well. In the area of physical education, the 1950s saw a significant shortening of uniforms, and in a growing number of fields, short pants (at times covered by a short skirt) were becoming obligatory.

But the 1960s also more intensely exposed the internal contradictions generated by the SF's physical education policy. The SF's instructors were sent to teach girls and young women how to care for their bodies and exercise muscles no one even dared to speak about. As a result, a space was created where short and relatively attractive uniforms, collective undressing and showering were considered legitimate. The organization's leadership now had to face the fact that such patterns of behavior, in combination with natural youthful curiosity, might lead to more liberal conduct than originally anticipated. As a result, one can find many documents from this period demanding that girls not be photographed standing too close together, holding hands, and so forth. Certain documents, such as this one written by SF's General Secretary Syera Manteola, insisted:

> In the dressing rooms one must take extra care when dressing and undressing together. The fact that we are all women does not mean we should forget our moral obligations . . . Under no conditions must men be allowed into the dressing rooms, even when all players are fully dressed.[50]

Providing a model for a more open and healthy way of life, while at the same time monitoring the moral and aesthetic preferences of the thousands of women who enjoyed the SF's physical education activities, was a complex task. This task was assigned to the SF's physical education and general instructors, whose relatively lengthy and arduous training attests to the importance accorded them within the organization. Although those women were at no time considered part of the SF's national hierarchy, the demands of their job were such that the majority of them chose to live in SF installations and, like the national delegates, to refrain from marriage.

Agents of Social Change – Health, Personal Care, and Theoretical Knowledge in the Training of the SF's Physical Education Instructors

No discussion of the SF's physical education policy is complete without a discussion of the women who spearheaded the organization's activities in this field. The personal experiences of the SF's physical education and youth instructors are of great interest, since they reflect many of the contradictions inherent in the SF's policy in this field. Moreover, the conflictive and problematic nature of their working conditions is perhaps the best proof of the tensions generated by women's physical education during the Franco era.

Luis Carrero Eras divided the professional history of those women into three major periods. The first began: during the Civil War and lasted until 1950, when their training took place in local centers loosely coordinated by the National Department for Sport and Physical Education. The second took place between 1951 and 1956, when an attempt was made to unify the training process by limiting it to the SF's national schools for general instructors *Isabel la Católica* in Avila and *Teresa de Jesus* in Madrid. The third occurred between 1956 and 1977, when all training took place at the National School for Physical Education *Ruiz de Alda* in Madrid.[51] The progressive change in the instructors' training process attests to the SF's attempts to centralize it and gain as much control as possible over the instructors' working conditions once they graduated. Since female physical educators hardly existed in Spain prior to the 1940s (unlike in Nazi Germany for example, where the party had to contend with "inheriting" experienced instructors with whom it had no ideological affinity), the SF's relationship with its trainees was totally reciprocal from the start. Training could take place only within the SF's institutions and the organization dictated the instructors' working conditions (hours and payment), as well as where they would work. In return, the young women who chose to become physical education instructors gained not only a new profession, but also official status within one of the regime's organs and the professional recognition of the Ministry of Education.

The first national course for physical education instructors was opened during the war, at a time when most teaching facilities were still closed. The course took place at Santander, but because of the lack of funding and other problems resulting from the war, it lasted a month and a half only (June 11, 1938 until July 29, 1938). The organization's insistence on holding the course when most teaching institutions had not yet opened their gates testifies to the great importance accorded it by the SF's leadership. The theoretical portion of the course included: two daily hours of anatomy and physiology classes, classes on the history of physical education and on sports theory. The part dedicated to the instructors' practical training is of special interest, since it included sporting activities that were to be banned by the regime in later years and would continue to be taught only within the SF's facilities. The sports activities trained for included gymnastics with apparatus, athletics, swimming, tennis, basketball, football, regional dancing and singing, hockey and children's games. Out of all these branches, only dancing and tennis fell under the definition of "beauty" sports. From the outset team sports instruction occupied a large portion of training time, as did different branches of athletics and gymnastics.

The category of children's games included not only games such as tug-of-war and catch, but also symbolic and imaginative activities, which made use of dolls and other accessories. The decision to include such activities in the training process points to a relatively advanced pedagogical outlook, which viewed the development of the child's emotional and psychological world as a prerequisite for its cognitive and social development. However, into this emotional and psychological climate the instructors integrated values based on a relatively rigid division of gender roles. Girls played with dolls and objects relating to family life and housework, while boys were given toy soldiers, weapons and work tools.

Thirty-four instructors successfully graduated from the first course, and a second course was already opened by September of the same year. The documents produced by the National Department for Sport and Physical Education do not provide personal information about the graduates prior to 1949, and it seems that the only entry requirement was a high-school diploma. With the opening of the SF's national schools – *Isabel la Católica* and *Teresa de Jesus* – new entry requirements were added, and the courses were extended, as can be seen from a document published by the SF in 1957. According to this document, students had to be single women, between the ages of 16–20 at registration, high school graduates and of Spanish nationality.[52] The studies now lasted three years and all students were required to reside at the school. From the list of general courses (which included religion, politics and civic studies, drawing lessons and either English or French as a second language), it is clear that the SF aimed at producing politically aware instructors with a relatively broad cultural background.

Theoretical courses included physiology and anatomy, as well as classes in movement analysis, hygiene, first aid and remedial physical education. The increased specialization of SF instructors reflects a growing interest in the field of physical education in many European countries at that time. The interest in the therapeutic nature of certain forms of physical education reflects the SF's growing interest in the field of special education and care for the disabled. The instructors' practical training included classes in all branches of sports taught by the SF, including compulsory athletics classes and, rather surprisingly, fencing.

The demanding workload throughout the three years of training at *Ruiz de Alda* was somewhat mitigated by the presence of foreign professors and excursions to physical education schools all over Europe, especially to Switzerland and Germany. M.J., a former student in *Ruiz de Alda*, told me of the time she spent in 1962 at McColine's, a physical education school in Switzerland. In addition to a variety of courses she attended there, she was exposed to the company of other young women who arrived from all over western Europe together with their different customs and fashions. One of her most vivid memories was of the French students:

> The French girls wore bikinis during swimming classes. During training, when the professor herself was in the pool, they changed to a one-piece bathing suit, but as soon as she came out – not when the class was over but

when the professor stepped out of the pool – they put their bikinis on again.[53]

It is not surprising that wearing bikinis during class, while in Spain the debate still raged whether women should even wear bathing suits in public, imprinted itself indelibly on M.J.'s memory. Years later (in 1974) she would cite this anecdote in order to make clear to her own students, not the neutrality of the use of a bikini, but rather the fact "that rules are rules", that is that even "the French" (*las francesas* as she called them) in McColine would wear a complete bathing suit when the professor was in the pool.

If the training received by the SF's physical education instructors was intensive, so were the demands made on them that went far beyond the teacher's role. Internal SF correspondence shows that these women were perceived as the organization's spearhead in an indifferent, at times even hostile, education system. Their task was to provide a personal and aesthetically pleasing example of the "New Falangist Woman". The physical aspects of this ideal woman did not manifest themselves through sporting activities only, but extended to personal hygiene and aesthetics. A letter written by the National Delegate for Sport and Physical Education addressed to the SF's instructors in 1952 stated the requirements from them:

> [The instructor] cannot wear in class the skirt, blouse or underwear she wears outside of the class. She must be clean and look clean. She must wear her hair short and if she does not, she must arrange it in an appropriate manner when teaching. She must, and this is of a special importance, watch her figure. It is important that the instructor maintain a refined and attractive look so as to encourage her students to perform the exercises she gives them. . . . [in order] to do so the instructor – who in the best of cases might no longer be young, and might even be married – must keep her body beautiful, agile and elegant.[54]

In order to accomplish all of this, instructors were required to maintain a strict diet and do exercises at home as well.

But good looks and youthfulness made little impression on "the system". In the interview I conducted with her, M.J. related to me that upon completing her training with the SF, she was sent to La Rioja and assigned to the school from which she had graduated ten years earlier. It was a private school run by the Church, and the headmistress was a young nun who had graduated the same year as M.J. At the end of her first teaching year, she organized a gymnastics display for her ten-year-old students. One of the exercises included handstands performed by the girls while wearing *bombachos*. According to M.J., most of the young nuns expressed their admiration at the girls' skills, but one of the older nuns was scandalized by the way they were exposing their legs in public. At the end of the day, M.J. was informed by the headmistress that as impressive as the display was, one must take the older nuns' feelings into consideration, so her students would henceforth not be allowed to do handstands in public. From M.J.'s testimony it appears that despite the SF's official position that the class curriculum was not be modified, she made a personal decision to sacrifice handstands for the sake of good working relations.

The pressure felt by the instructors during their working day affected their private lives as well. According to Magui León Llorante, another former SF physical education instructor, the instructors' workday, which went on until nine in the evening, sometimes even on weekends and holidays, was not compatible with married life. In addition to the long working hours, she also had to deal with inadequate facilities and the constant criticism generated by her lifestyle and choice of wardrobe:

> With my Vespa I was at least spared the difficulty of moving between the schools, but I was half frozen because I couldn't wear pants. They wouldn't allow it either at the schools or at some of the secular centers. And when it was a gymnastics class, you had to change in a hurry in whatever corner they set aside for you.[55]

But despite the difficulties, it seems that many instructors managed to win a special place in the hearts of their students. M.J. and Andresa Lopóz both agreed that this was partially the result of the nature of an instructor's job. Most instructors worked with the same students starting from their first year in kindergarten and up to their last year of high school. In the words of M.J.:

> Physical education teachers gave classes since kindergarten, since they were little . . . helping them take down their pants in order to go to the toilet. You cannot have a relationship with [a professor] you have in high school like the one you do with [a professor] you've had since primary [school]. With the physical education teacher, you usually had a good relationship, because when you were little she was the one shouting at you, or giving you a candy or wiping your nose . . . [56]

According to M.J. and Lopóz, the instructors' special standing resulted from a combination of this intimate relationship with the children and the ability to set clear limits:

> I used to get so fed up with this 'you just wait until M. got here', and when I did the children stopped running in the corridors, and do I don't know what. . . . We, the physical education teachers, did it (set limits) better than

anyone, because we were accustomed to giving orders. We were teaching in an open classroom and it's not the same as standing behind a desk. . . . You cannot imagine a physical education class without shouting at someone. You cannot plead with them 'children, children, please run'. You have to shout at them RUN OR ELSE. It's very different from sitting behind a desk.[57]

From the early 1950s onwards, the difficulties the instructors' job entailed, as well as the high entry-level qualifications and the lengthy training period required of them, were rewarded by relatively high salaries. According to statistics provided by María Luisa Zagalas Sánchez for the city of Jaen, it seems that at the end of the 1950s a high school physical education teacher's average salary was 3,000 pesetas, while that of an entry-level temporary teacher was 2,000 pesetas.[58] For the sake of comparison, one should keep in mind that the National Delegate's salary at that time was a mere 3,180 pesetas, while that of the different heads of national services was somewhere between 2,232–1,860 pesetas.

Summing up, the SF's physical education instructors taught several generations of Spanish girls and women born after the Civil War how to enjoy and take pride in their bodies. Furthermore, they instructed them how to nurture and even publicly expose their bodies in a manner considered acceptable in a conservative and a highly chauvinistic society. Such teachings, anchored as they were in the more open and progressive perceptions of the human body that were at the heart of fascist ideologies all over Europe, did not always go hand in hand with the Francoist moral system. The main tensions emerging from this could be felt in the organization's relations with the Church hierarchy, which saw the SF's physical education policy as a threat to its own control. Such tensions never disappeared, despite the instructors' continually paying "lip service" to a discourse that glorified women's modesty and their "universal" role as mothers.

On a practical level, one cannot ignore the fact that at the end of the Civil War, the number of Spanish women who took part in official sports activities was 2,800. By 1965 that number had reached 113,302. Such an increase reflected an unprecedented exposure of women to a variety of new branches of sport from which they had been banned in the past. This advance was achieved within the boundaries of an authoritarian regime and through a constant struggle against backward and chauvinistic mentalities.

At the same time, it must not be forgotten that it was not the yearning for individual freedom and new forms of personal expression that motivated the SF's physical education policy. It was rather the will to glorify discipline and the need to reach new populations within Spanish society, which "refused" to be converted to Falangist ideology. The very same resistance that the organization's policy encountered within the Francoist coalition turned it into a powerful recruitment tool by emphasizing the SF's uniqueness and establishing its position as an independent entity with a distinct political and social program. By presenting a more youthful and attractive facet of the regime and positioning its members as intermediaries between different female populations as well as public and private institutions, the organization proved its usefulness far beyond that of other organs of the *Movimiento*.

During the 1960s the number of women athletes was increasing, together with the attention being paid to competitive sports in general and to Spain's participation in international sporting events in particular. A large number of the women athletes who made a name for themselves during that period were initially trained under the supervision of the SF, but as we have seen, the organization itself was losing its monopoly in this area. However, in my view, such a loss of control did not result from the better services provided by private clubs or even from the general weakening of the *Movimiento*, but rather from a central paradox inherent in the SF's development. In the field of physical education, as in other fields with which this book is concerned, the SF managed to generate a more liberal value system and personal experiences than the ones promoted by other sectors of the Franco regime. But over time the organization proved unwilling and unable (both ideologically and structurally) to meet the changing needs and aspirations of thousands of Spanish women. While some had come to see the SF as too radical, for others it was not egalitarian and innovative enough. Despite the uniqueness of the SF's sports policy, and the effect it had on many women at specific junctures of their lives, in the long run even this attractive, and seemingly non-political, recruitment tool could not resolve the paradox and boost the organization's popularity and membership throughout the 1960s.

CONCLUSIONS

When I first started conducting my research on the SF de la FET, a colleague asked me a thought-provoking question. He wanted to know if I was writing the story of women in the context of 20th century Spain and the Franco regime specifically or perhaps that of the Franco regime from the perspective of women. A text entitled *The Making of a Female Political Elite in Franco's Spain* indeed begs this question. Having completed a thesis that in my mind at least is more about the story of women from a specific geographic and socio-political perspective than vice versa, I must now nonetheless answer two central, interrelated queries regarding both women and the regime.

Since the concept of "feminism" was first introduced in 1882 into European public discourse by French activist Hubertine Auclert, it has been almost inseparable from any discussion about women's lives and history.[1] But the relationship between feminism and women as a social group, or even between feminism and the promotion of women as a collective, is not a straightforward one. Having considered the distinction between "relational" and "individualist" feminism, Karen Offen defined as feminist any person whose ideas and actions show them to meet three criteria:

> A – They recognize the validity of women's own interpretations of their lived experience and needs and acknowledge the values women claim publicly as their own . . . in assessing their status in society relative to men. B – They exhibit consciousness of, discomfort at, and even anger over institutionalized injustice towards women as a group by men as a group in a given society, and C – They advocate the elimination of this injustice by challenging, through effort to alter prevailing ideas and/or social institutions and practices, the coercive power, force or authority that upholds male prerogative in that culture.[2]

But what do we learn from this revised, more flexible definition about the SF and its members? In the Introduction I discussed the fact that members of the SF rejected any attempt made by their adversaries at the time to present them as feminists. Are we as historians "overruling" their objections by considering the question of whether or not they indeed fit this label? Are we undermining, perhaps even ignoring, the very experiences our research sets out to explore? In my opinion, as long as we are mindful of the way the term "Feminism" itself evolved over the years, and are able explain why the subjects of our research recoiled from being classified as "feminists," we are doing neither.

Regarding the first trait of feminism, did the SF leadership recognize the validity of women's own interpretations of their experiences and needs and acknowledge the values they publicly claimed as their own? I think the answer to this is yes. As we have seen, the SF's discourse made use of a wide variety of biographies and historical models in an attempt to reflect the diverse experiences of women in Spanish society and their complex and changing interactions with different significant others (whether these be family members, colleagues, men, women or children). The emphasis placed on actions and interactions within this discourse reflects, in my view, an understanding of identity as changing, or at least as multiple, in nature. While women were encouraged to think of themselves in maternal terms, even this seemingly essential aspect of femininity was conceived of from a social perspective. Women were all assumed to have a nurturing side, which they had to access if they wished to explore their femininity to the full. However, nurturing did not necessarily mean a mother – child dyad; even in cases when maternal relations were discussed specifically, this was often done as a model for wider social engagement. "Motherhood" was often discussed interchangeably with "spiritual motherhood," that is, the nurturing and fostering of other women, younger colleagues and children who were not biologically one's own. The idea that women as a group had an inherent tendency to concern themselves with the welfare of others, and that this tendency was not necessarily expressed in terms of biological attachment, opened the way to women's involvement in all walks of life – in the workplace and the community and as active and productive daughters of the Fatherland.

As we have seen throughout this text, the *National Syndicalist Woman* as a discursive figure both shaped and was shaped by the everyday practices and experiences of SF members. The lives led by these women, the difficulties they faced and had to negotiate in their capacity as political activists, and the tensions their prominent presence within the Francoist system generated, all influenced the way they perceived their womanhood. While all members of the SF's national leadership that I interviewed saw themselves as devout Catholics and loyal Falangists, their everyday actions often put them at odds with both the Church hierarchy and their male counterparts. In this respect, one of the most empowering aspects of the organization's discourse lay in its insistence on the validity of the specific interpretations its members conferred on the concepts of nationalism and Catholicism. Wearing pants, exercising, moving unaccompanied through public spaces and challenging Church authorities in matters relating to education and gender relations did not make an SF member less of a Catholic. In much the same way, the constant bickering with local Falangist leaders, criticizing some of the major political decisions taken by the regime (such as the ones leading to the Unification or to the publication of the Law of Succession), and negotiating for more political and professional representation, did not lessen the members' loyalty to either General Franco or to the legacy of José Antonio.

However, as empowering as the SF's discourse on femininity was, it did not legitimize the experiences and values of every Spanish woman. Communist women, especially those of the communist militia, were denigrated and often ridiculed by the SF's rhetoric. In my view, this attitude, while more prominent during the early 1940s, was not solely the result of the ideological divisions generated by the experiences of the Second Republic and the Civil War. As previously noted, the SF, was for the most part founded and run by middle-class women. Furthermore, while claiming neutrality in class issues and publicly embracing all Spanish women, the SF nonetheless was heavily based on implicit class distinctions. This was evident in the aesthetics reflected in its uniforms and the demands it made on its youth instructors; in its sporting ethos; and finally in the equation of "positive" femininity and personal worthiness with formal education and a specific version of culture available and endorsed only by women of certain background and economic means.

At the same time, it is important to note once again the extent to which members of the SF were able to view "identity" as changing and multiple – as constructed and reconstructed by the everyday actions of women and the interactions between them and others. It was this notion of identity, combined with the organizational necessities explored above, that enabled the inclusion of "Leftist" women in the SF in the years immediately following the Civil War. While "on the ground" the massive incorporation of Republican and Socialist women into the organization was not always welcomed, the national leadership felt that through "re-education" these women would be able to acquire the necessary traits of "positive" femininity. It was hoped that by living and working in close proximity to Falangist women, their supposed belligerence and violence would be replaced by moderate forcefulness and quiet self-assurance and that their apparent lack of education and talent would be replaced by cultivation and nationalist commitment.

As for the second characteristic of feminism, can we claim that the SF's national leadership exhibited consciousness of or discomfort and even anger regarding institutionalized injustice towards women as a group by men as a group? Here again, in my view, the answer is a positive one. As we have seen in *Teresa*, men were criticized for encouraging women's frivolity and lack of professional ambition by forever reminding them of the threat any sign of intelligence or positive action could pose to their femininity. By viewing the family as the sole domain of women, the majority of men forced the majority of women into an impossible position whereby they had to choose between their motherhood and their social and professional lives. This line of criticism, often employed by writers in *Teresa*, singled out the deeply entrenched social patterns at work in the discrimination against women. Another line of argumentation, which was raised at the International Congress for Women, accused the Catholic Church of facilitating discrimination through its writings and activities. While the SF as an organization did not go so far as to call for a "canonical revolution," its members' everyday challenge to the Church's authority reflected their unwillingness to accept the either / or choice forced on them by this institution. By insisting on their devoutness and finding spiritual advisors who endorsed both their Catholicism and their nationalist activism, they refused to fall neatly into the categories of either Mary, mother of God, or Eve, the root of all evil.

While men were not the only ones to be criticized by the SF, the conscious choice to challenge discrimination against women as a collective drew the lines of battle in terms of gender-oriented issues. Therefore, even when men were not explicitly indicated as responsible for women's grim reality, situating women as collective victims had clear implications for men as collective oppressors. The fact that women themselves were called upon to consider their contribution to this situation – be it through educating other women towards submission or enabling their own husbands and sons to treat themselves and their daughters as less than competent – did not diminish men's blame.

Of the three components in Offen's definition of "Feminism," it is perhaps the last one – concerning the capacity and depth of social change – that is most problematic in our evaluation of the SF. Chapters 3 and 4 demonstrated the ability of the SF's national leadership to identify legislative and educational lacunae, discursive and operational spaces within which the organization could intervene in order to bring about change. But the SF as an organization never seriously contemplated working against, or even outside of, the "system." As mentioned in Chapter 3, it was precisely this characteristic of the SF – the fact that it was never viewed as a serious political threat – that enabled it to act as a pressure group within the regime and to continue promoting its own social and cultural agenda in a highly restrictive political arena.

When the SF's leadership identified the need for change, such as in the case of women's education or professional and political representation, it worked in order to find spaces within existing legislation that could accommodate such a change. All the rights guaranteed to women under the 1961

Law for Political and Professional Representation and the 1966 amendment of the same law, for example, had already been acknowledged by the Labor Charter published by the regime during the Civil War. Although extending each reference to *el español* or *los españoles* to include women was viewed as a highly subversive act by some, it was based on existing legislation. The same tendency was witnessed throughout the SF's struggle to institute female physical education. While the organization created spaces where nurturing and exposure of the female body were acceptable, it did so by constantly seeking legitimization within the National Catholic discourse. Exercising and taking pride in the female body was not advocated in terms of personal gratification or self-fulfillment, but rather as an act of obedience to the God that created that body or in the name of service to the nation.

While highly critical of the Franco regime and the Catholic Church, at no time was the SF's leadership prepared to undermine their authority completely. It is quite true that the SF's leadership led independent lifestyles and strove to formulate and implement an independent social and political agenda. It is also true that they fully understood the connection between the existing political and social institutions and women's discrimination. However, the SF gave priority to ideological considerations that dissuaded them from working towards the tearing down of the Francoist regime and its institutions. Change always had to come from within and female emancipation could not take precedence over the National Syndicalist Revolution.

This symbiotic, and at the same time highly conflictive, relationship with the Franco regime raises questions concerning the latter's nature and functioning. Social scientist Juan Linz, in a 1964 article entitled "An Authoritarian Regime: Spain", initiated a debate that still rages today concerning the character of the Franco regime.[3] Linz coined the expression "authoritarianism" in order to describe regimes whose members exhibited a limited degree of ideological heterogeneity. According to Linz, such regimes, did not present a specific, coherent ideology, but their different sectors were characterized nonetheless by a shared mentality (in the Spanish case that of National Catholicism). Linz claimed that totalitarian regimes strove to maintain high mobilization levels and attempted to penetrate and control all aspects of their subjects' everyday lives. Authoritarian regimes, on the other hand, presented low mobilization levels, except in times of major crisis. Furthermore, according to Linz, authoritarian leaders were often quite content to leave at least some aspects of everyday civic life in the control of different social groups, as long as these were perceived as having a vested interest in the regime's survival.

The current study, which examines the functioning of one of the Franco regime's organs from a gender and social perspective, supports Linz' general conclusions. As stated in the Introduction the amorphous unit that historians have called the "regime" was a bureaucratic apparatus whose policy was formulated through constant negotiation between its different sectors, each with its own ideological perspective and distinct personal and collective interests.

Throughout this text I have repeatedly referred to the social and political implications of public activism within the SF and to the personal gains and cultural capital attached to being a leading female Falangist. The women I interviewed led lives replete with personal and professional fulfillment, rich with empowering experiences and encounters. But despite the ability of its members to forge a place for themselves at the heart of Francoist power and to formulate and implement a socio-political agenda, the SF itself was viewed by the majority of Spaniards as a half-breed organization. While some people found it to be socially inclusive and culturally progressive to a dangerous degree, other felt it was conservative and backward, too middle-class in orientation and strongly attached to a chauvinistic and repressive regime.

This view of the SF persisted long after the organization itself and the regime it served were dismantled. In the Introduction, I referred to the Nueva Andadura Association. The ANA was formed by Pilar Primo de Rivera and Adelida del Pozo in 1987 in order to unite former SF members throughout Spain. The ANA's central aim was the conservation of the SF's legacy and memory, but it also had an important social role in post-Francoist society. After the death of General Franco and a "cooling-off period" of two years, most SF members returned to active professional lives, a fact that is not surprising considering their educational background and professional experience. But the easy way in which these women resettled into the job market only highlighted their ideological and cultural isolation. The ANA, then, kept alive some sort of an organizational structure, a place where former SF members could gather, discuss current issues and share personal experiences and memories with other women who had spent the majority of their adult lives in a manner similar to themselves.

In the course of my research in Madrid, I came into contact with four different organizations uniting former activists of the Francoist regime in the city. Two of these – *La Vieja Guardia* and *Plataforma 2003* – were considered to be Falangist in orientation. Yet the ANA did not maintain close working relations with either of them. As an organization, the ANA refused to take part in the majority of public events hosted by the other organizations and did not assist in their political campaigns. Andresa López, who headed the ANA in Madrid until her death in May 2006, commented on this lack of cooperation with a combined sense of pride and bitterness:

We always defined ourselves as *Joseantonianas* and our institutions kept a specific line. . . . There are many organizations and many Falanges [*muchas falanges*]. But we have nothing to do with the other organizations. There are members of those organizations who take part in our activities. They are used to making quite a bit of noise [on political matters], but they know that such discussions can be carried out there [within the other organizations], not here [at the ANA]. Here . . . no way!!!⁴

While the relative isolation of the ANA also resulted from less prosaic reasons such as personal conflicts and the struggle over funds allocated to different veterans' organizations, the sense of alienation reflected in López' words cannot be dismissed offhand. This feeling of alienation is perhaps the clearest evidence of the conflictive and complex nature of the SF. In perceiving themselves as *Joseantonias* – that is as women, Falangists and Catholics at the same time – the women with whom my work is concerned fought to reconcile that which was almost irreconcilable. In refusing to sacrifice any one aspect of their identity, they constructed a "whole" that, as in the best of Fascist terminology, was greater than the sum of its parts. But once severed from its base of political power, this unique "whole" – the organization and the discourse it upheld – no longer held much appeal for the majority of Spanish women. In the fields of physical education, political representation and labor relations, the SF managed to generate a more liberal value system than that promoted by other sectors of the Franco regime. But its members' refusal to modify in any way their complex set of allegiances and identifications left the SF unable to contain the changing needs and aspirations of thousands of Spanish women. Under such conditions this female political elite that was born within the stronghold of Spanish fascism, but had grown into one of Francoism's most dynamic organs, could not find a place for itself in the new democratic Spain.

NOTES

Introduction

1 For a discussion concerning the SF and its policies, see: M.T. Gallego Méndez, *Mujer, Falange y Franquismo* (Madrid, 1983); A. Jarne, *La Secció Femenina a Lleida* (Lleida, 1991); I. Blasco Herranz, *Armas femeninas para la contrarrevolución* (Málaga, 1999); J.M. Palomares Ibáñez, *La Guerra Civil en la ciudad de Valladolid – Entusiasmo y represión en la "Capital del Alzamiento"* (Valladolid, 2001), pp. 91–100; K. Bergès, "Pilar Primo de Rivera – Cause féminine, idéologie phalangiste, stratégies et enjeux politiques dans l'ombre du régime franquiste", Thèse de doctorat (L'université de Toulouse-Le Mirail, 2003); S. Rodríguez López, "La SF y la sociedad Almeriense durante el Franquismo: de las mujeres del movimiento al movimiento democrático de mujeres" (Tesis Doctoral, Universidad de Almería, 2004).

2 The Social Service was instituted during the Civil War as an alternative military service for women. It included six months of voluntary work for the state, as well as enforced daily religious and political classes. Completion of one's SS obligations was a precondition for receiving important state documents, such as passports, driver's licenses or work permits. Starting in 1939, the SS was overseen by the SF. For more information on the SS, see: I. Ofer, "A New Woman for a New Spain – the Sección Femenina de la FET and the Formation of a New Feminine Spanish Identity", pp. 74–94 (M.A. dissertation, Tel Aviv University, 2002); M. Orduña Prado, *El Auxilio Social (1936–1950)*, (Madrid, 1996).

3 For a discussion of the term "separate spheres" and its use in different historical contexts, see: N. Fraser, "Rethinking the Public Sphere: A Contribution to the Critique of Actually Existing Democracy" in *Habermas and the Public Sphere*, C. Calhoun (ed.), pp. 109–142 (Cambridge, MA, 1992); C. Pateman, "Feminist Critiques of the Public / Private Dichotomy", in *The Disorder of Women: Democracy, Feminism and Political Theory*, C. Pateman (ed.), pp. 118–140 (Stanford, 1989).

4 For the existing literature, see: M. Ugalde Solano, "Las mujeres nacionalistas vascas en la vida pública: gestación y desarrollo de Emakume Abertzale Batza 1906–1936" (Tesis doctoral, Madrid, 1991); N. Rios Bergantinhos, *A mulher no nacionalismo galego (1900–1936): ideologia e realidade* (Santiago de Compostela, 2001); I. Blasco, *Paradojas de la ortodoxia – política de masas y militancia Católica femenina en España (1919–1939)*, (Zaragoza, 2003).

Notes

5   M. Nash, "Experiencia y aprendizaje: la formación histórica de los femenismos en España", *Historia Social*, no. 20 (1994), pp. 152–172.

6   K. Offen, "Defining Feminism: a Comparative Historical Approach", in G. Bock S. James (eds.), *Beyond Equality and Difference: Citizenship, Feminist Politics and Female Subjectivity* (New York, 1991), pp. 75–76.

7   See for example: K. Millett, *Sexual Politics* (London, 1970); M. A. Macciochi, "Female Sexuality in Fascist Ideology", *Feminist Review*, 1 (1979), pp. 67–82; R. Bridenthal (ed.), *When Biology Became Destiny: Women in Weimar and Nazi Germany* (New York, 1984).

8   See for example: C. Koonz, *Mothers in the Fatherland* (London, 1987); V. DeGrazia, *How Fascism Ruled Women* (Berkeley, 1992); J.V. Gottlieb, *Feminine Fascism. Women in the British Union of Fascists (1923–1945)*, (London, 2000).

9   Linz, "An Authoritarian Regime."

10 For this view see: T. Medin, "Franco: the Seizing of Control and the Consolidation of Political Nothingness" in R. Rein (ed.), *They Shall Not Pass* (Tel Aviv, 2000), pp. 306–334.

11 Andresa López, born in 1922, entered the National Leadership in 1943 from the Falangist Teachers' Syndicate. Between the years 1944–1949 she was the provincial secretary of Teruel and the provincial delegate in charge of Youth. In 1949 she was appointed to the position of provincial delegate in that city, a post which she held until 1953. Between the years 1957–1978 López headed the Escuela Nacional Isabel la Católica for general instructors and was also a member of the SF's Central Committee between the years 1966–1972.
    Born in 1915, Vicky Eiroa joined the SF in 1934 following a meeting with Pilar Primo de Rivera at the University of Santiago de Compustela, where she completed a BA in humanities. Eiroa went on to become Santiago's first provincial delegate and the first National Delegate in charge of Administration.

12 L. Suárez Fernández, *Crónica de la Sección Femenina y su tiempo* (Madrid, 1993).

13 All the questionnaires began with a standardized section whose aim was the collection of personal background information (such as the name; date and place of birth; education, occupation and economic background of the interviewee etc.). The second section of questionnaire, also standardized, requested information about the initial contacts of each interviewee with the SF and her progress thereafter (the date of initial affiliation; the way in which her first contact within the organization was established; her initial position within the SF; her professional advancement; the year in which each woman left the SF). The first two sections were followed by a third one that was made up of open-ended questions that changed depending on the field of expertise of the delegate being interviewed.

14 Paul H. Lewis, *Latin Fascist Elites – The Mussolini, Franco and Salazar Regimes* (London, 2002), pp. 61–62.

15 C. Fuchs Epstein, "Women and Elites: a Cross-National Perspective", in C. Fuchs-Epstein and R. Laub-Coser (eds.), *Access to Power. Women and Elites: a Cross-National Perspective* (London, 1981), p. 5.

16 See, for example, Denitch's article about women in post-Second World War Yugoslavia: B. Denitch, "Women and Political Power in a Revolutionary Society:

the Yugoslav Case", in Fuchs-Epstein and Laub-Coser (eds.), *Access to Power*, pp. 115–123.

17　A. P. Moya, *Últimas conversaciones con Pilar Primo* (Madrid, 2006), p. 338.

Prologue – The Birth of a Female Political Elite

1　Gallego Méndez, *Mujer, Falange y Franquismo*, p. 26.

2　This was the estimate at the II National Congress, which took place in Salamanca in January 1937. As appearing in Ibid., p. 47.

3　Onésimo Redondo, a clerk at the Ministry of Finance and a law student, founded the JONs – Juntas de Ofensiva Nacional Sindicalista – in 1931 in the city of Valladolid. Redondo was one of the first individuals in Spain to combine radical nationalism with a call for social justice. Members of the JONs in Valladolid and supporters of the young ideologist Remiro Ledesma Ramos joined forces in 1934 with José Antonio's Falange and would comprise its left-wing flank regarding all social issues. Redondo himself was killed by the Communist militia a week after the outbreak of the Civil War.

4　The four studies that provide information on this issue are: Jarne, *La Secció Femenina a Lleida*; Blasco Herranz, *Armas Femeninas para la Contrarrevolución*; Palomares Ibáñez, *La Guerra Civil en la Ciudad de Valladolid*, pp. 91–100; Rodríguez López, "La SF y la sociedad Almeriense durante el Franquismo: de las mujeres del movimiento al movimiento democrático de mujeres".

5　R. Serrano Suñer, *Entre el Silencio y la Propaganda, la Historia como fue – Memorias* (Barcelona 1977), p. 42.

6　The Falangist poet and ideologist Dioniso Ridruejo was a faithful representative of this tendency. Historian Kathleen Richmonds has analyzed this process in detail. See: D. Ridruejo, *Casi unas memorias* (Barcelona, 1976), p. 103; K. Richmond, *Women and Spanish Fascism – The Women's Section of the Falange 1934–1959* (New York, 2003), pp. 33–45.

7　P. Primo de Rivera, *Discursos, circulares, escritos* (Madrid, s.a.), pp. 14–15.

8　Ibid.

9　Richmond, *Women and Spanish Fascism*, p. 72.

10　The organization's visiting nurses, for example, were paid by the Ministry of Health. The National School for Agricultural Studies at Aranjuez was financed by the Ministry of Agriculture.

11　For an analysis of the concept "Falangist existence" as understood by the SF, and its use of the concept of "silence", see: Ofer, "A New Woman for a New Spain", pp. 58–59.

12　Asociación de Nueva Andadura (henceforth ANA), Serie Azul, Carpeta No. 1B, Doc. 2.

13　A. Morcillo, *True Catholic Womanhood Gender Ideology in Franco's Spain* (Dekalb, 2000), chaps. 2, 3 and 5; M. del C. Agulló Díaz, *La educación de la mujer en Málaga durante el Franquismo* (Málaga, 1994), p. 177.

Notes

Chapter 1   Nurses and Students: Education, Professional Training and the Civil War Experience in the Shaping of Two Generations of Leadership

1   Agulló Díaz, *La educación de la mujer en Málag,* p. 167.

2   The term *hermanas pequeñas* is an adaptation of the expression *hermanos pequeños* taken from the work of Spanish historian Manuel Ruiz Carnicer regarding the Falane's Students' Syndicate. The expression refers to those students who joined the SEU between the years 1947–1951. Later on I will further explore the similarities in age, educational background and patterns of political mobilization between these young men and members of the SF's second generation of leadership.

3   Lewis, *Latin Fascist Elites,* pp. 61–62.

4   Ibid.

5   Teresa Loring, who was the last General Secretary of the SF, was born in 1912. Vicky Eiroa, the first National Delegate for Administration, and Mercedes Formica were born in 1915. Pilar Primo de Rivera, the oldest of the first generation, was born in 1906.

6   The most typical representative of this generation is Concuelo Valcarcel Burgos, which was to become in the 1960s the head of the Feminine Section of the SEU. Burgos was born in 1934.

7   K. Mannheim, "Generations", in P. Kecskemeti, (ed. and tran.), *Essays on the Sociology of Knowledge* (London, 1952), pp. 278–312.

8   A. J. Stewart, "2002 Carolyn Sharif Award Address: Gender, Race and Generation in a Midwest High School: Using Ethnographically Informed Methods in Psychology", *Psychology of Women Quarterly,* Vol. 27 (2003), pp. 4–5.

9   S. Ouditt, *Fighting Forces, Writing Women – Identity and Ideology in the First World War* (London, 1994), p. 41.

10 P. Summerfield, *Reconstructing Women's Wartime Lives: Gender, Memory and the Second World War* (Manchester, 1998), p. 42.

11 R. Merton, *Social Theory and Social Structure* (New York, 1957).

12 Fuchs-Epstein, "Women and Elites: a Cross-National Perspective", p. 8.

13 See for example Denitch's article about women post Second World War Yugoslavia: B. Denitch, "Women and Political Power in a Revolutionary Society: the Yugoslav Case", in *Access to Power,* pp. 115–123.

14 J. A. Primo de Rivera, *Textos de doctrina política* (Madrid, 1971), p. 664.

15 See: M. Carbajosa y P. Carbajosa, *La corte literaria de José Antonio – la primera generación cultural de la Falange* (Barcelona, 2003).

16 J. Kristeva, *Pouvoirs de l'horreur* (Paris, 1980), p. 15; L. Irigaray, *Sexes et parentés* (Paris, 1987); N. Jay, *Throughout Your Generations Forever: Sacrifice, Religion and Paternity* (Chicago, 1992).

17 Jay, *Throughout Your Generations Forever,* pp. 35–37.

18 M. Condern, "Sacrifice and Political Legitimization: The Production of a Gendered Social Order (Work in Progress)", *Journal of Women's History,* vol. 6 (4), 1994, pp. 165–167.

19 Ibid., p. 170.

20 P. Primo de Rivera as cited in Agulló Díaz, *La educación de la mujer en Málaga durante el franquismo,* p. 484.

21 For more information about the contribution of Falangist women to the war effort, as well as on the lives and death of its 59 members who fell during the war, see: I. Ofer, "A New Woman for a New Spain", pp. 40–44 & 65–68.

22 For such references see: D. Ridruejo, *Casi unas memorias*, p. 103; R. Serrano Suñer, *Entre el silencio y la propaganda*, p. 42.

23 For details concerning class affiliations of women in the fascist movements in Britain and Italy see: J. Gottlieb, *Feminine Fascism: Women in Britain's Fascist Movement (1923–1945)*, (London, 2000), pp. 74–77; V. de Grazia, *How Fascism Ruled Women: Italy 1922–1945* (Berkeley, 1992), pp. 268–269.

24 The most well-known was Angelita Ridruejo, sister of the Falangist ideologist Dionisio Ridruejo, who was appointed Provincial Delegate of Segovia and Consuelo Larruca, fiancé of the Falangist and young historian Antonio Tovar, who was the Provincial Delegate in Valladolid. Vicky Eiroa, the Provincial Delegate of the SF in Santiago de Compustela, and Rosario Pereda, the Local Delegate in Valladolid, on the other hand, were both SEU members.

25 From the testimoney of Carmina Montero, as cited by Rodríguez López, "La SF y la sociedad Almeriense durante el Franquismo", p. 249.

26 Of this group of war widows and "symbolic" war widows the best known are Pilar Primo de Rivera and Mercedes Sanz Bachiller, Onésimo Redondo's widow. Less well-known is Vicky Eiroa, who lost her fiancé in the first months of the war and Ricarda Canaleja, the first Provincial Delegate of La Coruña, who joined the SF after the death of her uncle, the Falange's Provincial Delegate in the area.

27 From the testimony of Gloria Cantero Muñoz as cited by Rodríguez López, "La SF y la sociedad Almeriense durante el Franquismo", p. 163.

28 Richmond, *Women and Spanish Fascism*, p. 106.

29 Table 1.1 is based on the analysis of a database compiled by the author. Regarding 55% of the SF members known to have joined the national leadership between 1934 and 1939, no background information was found.

30 ANA, Serie Azul, Carp. 73, Doc. h-3.

31 Ibid.

32 ANA, Serie Azul, Carpeta No. 169, Doc. 1.

33 P. Primo de Rivera, *Discurso general de la delegada nacional en el XIV Consejo nacional de la SF* (Lerida, 1950).

34 Enrique Sotomayor was the SEU National Delegate in the first months after the end of the Civil War, but resigned from this position after the censoring of his speech in the SEU's National Congress at the Escorial (in January 1941). The sections that were removed were those calling for university reform and those expressing the students' support of the economic plans of Salvador Marino, the head of National Syndicates. For more information about Soyomayor's term at the head of the SEU, see: Carnicer, *El Sindicato Español Universitario*, pp. 97–203.

35 Ibid., pp. 224–225.

36 An interview with the author (Madrid, 23.5.2003).
José Antonio Primo de Rivera did not belong to the Generation of '98 but to that of 1927.
Consuelo Valcarcel Burgos was an education and psychology student and was in charge of the SF's cultural activities in the Faculty of Humanities of the University

of Madrid between the years 1956 and 1959. Between the years 1959–1968, Valcacel headed the National Department for Professional Training for Youth and Adults. In 1968 she was appointed head of the Feminine Section of the SEU. Between the years 1973–1977 she was the SF's representative to the Ministry of Education.

37 Ibid.

38 For more information about the SEU-SF, see: Ruiz Carnicer, *El Sindicato Español Universitario*, pp. 476–491.

39 An interview with the author (Madrid, 23.05.2003).

40 ANA, serie azul, Carp. 73, Doc. h-3.

41 The information presented in Table 1.2 is based on a database collected by the author.

42 For the use of uniforms by the founding members of the Falange, see: M. Vincent, "Camisas Nuevas: Style and Uniformity in the Falange Española 1933–1943", in Wendy Parkins (ed.), *Fashioning the Body Politic: Dress, Gender, Citizenship* (Oxford, 2002), pp. 167–251.

43 All salaries were paid in pesetas. No information exists for the years in which no amount is indicated. The delegates were divided into five categories according to the size of the province they represented. See: ANA, serie Azul, Carp. 128, Doc. 3–27; Carp. 132, Doc. 1–42; Carp. 133, Doc. 1–41; Carp. 134, Doc. 8–35; Bergès, *Pilar Primo de Rivera*, p. 125.

44 C. Borderias, *Entre líneas: trabajo e identidad femenina en la España contemporánea. La compañia telefónica 1924–1980* (Barcelona 1993), pp. 123–124.

45 ANA, Serie Azul, Carp. 51, Doc. 31.

46 Starting from 1966, members of the SF's national leadership were entitled to higher social security payments, as well as to pension payments and health insurance. See: Richmond, *Women and Spanish Fascism*, p. 107; Suárez Fernández, *Crónica de la SF*, p. 408.

47 Until the mid-1940s, salaries comprised between 3.6% and 9.4% of the SF's total budget. During the 1950s, salaries made up between 21% and 25% of the total budget, and in 1966 they reached a new and final high of 34%.

48 Primo de Rivera, ANA, Serie Azul, Carpt. 51, Carta-circular, 15.7.1957.

49 M. Bordeaux, "Droit et femmes seules: Les piéges de la discrimination", in A. Frge & C. Klapisch-Zuber (dirs.) *Madame ou Mademoiselle? Itinéraires de la solitude féminine 18ème – 20ème siècle* (Montalba, 1984), pp. 19–57.

50 See for example: C. Dauphin, "Un excédent très ordinaire: l'exemple de Châtillon-sur-Seine en 1851", ibid., pp. 75–94; L. V. Chambers Schiller, *Liberty a Better Husband – Single Women in America: the Generations of 1780–1840* (New Haven, 1984); M. Vicinus, *Independent Women – Work and Community for Single Women 1850–1920* (Chicago, 1985).

51 M. R. Capel (coord.), *Mujer y sociedad en España (1700–1975),* (Madrid, 1986), p. 31.

52 For more information about these professions, see: F. Parent-Lardeur, "La vendeuse de grand magasin", in *Madame ou Mademoiselle?* pp. 97–110; P. Pézerat & D. Poublan, "Femmes sans maris: les employées des posts", Ibid., pp. 117–162; Y. Knibiehler, "Vocation sans voile, les métiers sociaux", Ibid., pp. 163–176; M.

Cacouault, "Diplôme et célibate: les femmes professeurs de lycée entre les deux guerres", Ibid., pp. 177–203.

53   Llona, *Entre Señorita y Garçonne*, p. 50.

54   E. D. Heineman, *What Difference Does a Husband Make? Women and Marital Status in Nazi and Post-War Germany* (Berkeley, 1999).

55   On the lives of female political activists of the Spanish Left, see: D. Ibarruri, *They Shall not Pass: The Autobiography of La Pasionaria* (London, 1966); S. Mangini, *Memories of Resistance: Women's Voices from the Spanish Civil War* (New Haven, 1995); M. Nash, *Defying Male Civilization: Women in the Spanish Civil War* (Denver, 1995).
On the life of Spanish female intellectuals, see: Mangini, *Las modernas de Madrid – las grandes intelectuales españolas de la vanguardia* (Barcelona, 2001).
On the life of leaders of the Feminine Section of Acción Católica, see: Blasco, *Paradojas de la Ortodoxia*.

56   P. Primo de Rivera, "Circular número 99 a las casadas", *Pilar Primo de Rivera – Escritos*, pp. 105–106.

57   Carmen Warner, who was born in Malaga, was a childhood friend of José Antonio Primo de Rivera and one of the first women to join the Falange. Between 1937 and 1941 Warner was the SF's National Delegate for Youth. Despite her marriage in 1941 Warner continued to hold several high-ranking positions within the organization (such as the National Delegate for Foreign Affairs and the National Delegate for Sanitation and Health). In 1966 Warner was elected to sit on the SF's Advisory committee, a position she held until 1977.

58   P. Primo de Rivera, *Recuerdos de una Vida* (Madrid, 1983), p. 17.

59   In an essay on the position of women in Francoist society, María Laffitte, Condesa de Campo Alange, claimed that in 1960 there were still a million more Spanish women than men. According to her, this demographic situation chiefly affected women who by that year were between the ages of 39 and 55, many of whom remained single. For the full text, see: M. Laffitte Condesa de Campo Alange, *La mujer como mito y como ser humano* (Madrid, 1961), p. 49.

60   Y. Knibiehler, "Vocation sans voile", in *Madame ou Mademoiselle?*, p. 171.

61   M. M. Castilla Gabriel, "La mujer soltera", Congreso Internacional de la Mujer, commisión 1, ANA, Serie Roja, Carp. 1.054.

62   An example of such fears can be found in the discussions concerning *la soltera* in the *International Congress on Women*. One of the participants claimed however, "that while friendship with men has its dangers, the same is true of too close friendships with women. It seems to us that the friendship of men is essential in order not to close oneself in an entirely feminine world." J. Marrugat, "La mujer soltera", Ibid.

63   P. Primo de Rivera, *Recuerdos de una vida*, p. 134.

64   D. Hymes, *Ethnography, Linguistics, Narrative Inequality: Towards an Understanding of Voice* (London, 1996).

65   A. Prometeo Moya, *Últimas conversaciones con Pilar Primo*, p. 184.

66   An interview with the author (Madrid, 25.05.2003).

67   An interview with the author (Madrid, 23.05.2003).

68   C. Gabriel, "La mujer soltera", Congreso internacional de la mujer, commisión 1, ANA, Serie Roja, Carp. 1.054.

69 Ibid.

70 For this image of nurturing spiritual motherhood, see a presentation given by an SF member, Asención Malero Sanz: M. Sanz, "La mujer soltera", Congreso internacional de la mujer, commisión 1, ANA, Serie Roja, Carp. 1.054.

71 An interview with the author (Madrid, 23.5.2003).

72 Ibid.

73 Ibid.

74 Ibid.

75 Ibid.

76 Ibid.

Chapter 2   *The National Syndicalist Woman*: The Genealogy of a Gender Identity

1 P. Primo de Rivera, in A. Prometeo Moya, *Últimas conversaciones con Pilar Primo*, pp. 194 y 19.

2 Coca Hernando, "Towards a New Image of Women under Franco", *International Journal of Iberian Studies*, Vol. 11, No. 1, p. 7.

3 Offen, "Defining Feminism: a Comparative Historical Approach", pp. 80–81.

4 B. Spackman, *Fascist Virilities – Rhetoric, Ideology, and Social Fantasy in Italy* (Minneapolis, 1996), pp. 36–37.

5 The SF had a diversified Press and Propaganda apparatus, which published a variety of journals aimed at different female populations. The main distinction was made between publications for members of the organization (of different ages and statuses), some of which I intend to analyze, and those aimed at non-affiliated women.

6 See for example: Leira, "Mujeres españolas en la historia universal", en *Medina*, 17 agosto de 1941; Serrano, "Lady Macbeth", en ibid., 8 marzo de 1942; "No hay nada más bello que servir – Azul", en ibid., 12 julio de 1942; Formica-Corsi, "Dos mujeres celebres y sus hijas", en *Y*, noviembre de 1941.

7 For the use made of the image of Saint Teresa of Avila and other Saints by the Francoist regime, see: G. di Febo, *La santa de la raza. Teresa de Ávila: un culto barroco en la España franquista* (Barcelona, 1988), pp. 63–71.

8 Ibid., p. 95.

9 Ibid.

10 "Recompensas" en ANA, Serie Azul, Carp. 8, Doc. 1.

11 For a further analysis of characteristics shared by the SF's gender discourse and that of conservative feminist organizations in early 20th century Spain, see: S. Rodríguez López, "La Falange femenina y construcción de la identidad de género durante el franquismo" (paper presented at the Universidad de Almería, 2000).

12 Historian Shirley Mangini studied the manner in which Curie's life story was used and publicized by the journal *Voz de la Mujer* of the *Union del Femenismo Español*, which belonged to the conservative sector of the Spanish Feminist Movement. For more details, see: Shirley Mangini, *Las modernas de Madrid – las grandes intelectuales españolas de la vanguardia* (Barcelona, 2001), pp. 96–97.

13 For the entire collection of articles dealing with the life and death of those 59 women, see: "Camaradas caídas", en ANA, Serie Azul, Carp. 18.

Notes

14 The dictionaries used include: José Casares (de la Real Academia Española), *Diccionario ideológico de la lengua Española* (Barcelona 1994); Maria Moliner, *Diccionario de uso del Español* (Madrid 1994); *Salvat Léxico – Diccionario de la lengua* (Barcelona 1991).

15 Altabello, "Entrevista con Beatriz Blesa Rodríguez, Registradora de la Propiedad" en *Medina*, 7 septiembre de 1941.

16 The interviewer, who identified herself by her first name only, claimed that she herself belonged to a different generation. "A generation where women's striving for a professional career would have been considered absurd". For the full interviews, see: "Muchachas en la Universidad", *Medina*, 7 junio de 1942.

17 Ibid.

18 Ibid.

19 For an analysis of the process undergone by Acción Católica, see: Blasco Herranz, *Paradojas de la ortodoxia*, pp. 197–306.

20 I. Nemirovsky, "El baile", en *Medina*, 17 de abril 1941.

21 On the use made of romance novels in consolidating "appropriate" notions femininity in Francoist Spain, see: Faura, Salvador, Shelley Godsland, and Nickianne Moody. "The Romance Novel or, the Generalísimo's control of the popular imagination", *Reading the Popular in Contemporary Spanish Texts* (Newark, 2004), pp. 46–57.

22 C. de Icaza, *Cristina Guzmán, profesora de idiomas* (Madrid, 1966), pp. 66–67.

23 Ibid., p. 242.

24 C. Bourland Ross, "Carmen de Icaza: Novela Rosa as Feminist Discourse?" (Unpublished paper), p. 11.

25 For other such examples, see: C. Mansfield, "Una taza de té", en *Medina*, 27 de marzo 1941.

26 I. Escobar Toresano in Rodríguez López, "La SF y la sociedad Almeriense", p. 79.

27 See for example: "Las mujeres quieren trabajar – las mujeres en las profesiones intelectuales", *Teresa*, núm. 24, diciembre de 1954; "Mujeres que trabajan", ibid., núm. 97, enero de 1962; "Carta abierta a veinte mil familias", ibid., núm. 150, junio de 1966.

28 "Piensa, escribe y habla bien – Doctora o doctor?", ibid., núm. 77, abril de 1960.

29 "Las mujeres quieren trabajar", ibid., núm. 23, noviembre de 1955.

30 See for example: "Las mujeres quieren trabajar", ibid., núm 42, junio de 1957; ibid., núm 73, diciembre de 1959.

31 "Teresa", *Teresa*, núm. 1, enero de 1954.

32 Ibid., núm. 5, mayo de 1954.

33 "Carta abierta a tía Mercedes, la más retrograda de la familia", ibid., núm. 224, agosto de 1972.

34 Cajide, "El hombre en la calle opina sobre la mujer", ibid., núm. 39, marzo de 1957.

35 See for example: "La vanidad de los hombres", ibid., núm. 1, enero de 1954; Guidandal, "La historia nos demuestra que el hombre es tan presumido como la mujer", ibid., núm. 39, marzo de 1957; "Carta abierta a nuestras lectoras", ibid., núm. 145, enero de 1966.

36 "Carta abierta a las mujeres españolas que se han negado a trabajar en Gibraltar", ibid., núm. 153, septiembre de 1966.

37 See for example: Martínez Romero, "La promoción de la mujer no consiste solo en trabajar fuera del hogar", ibid., núm. 189, septiembre de 1969.
38 Medina, "Las sufragistas Ingleses", ibid., núm. 61, enero de 1959.
39 Ibid.
40 "Carta a la Baronesa de Summerskill", ibid., núm. 170, febrero de 1968.
41 Dr. Antonio Combarros, "Concepto de la familia – fin social de la familia", Congreso Internacional de la Mujer, comisión 1, ANA, Serie Roja, carp. 1.054.
42 "La encíclica sobre el control de la natalidad, dos meses después", *Teresa*, núm. 177, septiembre de 1968.
43 Formica, "Vuestra misión de madres – crear un ambiente", ibid., núm. 6, junio de 1954.
44 See for example: Warleta Fernández, "Rincón Familiar – Usted tiene otro oficio", ibid., núm. 15, marzo de 1955.
45 Congreso Internacional de la Mujer, comisión 1, ANA, Serie Azul, Carp. 115, doc. H4 (1–2).
46 Ibid., Carp. 90, doc. 46.
47 "Algunas sugerencias sobre la educación de la mujer en España", Congreso Internacional de la mujer, ANA, Serie rojo, Carp. 1.057.
48 Ibid.
49 "Condicionamiento de la estructura sexual femenina en la participación social y cultural", ibid.
50 "La mujer en las ideologías contemporáneas", ibid.
51 "Promoción de la mujer en la Iglesia", ibid.
52 "La protección de la unidad bio-social madre-hijo", Ibid.

Chapter 3 Bridging the Gap between Elitist and Mass Politics: Gender Legislation of the Sección Feminina de FET

1 An interview with Monica Plaza, former head of the SF's National Service of Syndicates and a member of the Spanish Parliament. As cited by: Bergès, *Pilar Primo de Rivera*, p. 113.
2 Gómez Morcillo, *True Catholic Womanhood – Gender Ideology in Franco's Spain* (Illinois, 2000), chaps. 2, 3, 5; Agulló Díaz, *La educación de la mujer en Málaga durante el franquismo*, p. 177.
3 *The Economic Stabilization Plan* was launched in 1957 by the new ministers of Finance and Commerce (Mariano Navarro Rubio and Alberto Ullastres Calvo). The aim of this plan was to dismantle the last surviving vestiges of autarky. In order to control inflation, the regime froze both salaries and prices and the government's budget was drastically cut down. The Spanish peseta was devalued and foreign investors were called in to take over many projects that had until then been controlled and financed by the regime. Such reforms caused a grave economic crisis between the years 1957 and 1961, but starting from 1962, the Spanish economy started showing signs of consistent growth.
4 C. Valiente Fernández, "La liberalización del régimen franquista: la Ley del 22 de julio de 1961 sobre Derechos Políticos, Profesionales y de Trabajo de la Mujer", *Historia Social*, Madrid, no. 31, 1998, pp. 45–65.
5 When in 1959 the SF was trying to bring about the formation of an association

Notes

that would ensure the formal standing and working conditions of domestic employees, its proposal did not reach parliament due to the postponement of the government's approval. Pilar Primo de Rivera and Monica Plaza met with Carmen de Polo and presented to project to her and she promised that Franco himself would approve it. Three days later the project was indeed approved by the government. From an interview with Monica Plaza, see: Bergès, *Pilar Primo de Rivera*, p. 152.

6 Ibid., p.116.

7 P. Primo de Rivera, "Carta al General Franco de 23 marzo 1948", Archivo General de la Administración de Alcalá de Henares (henceforth AGA), Sección Presidencia del Gobierno, 17.02, caja 45.

8 Apart from the Primo de Rivera sisters and cousins, other examples were the sisters of the Falangist ideologist Dionisio Ridruejo – Lili, who headed the National Service for Administration and Cristina, who headed the National Service for Culture and the SF's National School for General Instructors *Isabel la Católica*. Teresa Loring, the last National Secretary of the SF joined the Falange in wake of her brother, who was a prominent Falangist figure in Malaga. Josefina Arraiza Goñi, the first Provincial Delegate of Navarra was the wife of José Elola, who was mentioned above. Those are only some prominent examples.

9 Carta del Secretario Nacional de la FET a la Delegada Nacional de la SF, 17.2.39, ANA, Serie Azul, Carp. 45a, Doc. 46.

10 Carta de P. Primo de Rivera, 26.5.64, AGA, Sección Presidencia del Gobierno 51.47, G3 N8, caja 16.

11 For official correspondence on these issues see for example: ANA, Serie Azul, Carp. 45a, Doc. 23; ibid., Carp. 45b, Doc. 27; ibid., Carp. 52, Doc. 7.

12 Ibid., Carp. 52, Doc. 68.

13 Ibid., Carp. 77, Doc. 21.

14 Carta de P. Primo de Rivera, 26.5.64, AGA, Sección Presidencia del Gobierno 51.47, G3 N8, caja 16.

15 Julian Pemartín was José Antonio's cousin and one of the leading Falangist ideologists. Jesus Muro was a veteran Falangist and the first Provincial Chief of Zaragoza. In 1959 both men were requested to vacate their seats in the FET's National Council. For Primo de Rivera's correspondence on this issues, see: ANA, Serie Azul, Carp. 52, Doc. 83; ibid., Carp. 97, Doc. 39.

16 The constitution of the Second Spanish Republic, along with that of the Weimar Republic, was the most advanced in Europe concerning women's rights. Women were given equal rights to elect and be elected to all public institutions; equal access to the job market; and the right to independently conduct their legal and financial affairs. The constitution also legalized divorce and abortions.

17 M. Basora Francesch, *Derecho del Trabajo* (Barcelona, 1964), pp. 126–127.

18 A. Fernández Heras, *Tratado práctico de legislación social* (Zaragoza, 1946), p. 153–154.

19 Borderias, *Entre líneas*, p. 22, 35.

20 ANA, Serie Azul, Carp. 2, Doc. 25.

21 Ibid., Doc. 18.

22 The first day care centers were opened by the SF in 1944, providing a full-time

solution (8:30–18:00) for children from the ages of 6 moths to 6 years for a minimal fee.

23 An interview with the author (Madrid, 15.12.2004). María Nieves Sunyer joined the SF from the SEU. In 1955 she was nominated Provincial Delegate of Madrid. Between the years 1957–1968 she was the National Delegate for Youth and in 1968 was appointed the Provincial Labor Delegate in Madrid. In this capacity, she worked side by side with Monica Plaza, the National Labor and Syndicates Delegate .

24 An interview with the author (Madrid, 15.12.2004).

25 ANA, Serie Azul, Carp. 2A, Doc. 159.

26 Ibid., Doc. 165.

27 For the experience of the Yellow or Catholic Syndicates for women in Spain of the first third of the 20th Century, see: Capel, *Mujer y sociedad en España*, pp. 258–259.

28 N. Milanich, "From Domestic Servant to Working-Class Housewife: Women, Labor, and Family in Chile," *E.I.A.L*, Vol. 16 (1), 2005, p. 23.

29 C. Warner, ANA, Serie Azul, Carp. 77, Doc. 9.

30 Ibid.

31 For the Francoist legislation concerning mutual aid funds see: Fernández Heras, *Tratado práctico de legislación social*, pp. 269–273.

32 For details concerning the electoral procedure, see an article in *Teresa*: "Elecciones del servicio doméstico," en *Teresa*, enero de 1961.

33 Mercedes Fromica, *instancia de parte*, (Madrid, 1991), pp. 36–37; Interview with Mercedes Formica in Richmond, *Women and Spanish Fascism*, pp. 87–88 and 155.

34 For the full report of Pilar Primo de Rivera before the SF's Committee of the Heads of National Services, see: ANA, Serie Azul, Carp. 77, Doc. 21.

35 Ibid.

36 T. Loring, *Promoción político-social de la mujer durante los años del mandato de Francisco Franco*, (Madrid, 1997), p. 593.

37 Davidson, *Politics, Policy and Propaganda of the Sección Femenina*, p. 203.

38 For the full text of the law, see: Suárez Fernández, *Crónica de la SF*, pp. 517–520.

39 Loring, *Promoción político-social de la mujer*, p. 599.

40 For the full text see: "Ley de 28/12/1966, que deroga el número 2 del artículo 3 de la ley de 22/6/1961: "Acceso a los cargos de Magistrados, Juez y Fiscal" en Suárez Fernández, *Crónica de la SF*, p. 521.

41 The SF's legal department was created in 1938, at the height of the Civil War, in order to enable the national leadership to oversee disciplinary measures at a local level and prevent hasty expulsions of ex-leftist activists such as the ones that took place within the Falange at the same time. Once the war was over, and under the supervision of its new head, Pilar Romeo, the department continued to function as the SF's disciplinary arm, using both negative incentives (fines and membership sanctions), and positive ones (*recompenses* or special decorations for outstanding and life long services). These *recompenses* were granted by the national delegate according to the department's recommendations.

42 ANA, Serie Azul, Carp. 102, Doc. 26.

Notes

43 For the full petition, see: Carp. 102, Doc. 2.

44 Ibid., Carp. 103, Doc. 77.

45 Ibid.

46 Ibid.

47 Ibid.

48 The last SF communication concerning the La Union petition I was able to find referred all the documents concerned to the SF's provincial delegate in Murcia and her legal advisor with a note indicating that if anything could be done in the matter they were better placed than the national delegation to do so. It is unknown what, if any, further measures were taken.

49 For such examples see a petition by María de los Angeles Fontao de la Vega, in ibid., Carp. 103, Doc. 6; petition by Josefina Perez Rodrigo, ibid., Carp. 102, Doc. 7; petition by Clotild Arnau Lartiga, ibid., Doc. 9.

50 Kathleen Richmonds points to the fact that in many cases, the official subordination of the SF to the Falange's male hierarchy was lost on the general public, since SF members were far more active than their male counterparts. Richmond goes on to cite Enrique de Aguinaga, a former Falangist, who gives the humorous example of a messenger boy who looked for the National Movement's offices in Madrid by asking the way to "the men's *Sección Femenina*". See Richmonds, *Women and Spanish Fascism*, pp. 112–113, 160.

51 The most radical example of such a case is a petition by a father of Spanish nationality to have the SF declared legal guardian of his six children residing in Spain, following his separation from their mother. See: ANA, Serie Azul, Carp. 103, Doc. 99.

52 Ibid., Doc. 58.

53 Ibid.

54 See: A. Cazorla Sánchez, *Las políticas de la Victoria: la consolidación del Nuevo Estado franquista (1938–1953)*, (Madrid, 2000), pp. 45–47.

55 For one such view see Josefina Perez Rodrigo's letter: ANA, Serie Azul, Carp. 102, Doc. 7.

56 See a letter by J. M. Castín, ibid, Carp. 103, Doc. 37.

57 Ibid, Doc. 6–7.

58 Ibid, Doc. 35.

59 For both petitions see: Ibid. Carp. 102, Doc. 246; Carp. 103, Doc. 59.

60 D. Ridruejo, *España 1963 – examen de una situación* (Barcelona, 1977), pp. 4–5.

61 For works dealing with the changing nature of the Spanish Catholic hierarchy and lay catholic organizations under the Franco regime, see: A. Murcia Santos, *Obreros y obispos en el franquismo: estudio sobre el significado eclesiológico de la crisis de Acción Católica Española* (Madrid, 1995); B. López García, *Aproximación a la historia de la HOAC 1946–1981* (Madrid, 1995); F. Montero García, *La Acción Católica y el franquismo: auge y crisis de la Acción Católica Española en los años sesentas* (Madrid, 2000).

For works dealing with the different sectors of the *movimiento*, see: J. Sáez Marín, *El frente de juventudes: política de juventud en la España de posguerra (1937–1960)*, (Madrid, 1988); Ruiz Carnicer, *El sindicato Español universitario (SEU)*; J. M. Thomás, *La Falange de Franco* (Barcelona, 2001).

Notes

Chapter 4 Am I That Body? Sección Femenina de la FET and the Struggle for the Institution of Physical Education and Competitive Sports for Women

1 ANA, Serie Azul, Carp. 41, Doc. 3, p. 3.

2 L. Carrero Eras, "La actividad físico-deportiva de la mujer en España 1938–1978", tesis doctoral, Universidad Politécnica de Madrid (Madrid, 1995), p. 865.

3 For the development of women's sports under liberal regimes, see: J. A. Mangan, and R. J. Park, *From "Fair Sex" to Feminism – Sport and the Socialization of Women in the Industrial and Post-Industrial Eras* (London, 1987); K. E. McCrone, *Sport and the Physical Emancipation of English Women: 1870–1914* (London, 1988); S. K. Cahn, *Coming on Strong – Gender and Sexuality in 20ᵗʰ Century Women's Sport* (Cambridge MA, 1994); M. A. Hall, *The Girls and the Game: a History of Women's Sport in Canada* (Peterborough, 2002).

4 C. Alcalde, *Muejeres en el franquismo: exiliadas, nacionalistas y opositoras* (Barcelona, 1996), p. 80.

5 In this respect I agree with Juan Linz, who saw the Franco regime as an example not of a totalitarian regime but of an authoritarian one. Its ruling elite manifested limited ideological heterogeneity, which only grew in time, with the lessening of repression and the different evolutionary path, which the regime's "families" (Falangists, Monarchists and the Catholic Church and its different representatives) took. See: J. J. Linz, "An Authoritarian Regime: Spain" in E Allardt and Y. Littunan (eds.), *Cleavages, Ideologies and Party Systems* (Helsinki, 1964). For works emphasizing the distinct political and social agenda of the regime's different political families, see: J. Tusell, *Franco y los católicos: la política interior española entre 1945–1957* (Madrid, 1984); Ruiz Carnicer, *El sindicato Español Universitario*; A. Cazorla Sánchez, *Las políticas de la Victoria.*

6 V. de Grazia, *The Culture of Consent – Mass Organization of Leisure in Fascist Italy*, (Cambridge, 1981); A. Krüger, "Strength through Joy: the Culture of Consent under Nazism, Fascism and Francoism", in J. Riordan (ed.), *The International Politics of Sport in the 20ᵗʰ Century* (London, 1999), pp. 67–89.

7 For details on female physical education under fascist regimes, see: De Grazia, *How Fascism Ruled Women*, pp. 162–163, 210–219.

8 A. Alcoba, *Auge y ocaso del Frente de Juventudes* (Madrid, 2002), pp. 56–112.

9 A. Hall, *The Girl and the Game*, p. 78.

10 Ley de 20 de septiembre de 1938 de la Jefatura del Estado, en Carrero Eras, "La actividad físico-deportiva de la mujer en España", p. 103.

11 Ley de 6 de diciembre de 1940, de la Jefatura del Estado, ibid., p. 105.

12 DAHIR de 31 de diciembre de 1940 y Orden de 6 agosto de 1943, ibid., pp. 107, 111.

13 Orden de 7 de junio de 1945 del Secretaría General del Movimiento, ibid., p. 121.

14 For details of the meeting between Agosti and the SF's leadership, see: M. L. Zagalaz Sánchez, *La educación física femenina (1940–1970): análisis y estudio en la ciudad de Jaén* (Jaén, 1997), p. 92.

15 McCrone, *Sport and the Physical Emancipation of English Women*, p. 101.

16 For the manner in which this school led the way in women's sports in the English-speaking world, see for example: ibid., pp. 100–126

Notes

17   SF de la FET (eds.), *Educación física en la escuela primaria* (Madrid, 1959), p. 141.
18   L. Agosti, *Gimnasia educativa (para las profesoras de Escuela Ruiz de Alda)*, (Madrid, 1948), pp. 719–723.
19   M. J. Inchausti y C. Gutiérrez Salgado, *Educación física femenina (texto oficial para las escuelas magisterio)*, (Madrid, 1955), p. 11.
20   C. Carbajosa Menéndez and E. Fernández Bustillo, *Manuales de educación física en el franquismo* (Oviedo, 2000), pp. 10–11.
21   Hall, *The Girl and the Game*, p. 4.
22   McCrone, *Sport and the Physical Emancipation of English Women*, p. 11.
23   "La formación moral y educación física de la mujer", ANA, Serie Azul, Carp. 41. Doc. 41. Amongst the first thinkers to write about the relation between sports and Christian values were Baron Pierre de Coubertin and Father Henri Didon. George Williams, founder of the YMCA in England, also wrote as early as 1850 about sports and its role in conquering the hearts of the youth for God.
24   M. de Miranda, "Instrucciones para la organización de cursos provinciales de educación física", ANA, Serie Azul, Carp. 41, Doc. 57.
25   "Discurso de Pilar Primo de Rivera en el primer Campeonato Nacional de deportes en Barcelona", ibíd., Doc. 14.
26   *Plan general de educación física*, ibíd., Carp. 80, Doc. 15bis.
27   M. de Miranda, *Necesidad de la educación física*, ibíd., Carp. 42, Doc. 49.
28   M. de Miranda, *Manera de servir*, ibíd., Doc. 44.
29   C. Sierra y Gil de la Cuesta, "El deporte – ocasión y promoción de la mujer en la sociedad", ibíd., Carp. 118, Doc. 45.
30   I have not been able to identify the specific work upon which this reference is based. However, its importance is less in the validity of the actual information and more in the SF's position, as reflected by its use, concerning the relation between the different components of social promotion of which physical education was one.
31   ANA, Serie Azul, Carp. 118, Doc. 45.
32   Ibid., Doc. 13.
33   Carrero Eras, "La actividad físico-deportiva de la mujer en España", p. 289.
34   ANA, Serie Azul, Carp. 118, Doc. 13; Serie Roja, Carp. 1084, pp. 221–238.
35   ANA, Serie Roja, Carp. 1084, pp. 818–819.
36   J. Esclava Galán, *Coitus Interruptus – la represión sexual y sus heróicos alivios en la España franquista* (Barcelona, 1997), p. 102.
37   An interview with the author (Madrid, 15.12.2004).
38   An interview with the author (Madrid, 15.12.2004).
39   ANA, Serie Azul, Carp. 42, Doc. 44.
40   Ibíd., Doc. 36; ibíd., Carp. 41, Doc. 66; ibíd., Carp. 43, Doc. 70.
41   Ibíd., Carp. 41, Doc. 27.
42   Ibíd., Carp. 117, Doc. 69.
43   Ibíd., Carp. 80, Doc. 26.
44   Ibíd., Carp. 83, Doc. 35.
45   Ibíd., Carp. 117, Doc. 27.
46   Ibíd.
47   Esclava Galán, *Coitus Interruptus*, p. 97.

48 ANA, Serie Azul, Carp. 84, Doc. 48.
49 Ibíd., Carp. 84, Doc. 40. In March 1954, following confrontations with several headmistresses, SF general secretary, Syera Manteola, published a decree that ordered instructors to suspend students who showed up in class without the required uniform.
50 ANA, Serie Azul, Carp. 83, Doc. 19.
51 An internal SF report from 1962 estimated the number of women who graduated from these different programs at 1,022. Of these, 452 graduated from *Ruiz de Alda* and another 570 from *Isabel la Católica*. Another 2,849 instructors received their training in local centers prior to the year 1950. For a full report, see: Ibíd., Carp. 117, Doc. 69.
52 Carrero Eras, "La actividad físico-deportiva de la mujer en España", pp. 221–238.
53 An interview with the author (Madrid, 15.12.2004).
54 Ibíd., Serie Azul, Carp. 81, Doc. 8.
55 Ibíd., p. 74–75.
56 An interview with the author (Madrid, 15.12.2004).
57 Ibid.
58 Zagalas Sánchez, *La educación física femenina*, p. 355.

Conclusions

1 As Karen Offen has pointed out, Auclert used the term to describe herself in her periodical *La Citoyenne* at least as early as 1882. Following the first "Feminist" congress in Paris in 1892, the term gained popularity. By 1895 it had crossed the channel to Great Britain and by the turn of the century was used in Spanish, Italian, Greek and Russian publications.
2 Offen, "Defining Feminism: a Comparative Historical Approach," p. 83.
3 Linz, "An Authoritarian Regime."
4 An interview with the author (Madrid, 15.12.2004).

BIBLIOGRAPHY

Primary Sources

Archives

Real Academia de Historia, Fondo de la Asociación de "Nueva Andadura", Serie Azul
and Roja.
Archivo General de la Administración de Alcalá de Henares, Sección Presidencia del
Gobierno, Secretaría General del Movimiento.

Periodicals of the SF

Medina – Seminario de la SF, 1939–1943.
Y – Revista para la mujer, 1940–1945.
Teresa, 1954–1977.

Interviews

Eiroa, M.V., Madrid, 20.5.2003.
Garcia Muñez, M.L. , Madrid, 28.5.2003.
J. M., Madrid, 15.12.2004.
López, A., Madrid, 15.12.2004.
Loring, T., Malaga, 29.9.2000
Nieves Sunyer, M., Madrid, 15.12.2004.
Pozo del, A., Madrid, 15.12.2004.
Salvo Guntín, C., Madrid, 26–28.5.2003.
Sierra, M., Madrid, 15.12.2004.
Suarez, J., Madrid, 26.5.2003.
Valcarcel, C., Madrid, 23.5.2003.

Speeches, official publications, memoirs and autobiographies

Agosti, L. , *Gimnasia educativa (para las profesoras de Escuela Ruiz de Alda)*, (Madrid,
1948).
Aragón Gómez, B., *Síntesis de economía corporativa* (Salamanca, 1937).
Ascanio de, A., *España Imperio: el Nuevo humanismo y la Hispanidad* (Avila, 1939).
Departamento Nacional de Propaganda del Frente de Juventudes (eds.), *Cartilla
Escolar de educación física* (Madrid, 1946).
Documentos inéditos para la historia del Generalísimo Franco, Tomo II–2 and IV.
Fernández Heras, A., *Tratado práctico de legislación social* (Zaragoza, 1946).
Formica, M., *A instancia de parte* (Madrid, 1991).

Bibliography

Ibarruri, D., *They shall not Pass: The Autobiography of La Pasionaria* (London, 1966).

Inchausti, M.J. and Gutiérrez Salgado, C., *Educación física femenina (texto oficial para las escuelas magisterio)*, (Madrid, 1955).

Legaz Lacambra, L. and Aragón Gómez, B. (eds.), *Cuatro estudios sobre sindicalismo vertical* (Zaragoza, 1939).

León Llorante, M., *Voces del silencio: memorias de instructora de juventud de la SF* (Madrid, 2000).

Loring, T., *Promoción político-social de la mujer durante los años del mandato de Francisco Franco* (Madrid, 1997).

Primo de Rivera, J. A., *Textos de doctrina política* (Madrid, 1971).

Primo de Rivera, P. , *Escritos* (Madrid, s.a.).

Primo de Rivera, P. , *Discursos, circulares, escritos* (Madrid, s.a.).

Primo de Rivera, P. , *Discurso general de la delegada nacional en el XIV Consejo nacional de la SF* (Lerida, 1950).

Primo de Rivera, P. , *Discurso, XVIII Consejo Nacional* (Malaga, 1956).

Primo de Rivera, P. , *Discurso, XIX Consejo Nacional* (Medina de Campo, 1958).

Primo de Rivera, P. , *Discurso, XXVI Consejo Nacional* (Murcia, 1972).

Primo de Rivera, P. , *Recuerdos de una vida* (Madrid, 1983).

Ridruejo, D., *Casi unas memorias* (Barcelona, 1976).

Ridruejo, D., *España 1963 – examen de una situación* (Barcelona, 1977).

Serrano Suñer, R., *Entre el Silencio y la Propaganda, la Historia como fue – Memorias* (Barcelona 1977).

SF de la FET (eds.), *Educación física en la escuela primaria* (Madrid, 1959).

Venero García, M. (ed.), *Testimonio de Manuel Hedilla – Segundo Jefe Nacional de Falange Española* (Barcelona, 1972).

Secondary Sources

Agullo Diaz, M. del C., *La educación de la mujer en Malaga durante el Franquismo* (Malaga, 1994).

Ahlegren, G.T.W., *Teresa of Avila and the Politics of Sanctity* (Ithaca, 1996).

Alcalde, C., *Muejeres en el franquismo: exiliadas, nacionalistas y opositoras* (Barcelona, 1996).

Alcoba, A., *Auge y Ocaso del Frente de Juventudes* (Madrid, 2002).

Alted, A., *Política del nuevo estado sobre el patrimonio cultural y la educación durante la guerra civil española* (Madrid, 1984).

Alted Vigil, A., "Las mujeres en la sociedad española de los años cuarenta", en *La mujer en la Guerra civil Español*, III Jornada de estudios monográficos (Salamanca, 1989).

Alvarez Bolando, A., *Para ganar la guerra, para ganar la paz. Iglesia y guerra civil: 1936–1939* (Madrid, 1995).

Barrachina, M.A., "Ideal de la mujer Falangista. Ideal falangista de la mujer", en *La mujer en la guerra civil Español*, Jornada de Estudios Monográficos (Ministerio de Asuntos Sociales, Instituto de la Mujer), (Salamanca, 1989).

Basora Francesch, M., *Derecho del Trabajo* (Barcelona, 1964)

Bellod, J.J., *José Antonio y el sindicalismo nacional* (Madrid, 1956).

Bibliography

Bergès, K., "Pilar Primo de Rivera – Cause Féminine, idéologie Phalangiste, strategies et enjeux politiques dans l'ombre du régime Franquiste", Thèse de doctorat (L'université de Toulouse–Le Mirail, 2003).

Bernáldez, J.M., *El patrón de la derecha. Biografía de Fraga* (Barcelona, 1985).

Bock, G., "Poverty and Mothers' Rights in the Emerging Welfare States", in G. Duby and M. Perrot (eds.), *A History of Women in the West. Towards a Cultural Identity in the Twentieth Century* (Cambridge, 1996), vol. 5, pp. 402–432.

Bordeaux, M., "Droit et femmes seules: Les piéges de la discrimination", in *Madame ou Mademoiselle? Itinéraires de la solitude feminine 18ᵗʰ–20ᵗʰ siécle* (eds.) A. Frge and C. Klapisch-Zuber (Montalba, 1984).

Borderias, C., *Entre lineas: trabajo e identidad femenina en la españa contemporanea. La compania telefónica 1924–1980* (Barcelona 1993).

Cacouault, M., "Diplôme et celibate: les femmes professeirs de lycée entre les deux guerres" in *Madame ou Mademoiselle? Itinéraires de la solitude feminine 18ᵗʰ–20ᵗʰ siécle* (eds.) A. Frge and C. Klapisch-Zuber (Montalba, 1984), pp. 177–203.

Cahn, S.K., *Coming on Strong – Gender and Sexuality in 20ᵗʰ Century Women's Sport* (Cambridge MS, 1994).

Carbajosa, M. and Carbajosa, P. , *La corte literaria de José Antonio – la primera generación cultural de la Falange* (Barcelona, 2003).

Carbajosa Menéndez, C. and Fernández Bustillo, E., *Manuales de educación física en el franquismo* (Oviado, 2000).

Carrero Eras, L. , "La actividad físico deportiva de la mujer en España 1938–1978", tesis doctoral, Universidad Politécnica de Madrid (Madrid, 1995).

Cazorla Sánchez, A., *Las políticas de la Victoria: la consolidación del Nuevo Estado franquista (1938–1953), (*Madrid, 2000).

Casino Muñez Repiso, J.M. and Lara de Vicente, F., "Sobre el pensamiento económico de José Antonio", en *José Antonio y la economía* (ed.) J. Velarde Fuertes (Madrid, 2004), pp. 214–216.

Cernuda, P., *Ciclón Fraga* (Madrid, 1997).

Coca Hernando, R., "Towards a New Image of Women under Franco: the Role of the Sección Femenina", in *International Journal of Iberian Studies*, vol. 11 (1), 1998, pp. 5–13.

Colomer, J.M., *La transición a la democracia: el modelo Español* (Barcelona, 1998).

Condern, M., "Sacrifice and Political Legitimization: The Production of a Gendered Social Order (Work in Progress)", *Journal of Women's History*, vol. 6 (4), 1994, pp. 155–167.

Costas Laguna, J.L. , *Hispanidad (1500–1558), (*Madrid, 1992)

Chambers Schiller, L. V., *Liberty a Better Husband – Single Women in America: the Generations of 1780–1840* (New Haven, 1984).

Chueca, R., *El Fascismo en los Comienzos del Régimen de Franco – Un Estudio sobre FET-JONS* (Madrid, 1983).

Chuliá, E., *El podel y la palabra: prensa y poder politico en las dictaduras. El regimen de Franco ante la prensa y el periodismo* (Madrid, 2001).

Dauphin, C., "Un excédent trés ordinaire: l'exemple de Châtillon-sur-Seine en 1851" in *Madame ou Mademoiselle? Itinéraires de la solitude feminine 18ᵗʰ–20ᵗʰ siécle* (eds.) A. Frge and C. Klapisch-Zuber (Montalba, 1984), pp. 19–57.

Bibliography

De Grazia, V., *How Fascism Rulled Women: Italy 1922–1945* (Berkeley, 1992).

De la Cierva, R., *La lucha por el poder: así cayó Arias Navarro* (Madrid, 1996).

Di Febo, G., *La santa de la raza. Teresa de Avila: un culto barroco en la España franquista* (Barcelona, 1988).

Echevarri Dávil, B., *La protección de la infania: educación sanitaria de las madres en la postguerra española*, El VII Congreso Español de Sociologiá de la Población, Madrid.

Ellwod, S., *Prietas las Filas – La Historia de Falange Española 1933–1983* (Barcelona, 1984).

Ellwood, S., *Spanish Fascism in the Franco Era: Falange Española de las JONS 1936–1975* (Basingstoke, 1987).

Esclava Galán, J., *Coitus Interruptus – la represión sexual y sus heróicos alivios en la España Franquista* (Barcelona, 1997).

Estruch, J., *Saints and Shemers: Opus Dei and its Paradoxes* (New York, 1995).

Fernández, J., "José Antonio y la reforma agraria", en *José Antonio y la economía* (ed.) J. Velarde Fuertes, pp. 341–379.

Fraser, N., "Rethinking the Public Sphere: A Contribution to the Critique of Actually Existing Democracy" in *Habermas and the Public Sphere*, (ed.) C. Calhoun, pp. 109–142 (Cambridge, MA, 1992).

Fuente, I., Golpe mortal: asesinato de Carrero y agonía del Franquismo (Madrid, 1984).

Fuentes Irurozqui, M., *Ideario economico de José Antonio,* (Madrid, 1951).

Fuentes Irurozqui, M., *El pensamiento economico de José Antonio Primo de Rivera* (Madrid, 1957).

Fundación Cánovas del Castillo, *Manuel Fraga. Homenaje Académico* (Madrid, 1997).

Gallego Méndez, M.T., *Mujer, Falange y Franquismo* (Madrid, 1983).

Gómez Morcillo, A., *True Catholic Womanhood – Gender Ideology in Franco's Spain* (DeKalb, 2000).

Gondrand, F., Al paso de Dios: Josemaría Escrivá de Balaguer, fundador del Opus Dei (Madrid, 1992).

González Calleja, E., *La Hispanidad como instrumento de combate: raza e imperio en la Guerra franquista durante la Guerra civil española* (Madrid, 1988).

Gottlieb, J., *Feminine Fascism: Women in Britain's Fascist movement (1923–1945),* (London, 2000).

Hall, M.A., *The Girls and the Game: a History of Women's Sport in Canada* (Peterborough, 2002).

Heineman, E.D., *What Difference Does a Husband Make? Women and Marital Status in Nazi and Post-War Germany* (Berkeley, 1999).

Herranz Blasco, I., *Armas Femeninas para la Contrarrevolución* (Malaga, 1999).

Herranz Blasco, I., *Paradojas de la ortodoxia – política de masas y militancia Católica femenina en España (1919–1939),* (Zaragoza, 2003).

Huneñus, C., *La unión d l centro democratico y la transición a la democracia en España* (Madrid, 1985).

Irigaray, L., *Sexes et Parentés* (Paris, 1987).

Jarne, A., *La Secció Femenina a Lleida* (Lleida, 1991).

Jay, N., *Throughout Your Generations Forever: Sacrifice, Religion and Paternity* (Chicago, 1992).

Bibliography

Knibiehler, Y., "Vocation sans voile, les métiers sociaux" in *Madame ou Mademoiselle? Itinéraires de la solitude feminine 18th–20th siécle* (eds.) A. Frge and C. Klapisch-Zuber (Montalba, 1984), pp. 163–176.

Kristeva, J., *Pouvoirs de l'horreur* (Paris, 1980).

Krüger, A., "Strengh through Joy: the Culture of Consent under Nazism, Fascism and Francoism", in *The International Politics of Sport in the 20th Century* (ed.) J. Riordan (London, 1999), pp. 67–89.

Lacalzada de Mateo, J.M., *Concepción Arenal: vida, ciencia y virtud* (La Coruña, 1997).

Laffitte Condesa de Campo Alange, M., *La mujer como mito y como ser humano* (Madrid, 1961).

Lewis, P. H., *Latin Fascist Elites – The Mussolini, Franco and Salazar Regimes* (London, 2002).

Leydesdorff, S., Passerini, L. and Thompson, P. (eds.), *Gender and memory* (Oxford, 1996).

Linz, J.J., "An Authoritarian Regime: Spain", in E. Allardt and Y. Littunen (eds.), *Cleavages, Ideologies and Party systems* (Helsinki, 1964).

Liss, P. K. *Isabel the Queen – Life and Times* (New York, 1992).

Loader, C., *The Intellectual Development of Karl Mannheim, Culture, Politics, and Planning* (Cambridge, 1985).

Lombardero, j., *Hacia una teoría del estado nacional sindicalista* (Madrid, 2000).

López García, B., Aproximación a la historia de la HOAC 1946–1981 (Madrid, 1995).

Mangan, J.A. and Park, R.J. (eds.), From "Fair Sex" to Feminism – Sport and the Socializatiom of Women in the Industrial and Post-Industrial Eras (London, 1987).

Mangini, S., *Memories of Resistence: Women's Voices from the Spanish Civil War* (New Haven, 1995).

Mangini, S., *Las modernas de Madrid – las grandes intelectuales españolas de la vanguardia* (Barcelona, 2001).

Mannheim, K., "Generations", in *Essays on the Sociology of Knowledge*, (ed. and tran.) Kecskemeti, P. (London, 1952).

Maravall, J.M., *Dictadura y disentimiento político: obreros y estudiantes bajo el franquismo* (Madrid, 1978).

Martín Aceña, P. and Prados de la Escosura, L. (eds.), *La nueva historia económica en España* (Madrid, 1985).

Mayor Martínez, L., *Ideologías dominantes en el sindicalismo vertial* (Algorta, 1972).

McCrone, K.E., *Sport and the Physical Emancipation of English Women 1870–1914* (London, 1988).

Messori, V., *Opus Dei: una investigación* (Barcelona, 1997).

Míguez González, S., *La preparación de la transición a la democracia en España* (Zaragoza, 1990).

Milanich, N., "From Domestic Servent to Working-Class Houswife: Women, Labor, and Familiy in Chile", *E.I.A.L*, Vol. 16 (1), 2005, pp. 11–40.

Montero García, F., *La Acción Católica y el franquismo: auge y crisis de la Acción Católica Española en los años sesentas* (Madrid, 2000).

Mora Bayo, M., *Desde el descubrimiento de la Hispanidad (la locura de España)*, (Huelva, 1998).

Bibliography

Muñoz Alonso, A., *Un pensador para un pueblo* (Madrid, 1971).

Murcia Santos, A., Obreros y obispos en el franquismo: estudio sobre el significado eclesiológico de la crisis de Acción Católica Española (Madrid, 1995).

Nash, M., "Experiencia y aprendizaje: la formación histórica de los femenismos en España", *Historia Social*, no. 20 (1994), pp. 152–172.

Nash, M., *Defying Male Civilization: Women in the Spanish Civil War* (Danver, 1995).

Núñez Díaz-Balart, M., *Mujeres caídas: prostitutas legales y clandestinas en el franquismo* (Madrid, 2003).

Ofer, I., "Fragmented Autobiographies: a Style of Writing or Self-perception? The Case of Pilar Primo de Rivera", *IberoAmericana*, Vol. 9 (2003), pp. 37–52.

Offen, K., "Definir el feminismo: un análisis histórico comparativo", *Historia Social*, no. 9 (invierno 1991), pp. 103–135.

Offen, K., "El cuerpo político: mujeres, trabajo y política de la maternidad en Francia, 1920–1950" en *Maternidad y polítcias de género. La mujer en los estados del bienestar europeos, 1880–1950* (eds.) G. Bock, G., y P. Thane (Madrid, 1996), (1st ed. English, 1991).

Orduña Prada, M., *El Auxilio Social (1936–1950),* (Madrid, 1996).

Ouditt, S., *Fighting Forces, Writing Women – Identity and Ideology in the First World War* (London, 1994).

Palomares, C., *The Quest for Survival After Franco. Moderate Francoism and the Slow Journey to the Polls 1964–1977* (Brighton, 2004).

Palomares Ibáñez, J.M., *La Guerra Civil en la Ciudad de Valladolid – Entusiasmo y Represión en la "Capital del Alzamiento"* (Valladolid, 2001).

Parent-Lardeur, F., "La vendeuse de grand magasin" in *Madame ou Mademoiselle? Itinéraires de la solitude feminine 18th–20th siécle* (eds.) A. Frge and C. Klapisch-Zuber (Montalba, 1984), pp. 97–110.

Pateman, C., "Feminist Critiques of the Public / Private Dichotomy", in *The Disorder of Women: Democracy, Feminism and Political Theory,* (ed.) C. Pateman, pp. 118–140 (Stanford, 1989).

Payne, S., *Falange* (Stanford, 1961).

Payne S. and Tusell J. (eds.), *La guerra civil* (Madrid, 1996).

Payne, S., *Fascism in Spain 1923–1977* (London, 1999).

Payne, S., *The Franco Regime: 1936–1975* (London, 2000).

Pecharromán, J.P., *José Antonio Primo de Rivera – Retrato de un Visionario* (Madrid, 1997).

Pereira Porto, C., *A aportación de Concepción Arenal no marco de estado liberal Español* (A Coruña, 1997).

Pérez, J., *Isabel y Fernando – los Reyes Católicos* (Madrid, 1997).

Perks, R. and Thomson, A. (eds.), *The oral history reader* (London, 1998).

Pezerat, P. and Poublan, D., "Femmes sans maris: les employees des posts" in *Madame ou Mademoiselle? Itinéraires de la solitude feminine 18th–20th siécle* (eds.) A. Frge and C. Klapisch-Zuber (Montalba, 1984), pp. 117–162.

Powell, C., *Reform versus "Ruptura" in Spain's Transition to Democracy* (Oxford, 1989).

Preston, P., *The Coming of the Spanish Civil War* (London 1978).

Preston, P., *The Politics of Revenge: Fascism and the Military in 20th Century Spain* (London, 1990).

Bibliography

Preston, P., *Franco. A Biography* (London, 1993).

Radcliff, P., "Citizens and Housewives: the Problem of Female Citizenship in Spain's Transition to Democracy", in *Journal of Social History*, Vol. 36, No. 1 (Fall 2002), pp. 77–100.

Raguer, H., *La espada y la cruz. La Iglesia, 1936–1939* (Barcelona, 1977).

Redero San Román, M., *Transición a la democracia y poder político en la España postfranquista (1975–1978)*, (Salamanca, 1993).

Requena, F.M., *Fuentes para la historia de Opus Dei* (Barcelona, 2002).

Richards, M., *A Time of Silence: Civil War and the Cultural Repression in Franco's Spain* (Cambridge, 1998).

Richmonds, K., *Women and Spanish Fascism – The Women's Section of the Falange 1934–1959* (New York, 2003).

Riordan, J., *Sport in Soviet Society: Development of Sport and Physical Education in Russia and the USSR* (Cambridge, 1980).

Riordan, J., *Sport, Politics and Communism* (Manchester, 1991).

Rios Bergantinhos, N., *A mulher no nacionalismo galego (1900–1936): ideologia e realidade* (Santiago de Compostela, 2001).

Rivas, A.M., *Concepción Arena* (Madrid, 1999).

Rodríguez Jiménez, J.L., "The Extreme Right in Spain after Franco", *Patterns of Prejudice*, vol. 24, winter 1990, pp. 76–89.

Rodríguez López, S., "La Falange femenina y construcción de la identidad de género durante el franquismo" (paper presented at the Universidad de Almeía, 2000).

Ruiz Carnicer, M.A., *El Sindicato Español Universitario (SEU) 1939–1965* (Madrid, 1996).

Ruiz Resa, J.D., *Trabajo y el Franquismo* (Granada, 2000).

Sáez Marín, J., *El frente de juventudes: política de juventud en la España de posguerra (1937–1960)*, (Madrid, 1988).

Saiz Barberá, J., *España y la idea de la Hispanidad – la lucha de las tres Españas* (Madrid, 1982).

Santos Rivero, V., *Unamuno y el sueño colonial* (Madrid, 2005).

Sepúlveda Muñoz, I., *El sueño de la madre patria: hispanoamericanismo y nacionalismo* (Madrid, 2005).

Soto, A., and Mateos, A., "El final del franquismo 1959–1975", *Historia-16*, no. 29, 1997, pp. 70–2.

Spackman, B., *Fascist Virilities – Rhetoric, Ideology, and Social Fantasy in Italy* (Minneapolis, 1996).

Stewart, A.J., "2002 Carolyn Sharif Award Address: Gender, Race and Generation in a Midwest High School: Using Ethnographically Informed Methods in Psychology", *Psychology of Women Quarterly*, Vol. 27 (2003), pp. 4–5.

Suárez Fernández, L., *Crónica de la Sección Femenina y su tiempo* (Madrid, 1993).

Suárez Fernández, L., *La España de los Reyes Católicos (1474–1516)*, (Madrid, 1969).

Summerfield, P., *Reconstructing women's wartime lives: discourse and subjectivity in oral histories of the Second World War* (Manchester, 1998).

Thomás, J.M., *La Falange de Franco* (Barcelona, 2001).

Tortella, G., *The Development of Modern Spain – an Economic History of the 19th and 20th Centuries* (Cambridge MA, 2000).

Bibliography

Tusell, J., *La dictadura de* Franco (Madrid, 1988).

Tusell, J., *Franco en la Guerra Civil. Una biografía política* (Barcelona, 1992).

Tusell, J., *Carrero: la eminencia gris del regimen de Franco* (Madrid, 1993).

Tusell, J., *La transición Española a la democracia* (Madrid, 1997).

Tusell, J., *Tiempo de incertidumbre: Carlos Arias Navarro entre el Franquismo y el transición (1973–1976),* (Barcelona, 2003).

Ugalde Solano, M., "Las mujeres nacionalistas vascas en la vida pública: gestación y desarrollo de Emakume Abertzale Batza 1906–1936", tesis doctoral (Madrid, 1991).

Valdés Larraoaga, M., *De la Falange al movimiento (1936–1952),* (Madrid, 1994).

Valiente Fernández, C., "La liberalización del régimen franquista: la Ley de 22 de julio de 1961 sobre Derechos Políticos, Profesionales y de Trabajo de la Mujer", *Historia Social,* Madrid, no. 31, 1998. pp. 45–65.

Vicinus, M., *Independent Women – Work and Community for Single Women 1850–1920* (Chicago, 1985).

Vincent, M., "Camisas Nuevas: Style and Uniformity in the Falange Española 1933–1943", in W. Parkins (ed.), *Fashioning the Body Politic: Dress, Gender, Citizenship* (Oxford, 2002).

Weber, A., *Teresa of Avila and the Rhetoric of Femininity* (Princeton, 1990).

Williamson, R., *Teresa of Avila* (London, 1991).

Zagalaz Sánchez, M.L., *La educación física femenina (1940–1970): análisis y estudio en la ciudad de Jaen* (Jaen, 1997).

Dictionaries

Casres, J. (de la Real Academia Española), *Diccionario ideológico de la lengua Española* (Barcelona 1994).

Moliner, M., *Diccionario de uso del Español* (Madrid, 1994).

Salvat Léxico – Diccionario de la lengua (Barcelona 1991).

INDEX

Acción Católica, 16, 29, 32, 64, 91
Agosti, Luis, 108–110, n. 149
Aparicio, Juan, 69
Arrese, José Luis, 82
Arriba (journal), 59
Auclert, Hubertine, 128

BDM (Nazi Youth Movement), 45
Blue Division, 33
BUF (British Union of Fascists), 28

Catholic Church, 27, 30, 55, 131, 132
   Church and Women, 2, 72, 76
   the Franco Regime, 6, 102, 103, n. 148
   physical education, 13, 83, 86, 105, 106,
      115, 116, 118, 119, 120, 124, 126
CEDA (Confederatión Espanola de
   Derechas Autónomas), 16, 32
Comunion Tradicionalista, 16, 29, 30
Cruz Hernández, Miguel, 83
Curie, Marie, 62, 142

De Beauvoir, Simone, 3, 71, 76–77
De Icaza, Carmen, 65–66
De Lara, Elisa, 67, 69, 70, 71, 109
De Miranda, María, 49, 112, 113, 119,
Decree of Unification, 16, 17, 18, 39, 130
Del Pozo, Adelida, 37, 133

Economic Stabilization Plan, 80, 120, n.
   144
Eiroa, María Victoria, 9, 11, 22, 31, n. 136,
   n. 138, n. 139,
Elola, José Antonio, 82, n. 145

Falcón Lidia, 95
Fasci Femminili, 28
Fascist Italy, 4, 10, 13, 28, 45, 58, 106

Feminist Movement, 2, 3, 4, 26, 57, 61, 62,
   71, 76, 95
Fernández Cuesta, Reimundo, 82
Formica, Mercedes, 11, 15, 22, 28, 73, 94,
   n. 138
Franco regime, 6, 32, 33, 35, 60, 61, 80,
   100, 102, 118, 130, 132, 133, 134, n.
   144, n. 148
   women, 1, 2, 3, 9, 12, 18, 19, 20, 24, 68, 79,
      81, 83, 87, 94
   Fascism, 4, 5
   physical education, 104, 105, 106,
      108, 110
Friedman, Betty, 3

Gímenez Caballero, Ernesto, 26
Gutiérrez Salgado, Carlos, 116

Haz (journal), 59
Hedilla, Manuel, 18
La Hora (journal), 59
Housewives Associations, 74
Huber, Aurora, 97, 99

Ibarruri, Dolores, 45
Institute for Political Studies, 94, 101
Internacional Union of Feminine Catholic
   Organizations, 76
Isabel I (Isabel la Católica), 60–61, 67

Labadie Otermin, Francisco, 97
Landaburu Gonzalez, Belen, 97, 99, 101
Law of Associations (1964), 74, 119
Law of Political and Professional Equality
   for Women, 13, 99
Law of Succession, 18, 81, 130
López Enseñat, Andresa, 9, 10, 50, 52, 53,
   117, 134, n. 136

Index

Loring, Teresa, 9, 11, 20, 22, 53, 61, 66, 84, 96, 99, n. 138, n. 145

Manteola, Sierra, 35, 84, 121, n. 150
Medina (journal), 12, 58, 59, 60, 66–70, 78
Medina Clubs, 32, 74
Montes, Eugenio, 26
Muro, Jesús, 86, n. 145

National Catholicism, 6, 56, 106, 112, 132
Nazi Germany, 5, 13, 45, 122
Neighborhood Associations, 74
Nieves Suñer, María, 89, 90, n. 146
Nueva Andadura Association, 9, 53, 133

Organic Law of the FET, 42, 101
Organization of University Women (Amistad Universitaria), 74

Pemartín, Julian, 86
Pereda, Rosario, 39, n. 139
Pla y Daniel, Enrique, 119
Primo de Rivera, Carmen, 15
Primo de Rivera Dictatorship (1923–1930), 11, 22
Primo de Rivera, Dolores, 15
Primo de Rivera, José Antonio, 1, 17, 26, 39, 139
  National Syndicalist doctrine, 9–10, 18, 25, 28, 29, 33, 34, 111
  Foundation of the SF, 15
Primo de Rivera, Miguel; 30
Primo de Rivera, Pilar, 7, 8, 9, 12, 14, 16, 17, 18, 19, 24, 27, 28, 32, 33, 37, 39, 42, 45, 46, 47, 48, 53, 55, 65, 82, 83–86, 88, 91, 94–97, 99–101, 109, 111, 116, 120, 133, n. 138, n. 139, n. 145

Ridruejo, Cristina, 28, n. 145
Ridruejo, Dionisio, 102, n. 137, n. 139
Rodríguez de Viguri, Josetina, 15, 28

Salinas Alfonso de Villagomez, Carmen, 97, 99, 101, 102
Sánchez Mazas, Rafael, 26
Second Spanish Republic, 5, 14, 16, 22, 45, 64, 87, 103, 130, n. 145
Second Vatican Consilium, 76
Segura y Sáenz, Pedro, 105
Serrano Suñer, Ramon, 17, 18
Sierra y Gil de la Cuesta, Concepción, 114
Social Service for Women (Servicio Social de la Mujer – SS), 2, 28, 34, 36, 85, n. 135
Solís, Luis, 82
Sotomayor, Enrique, 33, n. 139
Spanish Civil Code, 6, 13, 80, 87, 95, 101, 133
Spanish Civil War, 1, 5, 6, 8, 11, 12, 16, 17, 18, 20–22, 24, 26, 27, 29, 31, 33, 35, 39, 46, 51, 54, 56, 58, 60, 61, 62, 64, 91, 98, 103, 112, 115
Spanish Falange, 2, 6, 7, 16, 17, 18, 24, 25, 39, 55, 83, 84, 85, 89, 90, 111, n. 137, n. 139, n. 146, n. 147
  foundation, 11, 15, 28
  Students' Syndicate (SEU), 1, 15, 21, 28, 30, 31, 32, 33, 34, 35, 37, 51, n. 138, n. 139, n. 140, n. 146
  foundation of the SF, 15, 39
  the Franco Regime, 19
  Youth Movement, 32, 82, 106, 108
  physical education, 108
Spanish Work Charter, 95–96, 132

Teresa (journal), 12, 56, 58, 67–73, 76, 130–131
Teresa of Avila, 60, 61, 67

Valcarcel, Consuelo, 33, 34, 35, 37, 48, 50, 51–53, n. 138, n. 140

Warner, Carmen, 92–93, n. 141
World War I, 46
World War II, 5, 18, 23–24